PHOTO CREDITS

PREFACE

Interest in providing education for parenthood increases steadily. More and more schools are accepting responsibility for offering courses in the development and care of young children. Home economists consider child development an important subject. In Washington, D. C., the Office of Child Development and the Office of Education are encouraging educational programs among young people to help them become more effective and understanding parents in the future, and they are encouraging programs for training assistants in children's centers.

A welcome change in the field is that of giving boys and young men more opportunity to learn about children and to work with children. Young children need men in their day-to-day experience. It is to be hoped that more men will become teachers of young children.

There are other changes in the field. The matter of good day care or young children is beginning to get the attention it surely deserves. This has become more important than ever as more and more women are it work outside the home. Quality day care must be available for thee children if they, and our society, are not to suffer. Well trained staff, me and women who care about children and understand their needs, a essential for a good day-care center.

More parents and teachers are working together today, planning an taking responsibility for all the aspects of children's growth and develop ment. Teachers and parents gain as well as the children.

An appreciation of how much and how readily children learn from each other has grown in these last years, along with a greater respect for play and all that children learn through play. Every child seems to need some experiences in play with other children, especially experiences in which socio-dramatic play is freely possible. Along with a tendency in these last years to "push" young children's development, there has been some tendency to subvert play for adult purposes and thereby lose some of its important potential — the contribution it makes to personality growth as well as to cognitive growth.

third edition

Understanding and Guiding Young Children

Hi Lisa,
How are you?
I'm fine?
you) *See soon.*
Love,
?

third edition

Understanding and Guiding Young Children

KATHERINE READ BAKER

Former Head, Department of Family Life
and Home Administration
Oregon State University

XENIA F. FANE

Assistant Director of Home Economics
New York City Public Schools

PRENTICE-HALL, INC., ENGLEWOOD CLIFFS, NEW JERSEY

RELATED PRENTICE-HALL BOOKS

CAREERS: EXPLORATION AND DECISION, by Jack L. Rettig

EXPLORING HOME AND FAMILY LIVING, by Henrietta Fleck and Louise Fernandez

FOOD AND YOUR FUTURE, by Ruth Bennett White

LIVING WITH YOUR FAMILY, by Henrietta Fleck, Louise Fernandez, and Elizabeth Munves

MAKING HEALTH DECISIONS, by Ben C. Gmur, John T. Fodor, L. H. Glass, and Joseph J. Langan

PERSONAL ADJUSTMENT, MARRIAGE, AND FAMILY LIVING, by Judson T. Landis and Mary G. Landis

YOU AND YOUR FOOD, by Ruth Bennett White

UNDERSTANDING AND GUIDING YOUNG CHILDREN, Third Edition
Katherine Read Baker and Xenia F. Fane

Printed in the United States of America
10 9 8 7 6 5 4 3 2 1

ISBN 0-13-935825-0

Cover and title page photo by Carl Glassman

PRENTICE-HALL INTERNATIONAL, INC., *London*
PRENTICE-HALL OF AUSTRALIA, PTY. LTD., *Sydney*
PRENTICE-HALL OF CANADA, LTD., *Toronto*
PRENTICE-HALL OF INDIA PRIVATE LTD., *New Delhi*
PRENTICE-HALL OF JAPAN, INC., *Tokyo*

This edition of *Understanding and Guiding Young Children*, like the earlier ones, is written for young people who are interested in preparation for parenthood, but it gives more emphasis to work with groups of children than earlier editions did. It should serve as a background and introduction for the student who wishes to begin preparing for work in this field.

A new chapter has been added dealing with careers in child care. In other chapters there is more discussion of discipline in groups of children and discussion of group activities and equipment needed. There is an added section on the personal qualities needed by someone going into work with young children. These discussions have applications for parents as well as for prospective teaching assistants.

References at the end of each chapter in this edition have been limited to items of practical interest to the student. They are largely drawn from two journals, *Children Today*, published by the Office of Child Development and the Department of Health, Education and Welfare, Washington, D. C., and *Young Children*, published by the National Association for the Education of Young Children, Washington, D. C. Both journals are easily available and are sources with which students should become familiar.

The subject of understanding and guiding young children is important in this period of rapid social change. If, as seems possible, we are moving toward making our lives somewhat simpler and more livable, we may find ourselves better able to enjoy children and to give them understanding care. In spite of advances in knowledge about children, there remains a need for much more understanding of young children as persons and for greater skill in guiding them wisely. It is hoped that this volume will make some contribution toward the furthering of these goals.

KATHERINE READ BAKER
XENIA F. FANE

CONTENTS

7 Discipline, Punishment, Spoiling 203

8 Children Are Members of Families 223

11 A Look Ahead to Life's Work

293

Index

1

What Are
Children Like?

After studying this chapter, you will be able to

1. **Observe the differences among children.**
2. **Accept children as they are, with all their differences.**
3. **Distinguish between characteristics that are due to heredity and those that are due to environment.**

Each of us was once a child. Many of us, probably most of us, are with young children at some time or another. Children are fascinating to know and to know about. When they are newborn, they may *seem* to be very much alike; yet each will grow to be a distinct person, just as each of us is. By the time children start to school, each is unlike anyone else and is very different from a newborn. In spite of these differences, there are some things that every child needs, and there are some things we should know about children to help them grow up to be happy, well-adjusted adults.

This chapter introduces us to our study of children. We shall look for answers to questions such as what are children like? What do you yourself want to learn about children? List some of the questions you have about children. Check this list at the end of the course and see what answers you have found to your questions.

Good fathers and mothers watch over their babies
and respond to their needs.

Some of you may be planning to have a career in the child care
field. For you this will be an introduction to other courses later.
Most of you anticipate becoming parents some day. Some of you
may already be parents. For everyone, men as well as women, the
study of children is an important study.

Why Do We Study About Children?

It is only recently that people have really begun to study children
to learn more about how children grow and what they really need
to develop well.

Good fathers and mothers through the ages, of course, have
always watched over their babies and responded to their needs,
giving them food and loving them. They still do today. But today
we live in a different kind of world in many ways. There has been
an "explosion" in scientific knowledge in this century. There is
much more to be taught and learned. Patterns of family life are
shifting. Schools, with an organized and more extensive kind of

education, take the place of at least some of the teaching done earlier by parents and grandparents in the closely knit family group.

Today we know much more about health care and nutritional needs of infants and young children. We know more about how infants and young children learn and what helps and what hinders their learning. We know more, too, about the steps children take in mastering skills, in getting along with other people, and in discovering and valuing the kinds of persons they themselves are. We know enough to realize that there is much more still to be discovered about young children.

As our ways of living change, new problems have arisen such as the problem of pollution and the need to conserve our natural resources better. New discoveries have brought changes, for example, in our means of transportation. We have more contacts with people who live differently from ourselves. This makes new demands on us to adapt and to work cooperatively. By studying the new and yet very ancient subject of child development, we may find ourselves better able to develop and conserve our most important resource—the young child.

The best way to study about children is by observing them and working with them.

All of us will play a part in the lives of the children we meet. It may be the very significant role of a parent at home. It may be the significant role of a teacher, working in a day care center, or a nursery school, or a parent-child center, or perhaps in a church school, or on a playground, or in a summer camp. Everywhere there are children to understand and help in their growing. The more understanding each one of us has, the better we will each be able to meet children's needs.

How Do We Study and Learn About Children?

The best way to study about children is to learn from the children themselves by observing them and working with them. This means learning how to observe behavior carefully, thoughtfully, and in detail, noting the child's responses in situations and thinking about the meaning of those responses. We will discuss this more later. We also learn by observing experienced, skilled people as they work with children and by watching how the child responds to different kinds of guidance. We learn, too, from reading about what has already been discovered about growth and development, and we learn from discussing these findings in class with others. We ourselves may discover things about children.

Learning about children often increases our own insight into what *we* are like, for we were all children once. We went through these same stages in our own growth and development. We may come to understand ourselves better as we grow in our understanding of the children we meet.

Think of Children You Know

Think of the children you know. They may be children you see on your way to school in the morning, or in the grocery store, or on the bus. They may be children in your neighborhood or perhaps your own brothers and sisters.

They are all different. They may be round and plump or skinny and tall. They may cry a lot and often look unhappy. They may smile a lot and have sunny dispositions that make you feel like playing with them. They may be quiet or they may be active. They may often be naughty and difficult to take care of, or they may be easy to manage and fun to be with. Even the same child is different at different times.

In other words, children are people just as the rest of us are. They have feelings. They grow and change. They want to be understood. Each one is a little different from anyone else. He is *himself* or *herself*, just as each one of us is.

Things children do. When we watch children, we can see that they love to explore and to *discover* things. They discover things that may happen to water—how it splashes, how it spills, or how it disappears in sand. They are fascinated by funny things like a fly buzzing against a window pane. They *work hard* lining up a row of stones or filling a pan with dirt or carrying all their blocks from one place to another.

A child works hard making a tower of blocks.

A child discovers things that can happen to water and sand.

They like to *watch* cars go by or people on the street or to *listen* to the sound of a spoon banged on the table. It's an exciting world for them because so much is new and unexpected. They *get tired*, and they may fall asleep wherever they are, in the most uncomfortable-looking positions. Or they may climb up into someone's arms and settle down for a *rest*.

They *become frightened* easily by such things as sudden, loud noises or by being separated from the person taking care of them. They often *need help* in feeling safe or in actually being safe. They do not understand clearly what is dangerous and what isn't. They are often afraid of the wrong things! They *get angry* easily when they can't have what they want. They *find it hard to wait* for things and to be patient.

They are children, and things look different to children than to people who have lived a few years longer.

How we react to children. Every child is different and we may find ourselves acting differently toward each one. For example, Jane and Mary are both three years old but they are different.

Every child's personality is different,
and we may find ourselves reacting differently
toward each one.

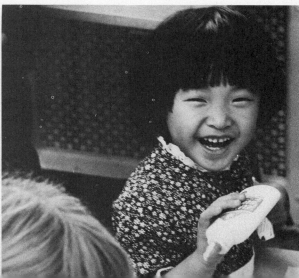

Jane stands quietly watching a group of children playing on the sidewalk. She is thin with blonde, straight hair and a wistful expression. The other children are not paying any attention to her. If you speak to her, she hangs her head and may put her finger in her mouth. She doesn't answer you.

Mary, on the other hand, comes running to the group. She picks up a toy lying nearby and plumps herself down in the midst of the children. She chatters away, paying little attention to the fact that no one seems to be listening to her. She looks up and calls "Hi" to you as you pass.

Would you act differently toward Jane and Mary if you were taking care of them? You probably would. Most people would.

You can hardly act the same toward a child who hangs her head and doesn't speak as you do toward a child who calls out a friendly "Hi." Children make other people behave differently toward them because of what they themselves do. Like everyone else, Jane and Mary, by their different ways of feeling and acting, make a different place for themselves in the world of people. In a sense each is building her own world.

Jane may feel, "No one wants me," when she is with people. When Mary is with people, she may feel, "Here are some people to play with. What fun!" Most people will act in a friendly way toward Mary. She builds that kind of world for herself as she says "Hi" and begins to play as though she expected people to like her and want to play with her. Jane is building a different world for herself. Most people will go on about their business and forget her. A few people may feel sorry for her and try to help her and perhaps tell her what she should do.

Because people act differently toward them, these children may go on becoming more "fixed" in their ways of acting. Mary may become more sure that people are friendly. Jane may become more sure that no one wants her or that others only try to boss her.

How did these children get started feeling and acting this way? *Can* they change? *Should* they change? What can we do about helping children become satisfied and happy, liking themselves and other people?

These are things we want to understand. We study children so that we can find some answers to questions such as these.

Children need to be understood.

Children Need to Be Understood

We all want to be understood. We all know how many times we are misunderstood. We know this from our own experience. It happens often to children, too.

Watch a small boy whose mother has just swept up the litter of sticks and stones on the walk. He weeps because for him the litter was a city with carefully laid out roads. She has ruined it. He does not understand that his mother is only trying to get things clean because company is coming. She is too busy to listen to what he is trying to tell her. He cries hopelessly. It isn't easy to be little!

Another mother calls her four-year-old daughter, "Come here this minute." By the time the child comes, the mother is talking on the telephone—a long conversation. The child waits and she may be wondering why she had to leave her play. She may wonder, "What's the matter with me when people don't pay any attention to me? Do they think that what I do is of no importance? Why do they interfere so often?"

It is often hard to feel valued and important when one is a little child. It is easy to get confused about what is expected. These kinds of things go on happening to us even when we are older, but then we are aware of some of the reasons, at least. Small children don't have the advantages of our experience. They need understanding from us.

Observing children carefully. To understand children we must learn to look at them as they really are, *to observe closely and with care* and not just glance at them and say thoughtlessly, "I know what that child is like."

We really cannot be sure what a child is like until we watch that child carefully over a period of time. And then there will still be a lot we do not know.

To understand children we must learn to observe them closely and with care.

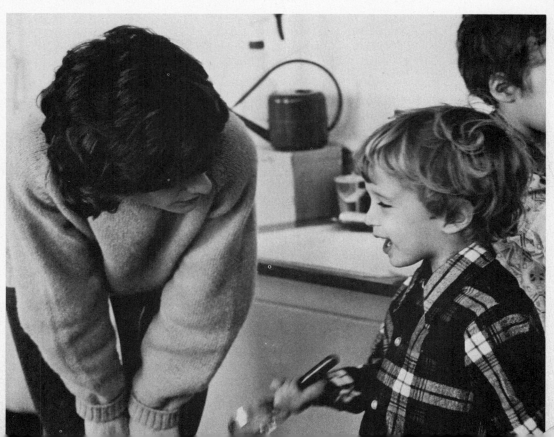

Do you think anyone could understand all about you even if this person had watched you for one whole day? You can act in so many different ways under different circumstances. It is sometimes hard to tell just what the real "you" is.

Certainly you are a lot of things. So is a child. The one advantage we have in learning what children are like is that children don't hide as much as older persons often do. Children really let us know how they feel by the way they act. And this is a good thing because children may not be able to put their feelings into words. They have to show us through the way they behave, the way they yell when hurt, or hit out when angry, or wiggle with joy when pleased. If we learn to watch closely, we can begin to learn to understand their behavior and some of its meanings.

We must train ourselves to observe details and not be content to describe in a general way what we think is happening. Maybe one bit of behavior is like something we saw another child do and we jump to the conclusion that the two children are alike, but this may not be true. Every child is unique, different from any other.

Understanding what you observe. What we *expect* to see may interfere with our seeing what is really there. All of us tend to have "images" in our mind of children and their behavior. We think of them as "cute" or "naughty" or "noisy" or something else. What we see when we look at them will often depend on what these "images" are or what we expect to see unless we are observing each individual child carefully. What we expect to see may interfere with our seeing what actually is happening. It may prevent our understanding the child's behavior.

Let us look at some of the ways children behave. Here is a child who fusses when he doesn't get what he wants. Is he "spoiled"? Another child cries hard when she falls. Is she a "crybaby"? Still another child grabs a toy from the child near him. Is he "selfish"? Another child calls you "stupid." Is she rude? What does she really mean when she says this?

It may be that a particular child is "spoiled" or "selfish," but it also may be your "image" of what this behavior means. You may be missing some important details. What looks like the same behavior in a general way may really be quite different in two different children or even in the same child at two different times.

For example, a child we might have labeled "selfish" may live in a neighborhood where there are a lot of children and most of them are older than he. They take things from him and he learns to grab to get what he wants when he plays with others. To him this is play and he thinks nothing of it. He doesn't get upset when someone grabs what he has. He expects to grab to get what he wants. He may smile in a friendly way as he grabs. He often gives something to another child. He isn't really "selfish." He is just behaving as he has learned to behave.

The child who cries hard over a small bump may be a child who is feeling lonesome and afraid. Perhaps her mother is away and has left her with an aunt who doesn't care about children. She wants her mother and does not understand why she has left her. She tries to be brave but when she trips and falls, all her miserable feelings of loneliness spill out and she sobs brokenheartedly. She is not a "crybaby" but only a child facing more problems than she can bear comfortably at the moment.

If you are going to do something for this child, it will make a difference whether you are responding to a real situation or to the "image" in your mind.

This is not a "crybaby" but only a child facing more problems than are bearable at the moment.

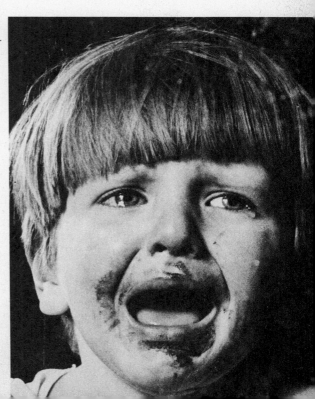

Children behave as they do because of many reasons, such as being hungry, being tired, being anxious or unhappy, being confused or not understanding what is expected of them. They may live under circumstances which produce patterns of behavior, as with the child who grabbed. A child may also behave this way because the behavior belongs with this child's age and stage of development. Being two or three or four makes a difference in behavior. Being two means having very little idea about property rights, for one thing. A two-year-old is likely to take any toy that appears attractive. A four-year-old is likely to have learned that toys may belong to a playmate. Labeling two-year-old behavior as "selfish" may interfere with our understanding of what the child is really like. It may interfere with our giving the kind of guidance that is needed. Observe what actually happens without labeling or judging the behavior. It takes careful observation to discover what a child's behavior is really telling us. We are wise not to pass judgment or speak in general terms about the kind of child we are observing.

It takes practice to learn to observe what actually happens. Only when we learn to observe with careful attention to details can we discover what children are really thinking and feeling and what they need from us. It makes a big difference to the child whether you respond to the real child or to your "image" of the child. We know we react differently if we think of a child as "naughty" rather than as someone who is scared, or if we think of a child as a "crybaby" rather than as someone who is lonely and bewildered. Avoid making snap judgments about children — or anyone.

Why Children Differ

We began by saying that children are people just as we are and that they need to be understood and respected. We pointed out that each child is different. We know that we react to these differences. We find some children easier to like than others.

You have probably wondered why people are so different. Where do these differences come from?

Children, like all of us, are different because of what they start out with and because of what happens to them along the way. We are all different because of what we inherit from our parents and because of our environments or the experiences we have from birth on. What do we mean by heredity and environment?

We start with heredity. As you probably know, each individual grows from the union of two cells, an ovum and a sperm. Both the ovum and the sperm contain chromosomes. These chromosomes are like rows of beads on a string and the beads are genes. The genes are carriers of inherited characteristics such as whether we are a boy or a girl or have blue eyes or curly hair or react quickly to stimuli. Incidentally, the gene which determines the sex of the child comes from the father's chromosomes.

Conception takes place when the sperm cell from the male penetrates the ovum, or egg cell, in the female and fertilizes it. The fertilized egg divides. In the process of division, the two sets of chromosomes pair off and divide, too. One cell becomes two, then four, then eight, then sixteen, and so on. Nine months later, when the infant is born, there are millions of cells and they have become very specialized—some making stomach muscles or eyes or some other special part of the body, all from the union of the sperm and the ovum at the moment called conception. All that is inherited is present in the genes in that first fertilized egg.

Combinations of genes in the ova and sperm are not apt to be exactly the same, so that no two children are exactly alike, not even identical twins. Identical twins come from one fertilized ovum.

In different environments, people may develop in an infinite variety of ways.

No two children are exactly alike.

A mother and father who are happy together create a favorable climate for a growing child.

Environment plays a part. We still have many things to learn about what genes contain, but we know that they play a part in determining what a person will be like as he grows. You notice the words, "play a part" rather than just "determine" what a person is like. For example, we know size is inherited. Genes determine how tall people *can* become, but how tall they actually do grow will depend also on what they eat, perhaps on illnesses they had and the age they were when they were ill, or the climate they live in. In other words, the environment plays a part along with the genes in setting the limits of possibility. Probably we seldom develop to the full extent of our capacity. Even though we are limited by what we inherit, we have plenty of room for change through improving our environment.

The Japanese people, for example, are shorter in height than Americans. But Japanese children born and raised in this country tend to be taller than those born and raised in Japan. The diet is different here. You can see how environment makes a difference even though inheritance determines the limits of growth.

There is an almost infinite variety to the ways that people may develop in different environments. Children learn to speak English or Eskimo or Russian depending on the country in which they happen to be reared. They are friendly or unfriendly depending on what kind of people they live with and what kind of expectations these people have for them. They are alert and interested in learning or fail to learn depending on the kinds of opportunities they have had to learn — all these things within the limits set by their individual inheritances.

Many things that people sometimes think are inherited are the result of environment. You may hear someone say, "He got that bad temper from his uncle," or "She inherited her clumsiness from me," or "Her lisp came from my mother." These are not true statements. There is no gene that carries "bad temper" or "clumsiness" or "a lisp." Living with a person with these characteristics means that the child may imitate these things. He follows the example of the adult in having a temper or a lisp or in being clumsy.

Another reason for the child's characteristic behavior patterns may be that the parent had this "image" of the child. The child may have dark hair and features like his uncle. When he gets mad, as everyone does at times, the mother may decide, "Here is a temper just like my brother's," and the child continues to act as she expects him to act. Her "image" helps produce the behavior.

We have seen how we can create a world for ourselves by expecting people to act toward us in certain ways. Parents also may expect children to behave in a certain way until they do. Then they blame it on heredity! Only physical features and general constitutional characteristics such as speed of reaction or sensitivity to sound or light are inherited. These characteristics are the basic building blocks from which the individual personality is fashioned by experiences that the environment provides.

Parents are part of the environment, too. Children inherit from their parents, but parents also provide the most important part of the environment in the child's first years of life. The people who care for the children influence them most and these people are usually the parents. A mother and father who are happy together and who can talk freely together about the things that upset them, little things and big things, create a favorable climate for growing. The care these parents give really nourishes the children. Whether the parents are rich or poor, have a big house or a small one, can give the children many material advantages or few, matters much less in their growth than does this matter of the personal relationship between the parents themselves. If they accept and respect each other, they create an environment in which the children are comfortable. They can be themselves and grow in their own ways just as their parents are growing in their own ways.

Family values and the respect accorded human relationships are reflected in the management of the tasks of homemaking. Wise management of time and energy as well as money are part of a favorable environment. A mother who finds time to enjoy her baby is building better relationships than is the mother whose time is filled with household routines. The years when children are young are crowded, busy years at best for both fathers and mothers. It takes good management and a sense of values to get the most from these years for parents and children. When this is successful, these years will be happy ones to be treasured throughout life.

A mother who finds time to enjoy her baby is building a better relationship with the baby than the mother is whose time is filled with household routines.

Why People Change

Differences in inheritance and differences in environment make each of us a *unique* individual. There never was anyone just like you or just like the child you see playing next door.

We can do nothing to change what a person has inherited as far as we know, but we can do a lot to change the environment in which people develop and in this way change the kind of people they may become. It is worthwhile understanding more about how these changes take place if we are concerned about children and about helping their personality growth.

People change, first of all, because of the strong impulse to grow and change which is present in all living things. It is one of the strongest forces there is. Have you ever noticed a tiny plant pushing its way between two heavy rocks or a morning-glory vine coming up through an asphalt driveway? Human beings, too, have strong impulses to grow, in spite of obstacles. Children grow without anyone's pushing them. In fact, they often do better if they are not interfered with too much. We may need to learn not to be obstacles to their growth.

Another reason people change is that someone *cares* for them and about them. Children who, because of unfavorable circumstances, have developed bad tempers, can change if they feel someone cares and wants to see them become different. They change because they love and want to please the people who love them. If they love and feel loved, they can change their pattern of behavior into one that is more acceptable to the people they love. They are not likely to change because they are nagged or scolded or threatened. They change because someone cares. *Loving makes the difference*. The people who fail to change are those who have lost their capacity to love or to feel close to other people or at least have had this capacity impaired or damaged by unfavorable circumstances. We know that most people can and do change.

Accepting Children as They Are

We help children most when we accept them as they are. We all need to feel that we are loved for what we are. This feeling gives each of us the courage to grow and improve. We are likely to want to change at our own rate and in our own way. It makes us uncomfortable or even unsure of ourselves to be pushed. Being pushed often makes it harder to change. Children feel the same way. Each child has different qualities or characteristics. Each child wants to be accepted and liked for what he or she is. All children need to be helped to grow in their own ways and at their own rates.

If we keep trying to change the way a child acts by saying, "Don't do that, silly" or "That isn't the right way, stupid," the child loses confidence, or rather fails to develop self-confidence. A child needs to feel that she or he is a person of worth. A child changes more readily when she or he feels liked and is not always being pushed to be different. We are part of the child's environment. As we care for the child, we want to build an atmosphere in which she or he grows easily and confidently.

There is a difference between accepting behavior and approving of it. Accepting means being aware and giving understanding, while approval means liking what is there. We should accept children as they are and then give our approval to the behavior we like and to their efforts to change in desirable directions.

A child needs to develop self-confidence.

ACTIVITIES

TO DO AND DISCUSS

1   What are some of the words you think of in describing children? Write these words down and compare them with what the others in the class have written. What kinds of "images" do members of the class seem to have of children? Where do you think these images came from (one child, many individuals, hearsay, etc.)? Combine some of the students' impressions and construct a "normal" child.

2   Watch a group of three or more preschool children for fifteen minutes while they are playing. List the kinds of behavior you see, such as sharing, quarreling, or playing alone. What did the children do that you liked? What did they do that you disliked? What kinds of behavior would you like to change or improve? Why? How?

3   List ten experiences a child might have and suggest how each might affect his or her personality.

4   Observe parents with their child. (They may be neighbors, relatives, or people for whom you baby-sit.) In what ways is the child like the parents (coloring, body type, friendliness, quietness, temperament, etc.)? Do you think these characteristics are inherited or learned? Compare your observations and conclusions with those of your classmates.

5   Try to bring to class several pictures of yourself as a young child, for use in a class exhibit. For each picture, prepare a brief statement which would help the viewer to understand the child in the picture.

TO THINK AND WRITE ABOUT

1   Think of something that happened to you when you were young, before you started school. Describe it as completely as you can. What did it seem like to you then? What do you think it might have seemed like to the adults you lived with? How do you think the same type of experience would affect you now?

2   Spend an hour quietly observing your own younger brother or sister or another young child. List the child's changes in activities and moods. What do you think contributed to these changes?

3   List some of the expectations your parents have for you. Be prepared to compare your list with those of your classmates. How have your parents' expectations influenced your behavior? Do you ever feel that they expect too much (or not enough) of you? Why do different parents expect different things of their children?

4 (a) Do you think some of the people you know should change their behavior? Why? Do some people appear to *want* to change their behavior more than do others? (b) How have you changed recently? What do you think caused the change? How would you go about getting a young child to change his behavior?

REFERENCES

CASE STUDIES

Axline, Virginia
Dibs: In Search of Self
Boston: Houghton Mifflin Co., 1964

Murphy, Lois Barclay
Colin — A Normal Child
New York: Basic Books, Inc., 1967

Phillips, Doris Campbell
"The One and Only Jimmy"
Young Children, Vol. 20, No. 3, pp. 164–175, January, 1965

EARLY CHILDHOOD EDUCATION

Landreth, Catherine
Preschool Learning and Teaching, Chapter 1, pp. 1–4
New York: Harper & Row, 1972

Senn, Milton
"Early Childhood Education — For What Goals?"
Children, January–February, 1969

Zigler, Edward F.
"A National Priority: Raising the Quality of Children's Lives"
Children, September–October, 1970

EDUCATION FOR PARENTHOOD

Education for Parenthood
Office of Education — Office of Child Development
Washington, D. C.: U. S. Department of Health, Education, and Welfare, 8 pp.
  1972 (Single copies free from OCD)

Kruger, W. Stanley
"Education for Parenthood and the Schools"
Children Today, March–April, 1973

SCHOOL PROGRAMS

Clayton, Marilyn, Peter Dow, and Jerome Kagan
"Exploring Childhood—A New Way for High School Students to Learn"
Children Today, March–April, 1973

Durbin, Louise
"A Day at Gaithersburg High School Child Development Laboratory"
Children Today, March–April, 1973

Kipcak, Ellen
"Six Graders Learn About Children and Themselves"
Children Today, March–April, 1973

OBSERVING CHILDREN

Cohen, Dorothy
"Learning to Observe—Observing to Learn"
The Significance of the Young Child's Motor Development, Georgianna Engstrom,
     Editor
     Washington, D. C.: National Association for the Education of Young Children,
     1971

Cohen, Dorothy, and Virginia Stern
Observing and Recording the Behavior of Young Children
New York: Bureau of Publications, Teachers College, Columbia University, 1958

Read, Katherine
The Nursery School, Chapter 9 "Making Observations"
Philadelphia, Pa.: W. B. Saunders Co., 1971

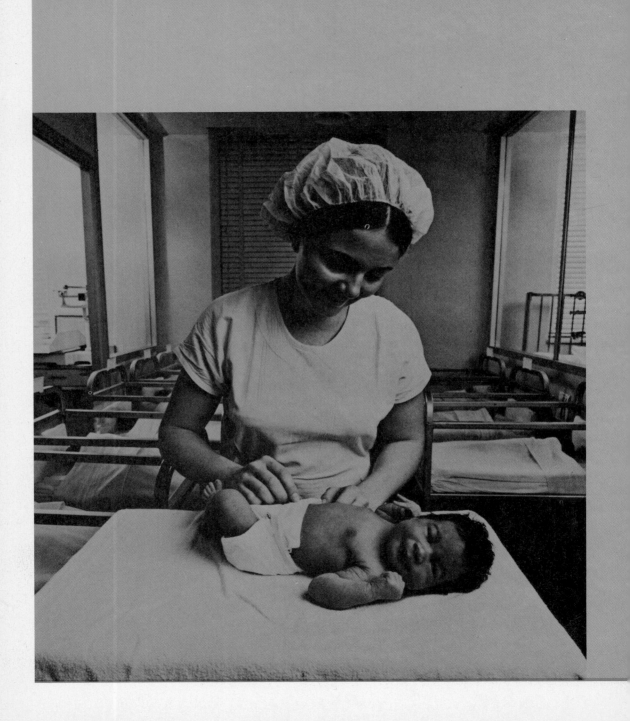

Let's Talk About Babies

2

After studying this chapter, you will be able to

1. Determine how parents can plan ahead to prepare for a new baby in the family.
2. Describe the characteristics of a newborn baby.
3. Analyze the role of the parents in adjusting to a new baby.
4. Discover the meaning of a baby's crying.
5. Evaluate different types of infant feeding and other daily routines.
6. Accept the natural stages in an infant's development.

The newborn is a very helpless, dependent being. The infant has a tremendous amount of learning to do before he can become at all independent. Yet babies learn very early how to let us know that they need something. It is up to us to understand the "language" of their behavior. They also find ways to tell us when their needs have been met. During their first year they become increasingly able to function as independent persons rather than as helpless beings

We shall look at the ways children grow and change, and try to find out what they may need from us if they are to be healthy. We shall start from the beginning, with babies. We shall learn some things about planning for a baby, preparing to become a parent, prenatal care, characteristics of the infant, crying, feeding and weaning, sucking—including thumbsucking, maturation, motor development, social development, and play.

Making Plans for a Baby

One of the most important decisions a couple has to make is the decision about adding to the family.

Babies take time, energy, and money. Babies are demanding. Parents must make changes in their lives with the coming of a baby. Most men and women need to take some time after they marry to share experiences together, to discover ways of resolving their differences, and to talk over important matters with each other before they are ready to become parents. They need time to enjoy one another, too, and to find satisfactions as a couple before they are ready to meet comfortably the demands a baby inevitably makes on them.

Babies take time, energy, and money.

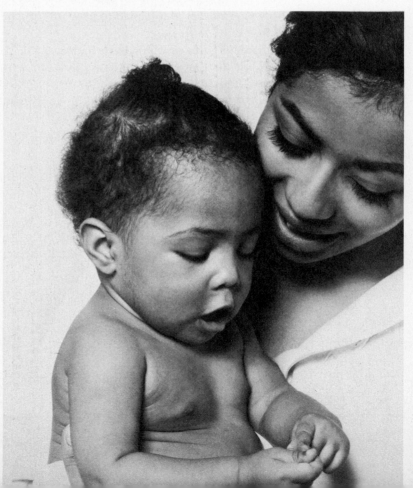

A baby is fortunate to come into a home where parents are ready for a baby.

For the husband and wife who have taken time to grow together, the coming of a baby usually adds richness and depth to their lives as they go on learning and growing through their new relationship with the baby. They come to respect each other more as they both shoulder their added responsibilities and see each other in new roles. A baby is fortunate to come into a home where parents are truly ready for a baby.

Not every couple will decide to take the step of adding a baby to the family. A husband and wife together may choose to find fulfillment in other ways than through children. For people today there are many ways of living satisfying, productive lives — through professional work, through community service, or through personally creative activity which also enriches the lives of others.

Most people will probably choose to have children if they are able. There is a strong maternal or paternal urge in us which we fulfill most readily in the way that is most direct, that is by having a baby, caring for him or her, and guiding his or her growth. Most people look forward to the role of a parent with all its joys as well as the trials it brings. Babies are wonderful.

Another decision a couple must make is about the number of children and the spacing of these children. There are many factors to consider in making this decision. Some of the factors are the money that is likely to be available (many wives hold jobs outside the home), their expectations for each child (a college education costs money but is important for many jobs today), their health and the circumstances of their jobs (such as the necessity of moving frequently), and their own goals in living (what they themselves want after their children are grown). Religious beliefs or the teaching of the church to which the couple belongs is another factor which will influence the number and spacing of children.

These factors are individual matters for families, but there are some general factors, too. The world is becoming more and more crowded. It takes more careful planning by both the parent and the community to give young children good learning and growing experiences under crowded conditions. It takes more supervision. The world no longer needs as many people to get necessary work done because machines have replaced people in doing many tasks. The world needs people with a much higher level of education and understanding and capacity to assume complex and difficult responsibilities. Parents and communities today must give more thought than formerly to providing well for children under these changing conditions. Providing well usually means planning to have a small family.

Providing well usually means planning to have a small family.

Preparing to become a parent. Babies are born. But birth is not the beginning of development. Important things happen through the nine months that a baby grows inside the protection of the mother's body. The baby does here the most rapid growing he or she will ever do. Growth slows down after birth.

The mother cares for the infant by caring for herself during the nine months of pregnancy. Good prenatal care means checking with the doctor each month. In the last month, the mother should check with the doctor every two weeks or oftener. The doctor advises her about what she may need to do to improve her physical health, checks the position of the fetus in the uterus, and makes plans for the delivery. The doctor listens to the heartbeat, which can be heard from around the fourth month.

It is not possible to tell the sex of the baby until birth, but the mother will know whether it is an active baby or a quiet one. She will begin to feel its movements around the fifth month. These movements get stronger and more frequent as the fetus grows.

During the prenatal period the father-to-be plays an important part through the support he gives to the expectant mother. He can help protect her from getting overtired. He can encourage her to follow a good health regime. Most of all he can give her the extra love she may need to carry her through the changes, both physical and emotional, which she faces, and he can share with her some of the miracle of growth before birth as the fetus becomes active.

Prenatal care. During the prenatal period the mother needs extra milk, a full quart a day at least, to provide calcium for the baby's fast-growing teeth and bones. The baby's first teeth are already formed at birth even though it will be months before they come through the gums. If the mother does not get enough calcium, her teeth will suffer. People used to think that mothers had to expect cavities or the loss of a tooth during pregnancy, but now we know better. Mothers just need to get enough calcium in the food they eat so they can supply both their own needs and those of the baby.

A mother does not need many more calories. She will have plenty of weight to carry with the growing baby, so she will avoid fattening foods such as sweets and rich, starchy foods high in calories. She will eat plenty of fruits and vegetables and plenty of protein foods. Diet is important during pregnancy for the health of both the baby and the mother.

In addition to watching her diet, the mother will be sure to get enough rest. She should rest whenever she feels tired.

Usually a woman feels very well during a pregnancy, except possibly in the first two or three months when so many changes are taking place. She is less likely to catch cold or be sick than at other times. Her immunity to disease tends to be greater. A certain number of women feel sick (nauseated) in the morning during these first weeks, but this can often be controlled by eating a cracker. In any event she should follow the doctor's suggestions. Many women do not have this "morning sickness."

If a woman has an adequate diet and good prenatal care, both physical and emotional, she is probably ready to enjoy the baby when it is born at the end of the nine months.

At Birth

The majority of babies born in the United States are born in hospitals. It is easier for the doctor to give the care there that may be needed. The mother usually stays in the hospital for four or five days. The part of the hospital reserved for mothers and newborn babies is called the maternity ward.

Some hospitals today are making provisions for the mother and baby to be in a room together. The baby's crib or bassinet is beside the mother's bed. This arrangement is called "rooming-in." "Rooming-in" gives the mothers a better chance to get acquainted with their babies and enjoy them from the beginning. When the mothers wish they can care for the babies themselves with the help of the nurses. They can nurse the babies when they are hungry rather than having them wait until the nurses are ready to bring them from the hospital nursery. When the mother takes the baby home, she knows what she or he is like and what she or he is likely to need. Hospitals which have this arrangement do not allow any visitors except the father. But it means that fathers, too, can get acquainted with their babies, not just look at them through a nursery window.

Fathers need to be considered for they face big changes with the birth of the baby. The mother is wrapped up in caring for the baby and in gaining her strength. It is easy for a father to feel "left out" unless he, too, can share in some way in enjoying and caring

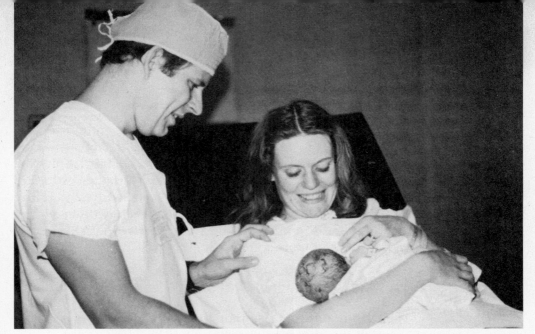

Childbirth is an experience
that should be shared
by father and mother.

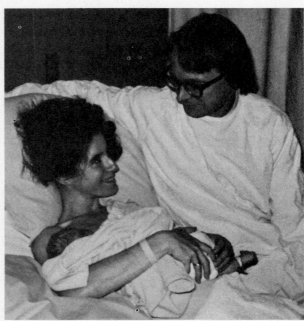

for the baby. He needs some attention, too. The couple must be
considerate of each other as the family goes through the pro-
cess of finding a new balance in their relationship and their
satisfactions.

Some things to observe about a new baby. Have you ever seen a newborn baby or at least a baby less than a month old?

If you have, you know that he or she may be red and wrinkled and old looking. The head may be rather out of shape and may be without much of a chin. The baby may have hair or may be almost bald, for babies are different from the first day of birth. We are often surprised at the way they look. They are so tiny and funny looking. But we are also surprised at how fast they change. The wrinkles fill out and the head changes shape and the baby begins to look more human before a month has passed.

Things to Notice About a Newborn Baby

1. The *head* is large in proportion to the size of the body. It is about ¼ of the total length. When the baby is full-grown, it will be only about ⅛ of the total length. The face is relatively smaller and the braincase is relatively larger than it will be later.

2. The *features* are different, a little nose and not much chin compared to what the baby will have later. The eyes are blue. The eyes may or may not be blue later.

Have you ever seen a newborn baby, or at least a baby less than a month old?

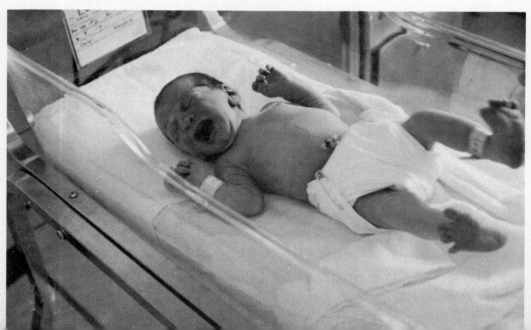

3. The baby's *arms* are longer than his or her legs at birth. The *legs* will grow and become longer than the arms when full-grown.

4. The *fingers* are short, too, but the hands will not change much in shape until he or she is in the teen-years.

5. The baby's *toes* fan out, almost like fingers, instead of curling up as they will do later when the bottom of the foot is touched.

6. At birth only about 25% of the total weight comes from *muscle.* More than 40% of it will be muscle when he or she is grown! The ligaments are not firmly attached, which makes the bones seem flexible. We can see why we must support a baby's large head when we hold the baby, for the muscles have not the strength to do it yet.

7. The *central nervous system* makes up about 15% of the baby's weight at birth but it will make up only 3% of the weight at maturity. No wonder the baby gets tired from any excitement!

8. The baby grows plumper very rapidly if healthy. He or she will usually *weigh* between 6–9 pounds when born and gain from 10–15 pounds in the first year. A baby weighing less than 5½ pounds at birth is considered "premature" and must have special care.

9. The baby is around 20 inches long at birth and will grow about 9–10 inches in the first year. Growth in *length* is less dependent on environmental factors than is gain in weight, although environment plays a part.

10. The *bones* of the infant are not very hard yet. All of the bone growth will not be complete until he or she is in the twenties. In the skull, for example, the baby has soft spots called "fontanels" that are covered with a membrane. One can easily see the soft spot at the top of the infant's head, especially if there is very little hair. The spots are filled in by bone by the 18th month. The head needs to be carefully protected at first.

11. The infant has no *teeth* in sight! But all 20 baby teeth are there in the gums, ready to start erupting when the baby is around six or more months old.

12. The baby *breathes* in a rapid, somewhat irregular way. The infant makes funny noises as she or he breathes. There is difficulty at first in managing to breathe and suck at the same time. The baby often has the hiccoughs and sneezes easily. During the first year the *heart* will grow rapidly and its beat will become stronger, slower and more regular. The breathing will become steadier.

13. The *ears* look like grown-up ears and the hearing is well developed. Some infants startle at sudden sounds more easily than do others.

14. The *eyes* are not fully developed at birth. The infant looks without seeing much in the first weeks and will not really focus on an object until around the third month. Binocular vision is not usually fully developed until after the child is six years old.

15. The *temperature regulating mechanism* is still poor. The baby chills easily or gets hot quickly and so must be covered, but not too much. The baby needs an even temperature.

16. When the infant *cries*, he or she moves all over, arms, legs, and body, and the baby's face may get very red.

During the first month. The infant under a month old is called a *neonate* or newborn infant. In the first month the infant sleeps most of the time if he or she is a healthy baby, waking to be fed and then sleeping again. The neonate has a big adjustment to make after birth. Life has changed. The newborn infant is on his or her own. At first, even breathing is a new experience and does not go

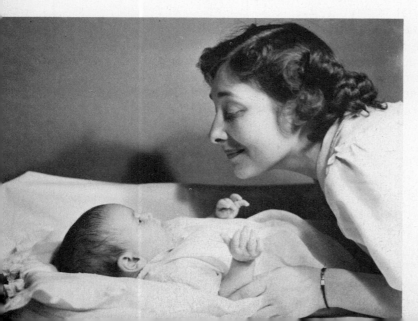

The important thing is to help babies discover that the world they have entered is a place where they will be cared for and where their needs will be satisfied.

smoothly. Listen to the funny noises a baby makes when nursing or taking the bottle as the baby tries to regulate breathing and swallowing—quite a feat! The infant learns quickly, but it does take some practice.

There is no question of "spoiling" babies in their first month. The important thing is to help them find that the world they have just entered is a place where they can be satisfied, a good place where they will be cared for and their needs will be met. It usually helps if the mothers try to follow the babies' rhythm, feeding them when they seem to indicate they are hungry. The acute hunger pangs babies feel are hard to bear. They need to be protected against acute discomfort if possible. They need to feel that the world is a comfortable, inviting place. A mother's job is to stay close to her baby in the first weeks and learn what he or she is like and what he or she needs.

Good mothers grow to understand their particular infants— whether they take their time nursing, dozing and then rousing for more feeding, or whether they suck strongly, vigorously gulping the milk, and then fall sound asleep. Each baby has a somewhat different schedule and usually develops in a more contented way if the mother fits what she does into the rhythm of his or her wants during these first weeks.

A mother's job is to stay close to her baby in the first weeks and to learn what her baby is like and what he or she needs.

In most babies, the hunger pangs come every three or four hours, but not like clockwork. In the first weeks, the intervals are often shorter. The baby may want frequent feedings in the afternoon and fewer in the early morning hours. Some infants occasionally sleep for six hours or more. Some settle down to a regular schedule fairly soon and some take quite a while. Schedules change, too, as the baby grows.

Only gradually do babies learn to regulate themselves so they can fit comfortably into a schedule which suits the whole family. This may take several months. If a mother does not have too many other duties, she can let her baby take his or her time fitting into the world and becoming a person.

It is a matter of *mutual regulation.* At first the mother fits herself to the baby. As she comes to know her baby and the baby comes to feel safe and sure of her and of her willingness to give the infant what she or he wants, the mother asks the baby to do a little more adjusting for her. The infant is better able to wait to be fed now, knowing that food will come eventually. The infant is not as distressed that food is not there the minute he or she feels hunger pangs. The baby is likely to stop crying when mother's footsteps are heard.

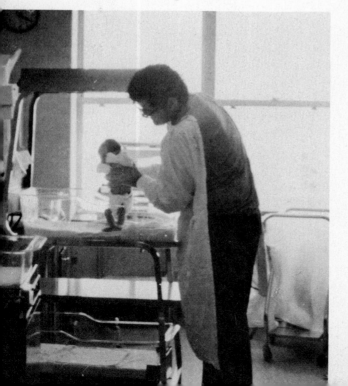

A father needs to get acquainted with his baby as soon as possible.

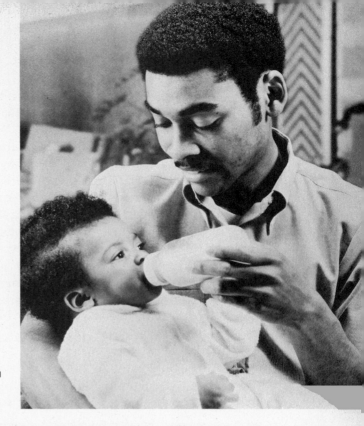

At first a baby needs a mother who can
adjust to her baby, and a father
who helps when he is home.

We have mentioned that we build up a picture of ourselves
from the responses of other people to us. It is true for babies, too,
and it will be easier for them to get an idea of themselves and of
the world around them as stable and trustworthy if they are cared
for by just a few people. At first a baby needs a mother who can
adjust herself to her baby with a father helping when he is home
and perhaps a third person relieving the mother and sharing in
the baby's care.

We think now that an infant who is taken care of by a succes-
sion of different people during the first year of life is not likely to
be as healthy in terms of physical, social, and emotional well-being
as the infant who has had the same people taking most of the care
of her or him.

In these first months it is easier for the baby to build a concept
of the kind of person he or she is or can become when only a few
people are responding to the infant. Later the baby's experiences
with people can be extended without confusing the baby or making
the baby feel bewildered and less sure of himself or herself. Too
many people caring for the infant in the beginning may slow the

process of the baby gaining a sense of having a separate, individual self. It may make it more difficult for the child to develop depth in later personal relationships. We may ask ourselves how important the capacity for intimate relationships may be or the sense of being a separate individual. We may not know the answers to such questions, but at least we should be aware of possible ways in which circumstances influence personality growth. Growth is a very complex process. Understanding it is not simple.

Babies are fortunate when their early experiences include relationships with children as well as adults. Babies need to discover themselves in relationships with other children, and in this way extend their ideas about themselves as people and the range of relationships that are possible. Brothers and sisters are a help to a baby for they see the baby as a very special person in the family.

Babies are fortunate when their early experiences include relationships with children and adults.

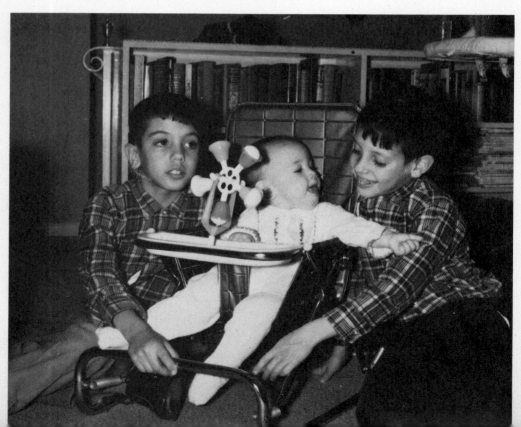

Watch a six-month-old child and you will notice that the baby is likely to respond with special interest and delight to the approach of another child.

Many states have laws which prohibit the care of infants in institutions such as "baby homes" or orphanages. These laws state that a baby whose parents cannot care for him or her must be placed in a family home. Studies done in institutions have shown that babies cared for in groups by a series of people are more likely to get sick and are less likely to have good relations with people later on in life. Babies need close, continuing personal relationships.

The baby's foundations for liking people are laid as the mother and father care for the infant in these first months, put the baby's needs first, feed the baby when he or she is hungry, pick up and cuddle the baby when she or he seems to ask for it, and let the baby rest undisturbed when she or he is sleepy. They keep their baby warm and clean and satisfied. They enjoy their infant. With this kind of care babies grow in a healthy way.

Growing in the First Year

In the first year the baby grows rapidly in a variety of ways. He or she takes important steps in mastering the process of communicating, in adapting to the environment and its demands, and in gaining control over his or her own body.

Crying. The first thing that a baby does is cry! The birth cry is the first breath taken. It gets air into the lungs and starts the baby breathing after being born. Crying exercises the lungs and all babies do some crying. In the first weeks the cry changes and gets stronger and more individual. A mother soon comes to know her baby's cry.

All babies do some crying and some of them do a lot in the first two or three months. It seems to be a part of the readjusting that follows birth when the infant's nervous system and digestive system are not completely in working order. The baby is getting used to eating, sleeping, and living in a strange new world. We try to make it as easy as we can. A pacifier may help or being held and rocked or perhaps another feeding. But fussing and crying are part of growing and exercising. Babies differ in the amounts they do.

Unhappiness in a family can make a baby irritable and fussy.

In the first three or four months of life some babies do quite a lot of crying with colic. Colic doesn't seem to have much to do with what the baby eats or how healthy he or she is. It just seems to be another case of individual difference. Some babies' intestinal tracts are more sensitive and they have a more difficult time making the adjustment to life on their own. They have more gas pains. In time the colic disappears.

Were you one of those babies who had colic? Find out from your parents. If you were, they spent a lot of time with you for a while!

A baby with colic may wake up crying shortly after being fed. Holding the baby over your shoulder and patting gently may help. Rocking and singing may distract the baby from the discomfort. Some babies love the motion of riding in a car. The worst part of colic, from the standpoint of parents, is that it often comes in the evening or at night and both baby and parents lose sleep over it. A mother needs plenty of extra daytime rest during this period.

Babies have their reasons for crying. Babies cry for reasons other than colic pains. Of course, the main reason they cry is because they are hungry. We can feed them and take care of this kind of crying.

But they may cry when they aren't hungry. They may want some comforting. Some babies are especially fussy when they are teething. They do a lot more crying just before a tooth appears.

They may cry, too, when things aren't going right with the important people in their lives. If a mother or father is tired or cross and unhappy about something, the baby is often fussy and may do a lot of crying. A baby doesn't understand these things in the same way that we do, but is very sensitive to the feelings of the people who care for him or her. Parents communicate their feelings to a baby by the tone of their voices and the way they touch him or her. A baby is miserable if he or she feels something is wrong. Unhappiness in the whole family may make a baby irritable and fussy.

It is important to be calm and rested when one is caring for a little baby. Angry feelings, anxious feelings, feelings of dislike are communicated to and disturb the infant. Some babies are more sensitive than others and find these things harder to bear, but all babies are influenced by how the people around them feel. If a baby of six months or older does a lot of crying for no reason that we can tell, maybe he or she is miserable because of trouble in the family.

The most seriously disturbed babies, however, may be those who do almost no crying. Of course there are happy, contented babies who do very little crying, but sometimes babies who do not cry very much are just not protesting or voicing their unhappiness. They may have given up asking for help. Babies without families, in institutions, frequently do almost no crying. They have found that no one cares. This is very serious and they will not grow and develop as they should. They are not healthy.

What *seems* like a lot of crying in an infant, of course, may only be the response of a vigorous, vocally active infant. Some babies exercise their lungs a lot more than others. They may really be quite content. Here again we accept the differences that exist among individual babies. Some babies are active, vigorous, and vocal. Others are quiet, less vigorous, and do less vocalizing. We need to get acquainted with them as individuals before we can be sure about the meaning of any particular bit of behavior. It is worthwhile making sure that nothing is really bothering a baby who does a lot of crying. Crying is often a baby's way of expressing herself or himself when something seems wrong.

During the second half of the first year, a baby is likely to do a lot of "talking" or vocalizing.

If we care for a baby, we must be comfortable about listening to some crying. Babies will sometimes cry and protest a thing like going to sleep. It will not hurt them to cry! If we know they are all right, we do not need to be disturbed by their exercising their lungs for a few minutes.

Vocalizing. During the second half of the first year babies are likely to do a lot of "talking" or vocalizing. The contented sounds they make as they play—their grunts, their cooing—have become real consonant and vowel sounds. They make all the sounds they will use later in speaking, and even a few which do not appear in the English language. Some babies give the muscles of speech plenty of practice during their first year. The pleased response of their parents may encourage these babies to learn to talk early. They seem to listen to themselves with real pleasure. They may be babies who are especially responsive to sounds. They enjoy listening to singing or to sounds of different pitch. Since language is an important form of communication, it is a help to enjoy using it and to achieve some mastery over it early.

All babies gain from being with people who talk to them in soft, pleasant tones, giving them plenty of chance to hear speech. They gain, too, from feeling content, from having new and interesting experiences which are not overwhelming but make them want to "talk," and from being sure there is someone who cares enough to listen with pleasure. Speech flourishes under these conditions, although individual differences remain in patterns and amounts of vocalization.

One sometimes meets a child whose vocalizing does not develop into intelligible speech sounds. One suspects a hearing loss here or perhaps some degree of mental retardation or an emotional disturbance. These possibilities should be checked.

Feeding the baby. Because babies need not only food, but also some cuddling, mothers will usually hold babies even if they are getting their milk from bottles. This body contact is almost as important as the food. It helps the baby feel safe and content. At first this contact and the feelings of comfort and security it gives come best at feeding time. The baby gets his or her very first ideas about the world and about how life will be from the feelings he or she has while being fed. The person who is feeding the baby is most important in establishing those feelings. The baby's world must include people!

The baby who is nursing probably feels additional satisfaction from contact with his or her mother.

Arrange to visit a family, if you can, and watch a baby while he or she is nursing or taking a bottle. Watch how the mother holds the baby to make him or her comfortable and to make it easy to get the food.

It is usually more satisfactory to nurse a baby for the first few months than to depend on bottle feedings. Breast milk is designed for infants. The baby who is nursing gets more contact with his mother and probably feels more satisfied by it. The mother who is nursing a baby, however, must pay attention to her diet, drinking at least a quart of milk a day and eating plenty of fruit and vegetables, meat, poultry, or fish once or twice a day, taking some vitamin D.

A mother may wish to give the baby an occasional bottle to make weaning easier. She or he gets used to something other than the breast before weaning starts. A mother changes from breast feeding to bottle feeding if she finds she does not have enough breast milk or for other reasons such as having to return to outside work. Some mothers may continue to nurse their babies for eight or nine months and then change to a cup rather than a bottle.

After a baby has had a feeding and, with some babies, during the feeding, she or he will need to be "bubbled" or "burped" by holding the baby over your shoulder and patting gently to get out any air bubbles which may give the baby a stomachache and prevent sleeping comfortably.

After the baby is fed, he or she will need to be "bubbled" to get out any air that may have been swallowed.

In addition to milk, an infant is usually given vitamin D. A baby may also have strained orange juice beginning in the first month. By the time she or he is three or four months old, some solid foods such as cereal and perhaps strained fruit will be added to the diet. Baby may also be eating some egg yolk. Pureed (mashed) vegetables will be added, followed by meat. With canned foods available for infant feeding, a mother's job of preparing food is much easier than it used to be.

Research findings have shown us the importance of a good diet during a mother's pregnancy and during the first two or three years of a child's life.

A young child whose diet or whose mother's diet during pregnancy has not had enough protein suffers. Both mental and physical development are harmed. The child's ability to learn will be affected. It seems that this damage cannot be overcome in later years. Good nutrition for the mother during pregnancy and for the child during early childhood is of the greatest importance.

Many adults have trouble controlling their weight. It has been discovered that this may be due to having too many fat cells. Children who are overfed during their early years develop too many fat cells. Children who are kept thin during their early years do not develop many fat cells. In adult life, those persons who have many fat cells find it very hard to control their weight. Those who have fewer fat cells find it much easier to control their weight.

For a young child it is important to have a diet which combines good nutrition with staying thin. For best health, this is true at all ages. However, the eating habits of a lifetime are started in early childhood. Also, the body that develops during early childhood is the one a person will have all through life.

Children react to their food with a variety of emotions.

Babies will like some foods more than others. A wise parent adjusts to the baby's preference but keeps offering other foods to help get the baby accustomed to them. Some babies do better if they are given their solid foods first, while others like some milk first and then their solid food. Parents will discover what works best with their individual baby. They will never force him or her to eat what the baby seems to dislike, or force the baby to eat more then he or she wants at any one time.

As they progress in development, babies usually enjoy playing with their food. It is one way to find out what food is like. It is often a step in learning to enjoy it. They will try using their fingers to get food into their mouths along with the spoons. It helps if parents can feel comfortable about the "messiness" that is part of eating for most young children. Babies feel better about themselves and eating goes more smoothly.

Weaning the baby. *Weaning* refers to the baby's giving up taking milk from the breast or bottle and taking milk from the cup instead. Weaning should be done gradually. It is a "giving up" of something which has been really important. We all know that it isn't easy to leave behind things we've liked. It makes us feel unhappy.

A baby should not be weaned at a time when he or she has had other upsetting things happen such as moving to a new house or an illness. A baby needs to feel good at the time of weaning. Babies show they are ready for weaning in many ways. They enjoy and are increasingly successful in drinking from a cup. They seem to be trying out giving up things of their own accord as they drop objects in their play or even offer them to adults.

Weaning may take a good many weeks and a child may continue to want the bottle at bedtime long after having stopped taking it any other time. Mothers need to *help* children learn to like using a cup but not force them or get impatient with them. It takes time, but they will learn. Here is another place where we see how different each child is. Each child will carry through this weaning process in a different way and at a different rate. For one child it may be harder than for another. In this case the mother herself must feel sure when she starts weaning that, at this point, it is possible and necessary. Her sureness that it can and should be done will help her to bear the child's protests. She will be better able to help him or her feel that giving up nursing and beginning drinking from a

Some babies take time to develop regular sleep habits.

cup can be a good thing. All through life the child will face the necessity of leaving behind things that he or she has liked in order to go on to new experiences. Weaning is likely to be one of the first, as well as one of the most significant, of these experiences. By managing the weaning process in such a way that they can accept it, mothers help children to face and accept more comfortably later experiences of leaving behind what they have enjoyed to go on to other experiences. Giving up one thing to gain another is an aspect of the growing process that we all continue to face through life.

Sleeping. Regular sleep habits take time to develop in some babies. Most babies go through occasional wakeful periods at night. It usually is easier for them to develop good sleep patterns if they are put to bed in the same place about the same time, especially after they are four or five months old.

If the baby's room can be kept at about the same temperature, he or she will need only a light-weight blanket. The mattress of the crib should be firm, and there is no need for a pillow. Most babies prefer to be on their stomachs for sleeping—it seems to take care of gas pains better.

Many babies by the end of the first year have a special blanket or object which seems to be associated with sleep and makes it easier for them to settle down. Babies as well as older children often like the security of having familiar things around them and going through the same routines at bedtime.

A baby is fortunate if the bedtime routine includes some time with her or his father. A father needs to spend time caring for his baby if they are to become really acquainted. Fathers who know their children through caring for them can follow and enjoy the

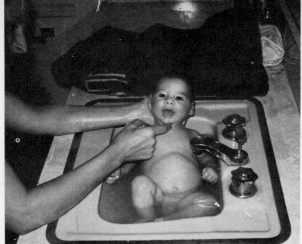
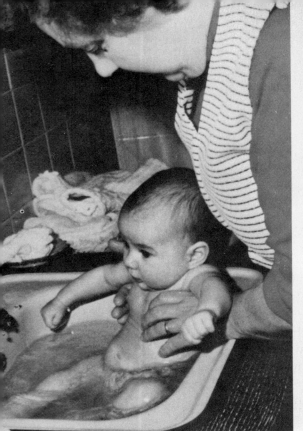

Bath time may become the most fascinating part of the day.

developmental changes taking place. A baby responds well to a change of person at the end of the day and to quiet play with father. A baby learns to know and feel safe and secure with father as well as with mother. The baby begins to discover the differences between the male person and the female person. A mother is also helped if the father shares in the baby's care. It gives her a rest and it also helps her in the process of beginning to let the baby grow away from dependence on her. The mother may need to give encouragement to the father in taking over a routine such as play before bedtime or undressing or perhaps the bathing. When the father does this, it is important that the mother accept the father's way of doing things with the baby so that the two may be comfortable together and really enjoy the time they spend together.

Bathing the baby. Some babies have skin that is easily irritated by the acid in urine. Parents of such a baby must use special care to see that he or she is completely dry when diapers are changed

The baby is fascinated by "the baby" in the mirror.

and that the diapers are thoroughly rinsed. The baby may need to be rubbed with some kind of ointment. Each baby is a bit different.

In the first months the infant will often cry when being given a bath. A baby gets tired. He or she may not enjoy being disturbed this way at first. Later baby will enjoy the bath. Bath time may become the most fascinating part of the day. Babies splash with their arms and kick. Before the end of the first year, they are exploring many aspects of water and its wonderful properties.

Elimination. Each baby will have his or her own pattern of elimination. A baby may have several bowel movements a day or may have a movement only every two or three days. The stools of breast fed and bottle fed babies will be different in color and texture, too. Stools of babies change after they begin eating solid foods, and their patterns of eliminating will change then.

"Toilet training," as it is called, is not usually undertaken in the first year, so it will be discussed in a later chapter. We just accept the necessity of washing diapers every day or two when there is a baby in the house!

Clothing. Clothes for babies today are a simple matter. The baby will wear a diaper, a shirt, and a short wrapper of some kind. In colder weather a gown with a drawstring bottom may be worn. The clothes are usually of cotton material which is soft and easily washed. The popular cotton knits require no ironing.

The big item of laundry is the diapers. Soiled ones should be rinsed in the toilet and then put to soak in a diaper pail until washing time. Hot water and soap and plenty of rinsing will keep the diapers clean and soft. People used to think that diapers had to be boiled, but with the hot water possible in an automatic washing machine boiling is not considered necessary today.

Disposable diapers are useful when one is traveling or even away from home for a day. One does not need to carry wet or soiled diapers. Some communities have satisfactory diaper services. These services supply diapers with pickup and delivery service as required. Using the diaper service may be a help to the family, especially at times when the mother is ill or has extra responsibilities or when laundry facilities are not adequate. Disposable diapers or diaper service may seem expensive but may be a wise use of money under some circumstances.

Learning motor control. In the beginning the infant makes many random, uncoordinated movements. The baby wiggles all over when excited. The infant shakes with rage and her or his arms and legs wave. As the weeks pass, the movements gradually become less diffuse and less undifferentiated. Instead of merely being random they become more direct and purposeful. The baby turns her or his head toward the door when expecting a bottle. Arms wave. The baby is gaining control over body movements. Control proceeds in an orderly way. Some control is gained over arm movements, then hand and still later finger movements. The baby gains control over head movements before controlling leg movements. Infants can turn their heads early. When they are held, their heads need support for they wobble at first, but gradually they hold them up more firmly and turn them in the direction they wish. Much

By six or eight months, a child attempts to crawl.

later they draw their legs up under them and raise themselves off the floor or push themselves forward, scooting over the floor.

A baby not only has to learn what belongs to her or his body but also has to learn to control that body. Watch three- or four-month-old babies playing with their hands and fingers. They get them in front of their faces and move them around, fascinated by what they do. They may stick fingers into their mouths. It gives a baby a different feeling from sticking a toy into her or his mouth. The baby is finding out more about what is the "me" and the "not me" in the world.

We support babies' heads carefully when we pick them up, even at three months. But by this time they will raise their heads when they are held over a shoulder, and by the time they are four to six months old they can lift their heads and chests when they are placed on their stomachs. Their head and body control are good enough by six months so that they will be comfortable sitting with support. But posture will be better later if they do not do much sitting while their bones are still soft. They are better off lying on their stomachs raising their heads and strengthening their back muscles while they watch things.

By six or seven months babies can turn over. They should *never* be left on a bed without sides even when they are only three or four months old. By six or eight months, too, they may be attempting to crawl or creep.

By the time they are eight months old they can usually sit upright for a time without fatigue. They may soon pull themselves to standing positions and take steps with support.

The stretching and kicking and waving of arms which baby has been doing are exercises in preparation for standing and walking. Most children are walking by fifteen months. Then they are on their way! They are entering the toddler stage!

Learning to grasp objects is an important milestone in babies' development. Their own fingers will fascinate them for a long time. They began observing them at three or four months. At six or eight months they begin to use them. Watch them work to acquire skill in picking up objects. It is like the process that you go through in learning to play tennis or basketball. It takes lots and lots of practice to control the muscles and to develop the eye-hand coordination needed to make picking up an object or playing a complicated game like tennis a smooth and efficient process.

It is easy for us to reach out and pick up a small object. Notice how clumsy the baby is about it at first. Just reaching out and getting near the object is hard. The baby's hand lands near it but not on it. Sometimes in his or her efforts the object is pushed away rather than brought closer. When the baby does reach it, it is scooped up with the palm of the hand at first rather than with the thumb and fingers as we do.

Before babies are a year old they begin to use their thumbs, not just as something to suck, but as useful things for grasping. With the thumb and forefinger they develop a "pincer grip" which gets results and which will serve them the rest of their lives. It has taken weeks of practice. Now they reach for everything, the tiniest speck of dust or a bit of paper. They give themselves plenty of practice. We need to watch carefully—the object picked up usually goes into baby's mouth.

Babies must feel great satisfaction in being able to accomplish this feat of controlling their thumbs and fingers to get what they set out to get. How discouraging to them if someone always snatches the things away from them, with no appreciation of their achievement. They will continue to work at practicing this skill but the effort may seem less satisfying if they feel that people don't appreciate what they are trying to do. You may need to give a baby another object if you take something away.

Sucking and thumbsucking. Since babies need to do a lot of sucking, some babies may like a pacifier to suck on when they feel uncomfortable or restless. Sucking on a pacifier may mean they do less crying which makes them easier to live with. Some babies do a lot of thumbsucking. We are not sure why they differ in the amount of thumbsucking they do.

Children may suck a thumb when they are sleepy or tired or not feeling well. This comforts them. They need comfort for they are in a new, strange world. They may feel more safe and secure with a thumb in their mouth. Watch how a child confronted with a new person or an unexpected noise or a strange situation may put a finger into his or her mouth. As they grow older, they will feel safer and more confident. They may no longer need this kind of support.

In some cases a baby or an older child who sucks a thumb is having trouble feeling that the world is a good place, so the child

Boxer

Through play a child discovers
how things work.

C. Glassman

Boxer

By three years of age, a child
is ready to question the
discoveries he or she has made
about the world.

D. Funt

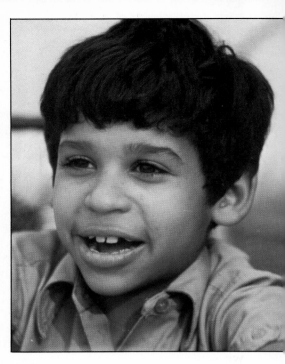

A healthy, happy child is a joy.

D. Funt

Children may suck a thumb
when they are sleepy, or
tired, or not feeling well.

retreats to the comfort of a thumb. He or she knows that the thumb can be depended upon. It is always available. It is easy to see that we only make matters worse for this kind of child if we pull the thumb out of her or his mouth or cover it so the child can't get to it. Sucking a thumb seems to be a natural safety valve which children use. It may do harm to deprive them of it.

It is better just to feel comfortable about letting infants suck if they want. We can try, too, to make sure that their world is really comfortable, without too much strain in it and with plenty of love and attention. When they are older, we can help them find other things to play with and other ways of finding satisfaction, so that they need their thumbs less and less. If children give up thumb-sucking before they are five or six years old, their teeth are not likely to be made crooked by their sucking. Thumbsucking may be a sign of emotional trouble in an older child, but is not apt to be serious for a toddler.

Often it is the children whose parents have fought with them over the habit who keep on sucking the longest and hardest. As we know, the toddler is trying hard to assert herself or himself and be independent. If someone tries to *make* a toddler take a thumb out of his or her mouth, the toddler may use this as the issue to take a stand on. A flag of independence is raised. The toddler insists on having his or her thumb.

One quiet little girl of three who sucked her thumb when she was tired or unhappy was taken to the dentist. The dentist happened to be one who tried to discourage any thumbsucking. He told her she must stop the "bad habit." Her mother kept reminding her when she saw the thumb go into the child's mouth. The child's answer was to keep the thumb in her mouth more and more of the time. As a quiet, timid child, she didn't feel brave enough to assert herself in many other ways, but she could defiantly suck her thumb. She did less thumbsucking when the family dropped the issue, leaving the matter up to her.

Our feelings about thumbsucking usually come from the feelings our parents had toward it. Our feelings may be especially strong if we happened to have been scolded by our parents for sucking our thumbs. If we had to try hard to overcome the habit, we aren't likely to enjoy seeing someone else thumbsucking contentedly!

Readiness and maturation. Learning things like grasping an object is more than just a matter of practice. It is a developmental matter, too. A baby or a young child gains control over her or his body because there are changes taking place in the muscles, the bones and the skeletal system, and the pathways in the nervous system which make it possible for the child to acquire the skill. The possibility of using the thumb in opposition to the fingers in a "pincer grip" appears as a child nears the end of the first year because of the child's physical development then. The body is "ready" for the child to learn to grasp objects. Every chance is seized to practice and perfect the skill.

We call this readiness *maturation.* Maturation means that growth has taken place which now makes it possible to do a thing, such as opposing the thumb and forefinger, that has been impossible before a certain level of development was reached. Doing the thing then becomes easily possible. It gives the child satisfaction to perfect this control over muscles.

Stair-climbing is a good example of a skill which depends on maturation. Most children are nearly four years old before they walk up and down stairs smoothly the way we do, one foot to a step. Before the maturation of this capacity (which depends on physical growth in the body), children use two feet to each stair step. The adult way of walking up and down stairs appears in a child not because of our efforts to teach the child, but because she or he has matured to the point where it is possible to do it this way easily.

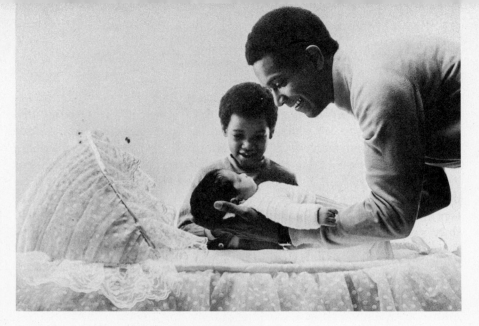

At first a baby knows people by their voices or
by the way they pick her or him up.

A child will usually practice those skills for which the child is developmentally ready. It helps a child to have opportunities to practice when he or she is ready. It is discouraging to a child to be urged to practice skills for which he or she is not ready, like trying to catch a ball when only two or three years old. The child likes to throw the ball but catching it is difficult. Left alone, with plenty of chance to do what he or she wishes, the child will usually work at what is most appropriate to learn at the time, from sucking to picking up things, to sitting alone, to standing and then walking and throwing balls.

Maturation, or the "readiness" to do a thing, and then a chance to practice doing it are what a child needs in developing motor skills. Satisfaction is found in exercising these skills as well as in our pleasure at seeing the child be successful. The child likes to know that we approve and are pleased with her or him. The child begins to feel good about herself or himself.

Social relationships. At first a baby knows people by the way they pick her or him up or by their voices. A baby's eyes do not focus well enough at first to see people as we do. But babies soon begin to know special people such as their mothers and fathers. They stop crying more readily in that person's arms or even when they hear his or her step.

By the end of the first two months a baby is beginning to smile. By the time a baby is three or four months old he or she usually smiles at a person who makes a friendly approach. Babies become more discriminating at five or six months. They show more pleasure in being greeted by people they know than by a strange face. Around eight or ten months they may even cry if a stranger approaches. This means they are realizing the significance of the differences between familiar people and ones strange to them. Later they will be friendlier and more interested in strange people.

Almost from the beginning babies begin to show their own individual patterns of making contacts with people. Some babies are very ready to smile and invite approaches. Others want to take their time with people. Some babies may be busy exploring so many other aspects of the world that they don't want to be bothered by attention except when it's needed. But most babies like attention and like to watch other people, especially children.

By the end of the first two months,
a baby is beginning to smile.

Most babies like attention and
like to watch other people.

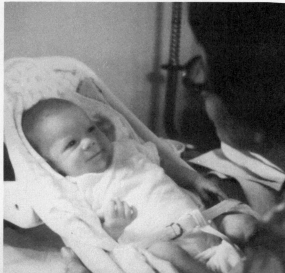

Play. Toward the end of the first year most babies have begun to enjoy simple games like "pat-a-cake" or having someone cover up a face and then reappear. Too much of this kind of play makes them tired and may lead to crying. Babies should be played with for only short periods of time. One of the best times for playing with a baby is while the baby is being bathed and dressed. Here is an opportunity for that extra bit of attention. It is good to allow time for splashing in the bath, for talking and singing while you bathe and dress the baby and while you are getting her or his cereal ready. It will be fun for both of you.

Things to Play With

Watch a baby and see what he or she plays with. A baby should have:

something that can be *safely put into the mouth and can be washed* and easily kept clean, such as a terry cloth animal;

something that is *hard* and feel good on the gums when the baby bites on it, such as a hard rubber teething ring;

something that is *soft* and feels good when the baby squeezes it and bangs it with her or his hands, such as a soft rubber doll;

something that is a *bright color*, such as colored plastic cubes;

something that *moves*, such as a mobile;

something that makes a *sound*, such as a rattle;

something that can be *grasped* in her or his hands, such as a small lid;

something *light in weight* without sharp edges or points.

At the end of twelve months. By the end of the first year, the baby has changed from an unknown and unknowing newcomer to an individual admired and admiring. The baby has progressed from a milk diet to one including some solid foods. Discoveries have been made about himself or herself—hands, toes, how to manipulate himself or herself to crawl and, perhaps, to take a few steps. The baby has discovered some things about the world—the security and affection of parents, the fun and play of brothers and sisters, that a smile gets a smile, and that crying also gets a response. The change and growth in a baby during the first year is amazing.

ACTIVITIES

TO DO AND DISCUSS

1 Visit a home where there is a baby. Before you visit, decide what you will want to observe and what you will want to ask the parents about the baby. Afterwards write a report of what you learned. Be sure to mention the age of the baby.
   a. What did you learn from your observations of the baby?
   b. What additional information did you obtain from the parents?
   c. How much control does this baby have over her or his body? hands? arms? legs?
   d. How does the baby respond to people? What are the differences in responses to familiar people and strangers?

2 Arrange to watch a parent as he or she gives a bath to a baby less than a year old. Describe what the baby does. What are the steps the parent takes in bathing and dressing the infant? List the things used at bath time.

3 Visit a baby who is being bottle fed; watch the parent prepare the bottle. Find out just how it is done. You may need to know about getting a bottle ready if you are taking care of a baby. Watch how the parent holds the baby when he or she gives the baby a bottle.

4 Make a list of some play materials which are safe, such as rubber rings. What makes these things safe? Observe a baby at play. Did the baby you observed have any playthings which seemed unsafe?

TO THINK AND WRITE ABOUT

1 What are five changes married couples can expect in their lives when their first baby is born?

2 What are some of the things a pregnant woman does to insure the best health for her child and for herself?

3 Which daily activities may a pregnant woman safely continue to do? What activities would better be suspended until after the baby is born?

4 What are some of the reasons that breast feeding of babies is recommended when it is possible?

5 How does the mother of a newborn baby make the baby feel that the world is a nice place?

6 Why is it important for a baby to live at home with a family rather than in an institution?

7 List at least ten ways in which a newborn baby is helpless and must depend on others.

8 What are some reasons babies cry? Why do some cry more than others?

9 What is a three-month-old baby like? a six-month-old baby? a twelve-month-old baby? What are some ways babies of each age show that they are individuals?

10 What differences have you observed in the way babies respond to your approaches to them? Does the same baby always respond in the same way to you? If not, what seems to make the response different at different times? For example, who is holding the baby at the time you approach her or him?

11 How do you feel about seeing a baby or a small child sucking a thumb? What do you remember about your own experiences in connection with thumbsucking? What differences in attitudes are there among members of the class?

REFERENCES

Carson, Ruth
Your New Baby
Public Affairs Pamphlet No. 353
New York: Public Affairs Committee, Inc.

Food for Your Baby's First Year
Leaflet for Parents
New York: Child Study Association of America (5 cents)

Lowenberg, Miriam
Feeding Your Baby and Child
New York: Pocket Books, Inc.

Spock, Benjamin
Baby and Child Care, Revised Edition
New York: Pocket Books, Inc.

Infant Care
Children's Bureau Publication No. (OCD) 73–15, 72 pp., 1973 (75 cents)
Washington, D. C.: U. S. Superintendent of Documents

Prenatal Care, Revised Edition
Children's Bureau Publication
Washington, D. C.: U. S. Superintendent of Documents

Winston, Shirley
The Premature Baby
Children's Bureau Publication No. 40, 9 pp., revised 1971 (40 cents)
Washington, D. C.: U. S. Superintendent of Documents

3

Children Who
Are One and
Two Years Old

After studying this chapter, you will be able to

1. Encourage a toddler's growing independence.
2. Accept the importance of a little child's play.
3. Help a child develop a favorable self-image.
4. Analyze the development of a one- or two-year-old.
5. Provide safe opportunities for a toddler to learn and succeed at his or her tasks.

The child who is one or two years old is beginning to learn about the world. The child is discovering he or she is a person, and it is important for the child to feel that he or she is a person of worth. Children have a strong urge to be independent, but they feel safe and are safe only when someone is near to care for them. They need discipline that is gentle but firm. They are learning to fit into a world of other individuals by talking, walking about, and acquiring some social customs.

Curiosity and play are very important to the toddlers' development. Exploring may lead them anywhere—they like to wander and to touch everything within reach. A wide variety of play experiences help to develop their muscular coordination, as well as providing the basis for future learning.

What Are Toddlers Like?

"I'm really somebody." The toddler presents us with a challenge. Caring for toddlers is a full-time job. They are active. They are learning to walk and do some things by themselves. He or she often says "No," which usually means that the toddler is trying to say, "I'm discovering I'm really somebody. I want to do things my way."

In spite of feeling they are somebody, they depend on us to protect them and keep them safe. We have to see that they don't fall into holes, get into the street, pinch their fingers in the door, or eat inedible things. We have to be very alert to keep up with them.

We need to help the toddler but we want to do it in such a way that we leave her or him with that wonderful feeling, "I'm really somebody!" This is a good feeling for anyone to have. We all do better when we feel we are "somebody." We want the toddler to keep the feeling that she or he can assert herself or himself and be somebody.

"I'm really somebody."

When we protect them, we want to be sure that we do it in such a way that toddlers do not feel afraid to try new things, or afraid to be wrong (this is a terrible way to feel), or do not feel that they are just little and worthless. We want them to keep the feeling that it is wonderful to explore on their own. We want them to find out how to do it safely, when to use help, and what the limits are. Young children aren't very "realistic" when they begin trotting around. It takes experience to learn about the world and what's in it.

The desire to be independent versus the need to be babied. Children have a strong desire to be independent. They may run the other way when we want them to come with us. They may refuse to put on shoes when we are trying to dress them. They may turn their heads away when we try to feed them.

It helps to remember that we can expect them to act like this many times. It is part of being a one- or two-year-old or even three or four. It has little to do with us or our methods of managing them. It is not the beginning of "bad" behavior. They have just learned that they *can* run away or refuse things. They are practicing their independence. Perhaps the shoe doesn't really need to go on just at this minute. We can wait. Five minutes later the child is delighted to put the shoe on — provided we have not been too insistent the first time.

We can wait with the spoonful of food when the child turns away. The last mouthful may not be completely down. There is just not room. Maybe this is a child who likes to take his or her time and we are hurrying matters. Maybe the toddler has really had enough. Forcing the child only makes her or him more resistant and the child will eat less rather than more. After all the child is the authority on how much she or he needs to eat. We do well to accept this decision and not push. Giving a two-year-old many chances to be independent and to make the decisions which he or she is able to make encourages healthy personality growth.

Watch a toddler run away from her parents. She runs a little way and then turns and looks back. If her mother or father waits and smiles reassuringly, the child may run happily back into her parent's arms. She is learning that it is all right to go away on her own. She is learning that her parents feel all right about it. A wonderful bit of learning!

Toddlers are independent at times but are often babies, too. In the process of growing up they need to be free to retreat to babyhood when they find the world a bit too frightening without feeling ashamed of acting this way. They may hang on to their mothers' skirts and refuse to leave her in a strange place or they may cry bitterly when something startles them. Yet they are the same children who were climbing up high or pulling a wagonload of leaves or wearing a big cowboy hat a few minutes earlier. But now they want to be accepted as little just because they *feel* little.

We should approve of them when they act in grown-up ways, but we do not disapprove of them when they act like little children. In this way they can be comfortable about their ups and downs of feelings and become better able to manage *all* their feelings.

It is important for us to know how they feel because we are better able to help them when we understand. If they hide their feelings from us, they are showing us that they do not trust us or themselves as they should. If they are angry at us, for example, it is better for us to know it and better for them to tell us directly. Anger is hard to bear alone. We will talk more about this later on.

Children like to take their time. The child needs *time*. When he goes walking, he really strolls — if he isn't running! He stops to touch the fire hydrant and feel its knobs or pick up a stone and then drop it for the next one. He stands and watches. Sometimes it is hard to figure out which way he wants to go. He really enjoys a walk when he can go at his own rate. We can't always go at this rate, of course, but he is entitled to do it whenever it is possible.

She is learning that
it is all right to
go away on her own.

Toddlers are independent at times, but they are often babies, too.

Having to hurry makes a child irritable for he or she sees no purpose in it. Only later can the child understand about being "on time." It makes no sense to a child at this age. He or she is busy learning about other things. Children want time to play with the crackly leaf or the crumbling clod of dirt and poke their fingers into the cracks as they walk along. We will enjoy giving them this time if we appreciate how important it is to their development. They are laying foundations for understanding and living.

The magic of distraction. When parents manage the toddler's wandering, exploratory gestures in an understanding way, they satisfy the urge to test out her or his independence. During a walk, the child may then become interested in a bright flower or a stick along the way, thoroughly exploring this fascinating object. It becomes a scientific adventure. The objective of the walk has taken a different form. This change suggests an important principle in guidance —the magic of distraction.

Young children are easily distracted. They may be sobbing one minute because they can't have a shiny pair of scissors, but their tears stop and a smile breaks through at the sight of a shiny lid from a cottage cheese carton which can be set spinning. If one can't have one thing, there is often another. The world is still a good place.

It seldom gets us anywhere to beat our heads against a stone wall, as the saying goes. If we keep insisting, "No, you can't have the scissors," the child will be unhappy. She or he may become less likely to want things—a pretty unfortunate way for anyone to feel. With a little imagination and resourcefulness, we can usually think of something to substitute or some way to distract the child and make life livable again for all of us. We are helping the child, too, with an important step in personality growth. Everyone has to learn to live within some limits and feel *comfortable* about doing it.

Play makes children healthy. The children of this age need plenty of time and opportunity to play. Play keeps them healthy. It may sound strange, but play is essential for a child's health.

At this age, they will usually need to play near us or keep in touch with us, reassured by a smile or a word and knowing that we feel interest and pleasure in what is happening and that we can be depended on to see that all goes well. They need this if they are to play freely. Notice how much more freely some children play than others.

Play is a way of feeling big even when one is still little. It is a way of making things happen as one wants, quite different from the world the child lives in. It is a way of overcoming fears. For example, the child can make things disappear and reappear in play by covering them up and then uncovering them. The child grows less afraid that people will leave her or him. Play is a way of anticipating things and getting prepared, trying to understand what it is like to be a mother or a father or a doctor or a policeman. In play the child can act as if she or he were these people and feel bigger.

Toddlers like mud and sand.

Although the interest spans of two-year-olds are usually short, children will be satisfied to play in water for long periods of time.

Play is a way of learning what all kinds of things are like, and how one solves the problems they present; for example, how to keep the tower of blocks from toppling over, or how to build the bridge, or fill the hole. It is absorbing business and the child needs plenty of time to lay a good foundation. The child creates through play, stretches the imagination and brings fantasies in touch with the real world through play.

Children do not need many playthings. They play best with just a few things at this age. They repeat things over and over. They are mastering their world. Although their interest spans are usually short at two, they will be satisfied to play in water for long periods of time. They like mud and sand and sticks and stones and pans and perhaps something to serve as a doll. Simple activities entertain them, repeated over and over. They watch moving objects and people. They listen to sounds and make some themselves. They try to pick up tiny objects. They examine every article they find. They are two and are discovering the world in their own ways.

Two-year-olds enjoy the company of other children. They like to play near others, but they tend to treat other children like objects, pushing them down or out of the way. They take things from each other and seem surprised if the response is tears. They are learning that children are not like adults. When two-year-olds play together, they need some adult supervision.

Attitudes And Developmental Tasks

"What's it all about? Who am I?" the child wonders. What is the answer? Will the child find he or she is a person who manages pretty well, who can discover, who lives in an interesting world, who can depend on people and yet is not being interfered with all the time? Or is the answer—a person who is always in trouble, who lives in the kind of world that is always hurting one, who lives with people who are always interfering and do not comfort one or keep one safe?

Attitudes are learned early. Attitudes toward herself or himself and the world are among the most important things that the toddler learns. Out of all the many experiences in these first years of rapid growth, the child builds up ideas about the kind of person he or she is, about what others are like, and about what he or she can expect in the world.

If fortunate, a child learns to feel that he or she is an important person, a lovable person, a successful person; one who can explore and discover, enjoy and create; one who can have things and do things. In other words, the child develops self-confidence and self-respect. These attitudes grow out of experiences of being treated with respect from the beginning. Of course she or he will have many kinds of experiences, but it is important that the largest number of these experiences be the kind that help the child feel confidence in herself or himself and trust in the people around her or him.

A mother was talking about her daughter who was attending college. The daughter was having real trouble because she thought that she could not do anything successfully. She would sit and look at her books and try to study, but she always thought, "I'm just stupid. I can't learn. I always fail. Other people are so much better."

As she talked, this mother began to remember certain things. She remembered that when the girl was quite small, she had been given a tricycle. It was really too big for her. The family lived in the country where there was no sidewalk. Her parents tried to teach her to ride the tricycle but it would tip over. She couldn't make it go. She would cry and try pushing it around, but she was told that wasn't the right way. Her older brother laughed at her. He could

It is important that most experiences be the kind that help children feel confidence in themselves and trust in the people around them.

ride it easily. This girl finally learned to ride the tricycle, but, unfortunately, she developed some ideas about herself. She learned to feel that, regardless of how hard she tried, she would fail, even when she wanted very much to feel big and to please her parents.

Probably many other things like this had happened to this girl as she was growing up. The ideas she built up about herself did not happen to be true in many respects. She really was not stupid. She did not need to fail, but because of her early experiences, she felt convinced that her efforts could lead only to failure. Later she did change her attitudes about herself. She was able to build a different "image" of herself, but only after someone else had helped her see more clearly what things had really been like for her. And she had been pretty unhappy and discouraged for a good many years.

Attitudes about the kind of person one is are learned early in life. Many experiences of failing to please one's parents or of failing to get approval result in handicapping attitudes about oneself, as with the girl who found it so difficult to ride her tricycle. She could not trust herself to be successful in anything.

You may have seen a child who seems to feel that the only way to get attention and feel important is to act silly and make people laugh. Perhaps he is really a quiet, timid child who never received much notice. One day he happened to put his father's hat on backwards. To his great delight everyone laughed. No one had paid attention when he succeeded in opening a door by himself or in building a big tower. No one seemed to value the things that were important to him. From the response of other people he learned that one gets attention by showing off, so he continues to try it. But he does not get the satisfaction he should.

We all need attention, especially when we are young. You may know a child who has found that the best way to get attention is to be noisy and disturbing, forcing people to notice him or her. Another child may be very quiet, seeking attention by climbing into the adult's lap and sitting. If this child is a slow-moving, placid child, he or she may be content in doing this. If this child is an active, impulsive child, he or she may do this only because of being unhappy. These children have found different ways of coping with the problem of finding attention and approval, but not all the ways are healthy ways of finding one's place in the world.

Attitudes and patterns of eating. "By two years of age many children can do a pretty complete feeding job, if not a neat one." (*Your Child from One to Six,* p. 11.) They are far less messy than they were earlier. They still use their fingers a good deal. They still play with food in a purposeful way to find out more about it, such as its texture or temperature.

If they are fed toward the end of the meal, two-year-olds may eat more. But we need to be sure that we do not try to get them to take more than they want. The rule is *no urging or coaxing.* The extra mouthful gained this way may be more than lost if it lessens the appetite or gives a distaste for the food or builds a resistance to eating. Remember two-year-olds have a strong urge to be independent and to resist pressure! Relax and let them be the judge of the amounts of food they need.

Our part as adults is to serve simple, attractive, well-balanced meals to the child under comfortable conditions. This means a chair which fits the child, with a support on which the feet can rest if they do not reach the floor. It means a spoon, a fork, and a glass the child can hold easily. It also means avoiding issues about eating. Appetites fluctuate in young children. They may eat a lot one day and want very little on another day. We need to let the child be the judge of how much is wanted at any meal. Likes and dislikes change, too, and there are big individual differences here. Some children are eager to taste new foods while others are very conservative. They stick to the familiar and only slowly learn to enjoy new tastes. Some children go on food "jags," eating a lot of one food day after day until they are satisfied. Wise parents accept most of these individual idiosyncrasies. They know there are many ways of getting the nutrients one needs. If a child dislikes one food, they serve another he or she likes which has about the same food value.

(Top) Many finger foods are easy for
a child to eat.

(Right) By two years of age, many children can do
a pretty complete feeding job, if not a neat one.

(Bottom) Parents are not too concerned with
table manners at this age.

While they do not cater to the child's preferences alone, the parents try to serve some of the foods he or she likes. Many finger foods are easy for the child to eat—carrot sticks, raw cauliflowerlets or broccoli, strips of celery or turnips, apple slices, meat in bite-sized pieces.

Appetite is related to growth spurts and becomes more stable with age. Acceptance of a variety of foods becomes easier with experience. A healthy child enjoys eating. While individual differences are present in what is preferred, the child learns to like an increasing number of the foods which are served unless there are issues about foods, or the child has examples of finicky adults to imitate.

Some children satisfy their hunger by drinking a lot of milk so that they eat less of other foods which they need. In this case it may be necessary to limit the amount of milk they drink before they have eaten other foods. On the other hand, if the child drinks only a small amount of milk his parents will serve milk in other forms such as custard, ice cream, or by adding powdered milk to other foods to make sure the child is getting a quart every day. Sweets or rich foods which take away the appetite are avoided. Desserts are usually fruits or custards. Parents are not too concerned with manners in eating at this age. They give the child time to master the whole process of eating at a table, using implements some of the time, and learning to like a variety of wholesome foods.

Learning to talk. The two-year-old is learning to talk. He or she has been making speech sounds since only a few months old. Babbling and vocalization precede using these sounds as speech to communicate wishes.

Progress in learning to talk depends on hearing speech. We mentioned earlier the importance of talking as we care for a baby so that she or he is familiar with the sound of voices and patterns of communication. Most two-year-olds love the sound of words and repeat them over and over. They practice talking. They are pleased with any success in using speech to get what they want. We need to pay attention when they try to communicate something to us in words. Our response and our approval are important in encouraging them to learn to use language.

The two-year-old loves simple stories of a few sentences— repeated—about what he or she did. Try making up one about what

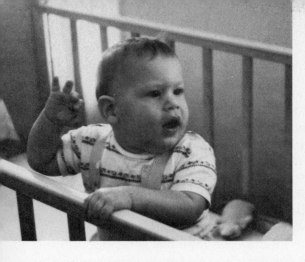

The two-year-old is learning to talk.

the child did. Repeat it as you are dressing him or her. Tell the child in simple words what is going to happen:

> "Bobby is getting dressed now—first his shirt—now his pants—now his socks, one on this foot, one on the other foot—next his shoes, one for this foot, and one for that foot—then his sweater, over his head."

In this way the child learns about language and how to use it this way. The child learns how things are put into words.

Here again there are individual differences. Some children enjoy sounds of words more than do others. They are fascinated by almost anything they hear. They listen for quite a long time. Other children will not listen as long. But they all need to *hear* speech if they are to develop well in using language. It will help if we speak slowly so that they can understand more easily.

It is important to learn good patterns of speech. People are handicapped if they use incorrect grammar and speak in harsh, unpleasant voices. These habits are hard to change, so we need to be careful to set an example in using correct grammar, enunciating distinctly, and watching the quality of our voices. The child is a great imitator. He will copy our speech habits.

We give the two-year-old plenty of opportunites to use speech, but we do not call attention to the child's mistakes. We know the child will learn correct speech in time if he or she hears it. Correcting the child, trying to make the child repeat words, may only interfere with learning. If speech does not develop, the reason may be in conditions such as defective hearing or slow mental growth or even an emotional blocking in growth. These conditions require special treatment.

Toilet training. *Learning to control elimination is a step toward independence.* For a child at this age, learning to follow the customs of adults in the use of the toilet is a real accomplishment.

Some parents take pride in seeing how early they can "train" a child to stay "dry" or "clean." We know now that while this may be convenient for the parent, it may not be good for the child. A wise parent will usually wait until after the child is walking before starting her or his toilet training. Parents may try to "catch" a bowel movement much earlier than this if the child's movements come at a regular time, but this is a matter of convenience for the parents.

The child needs help in learning to use the toilet properly, but the child needs the right kind of help. Just responding to the contact of a cool potty on a warm bottom is a passive process in learning. It is an active kind of learning when the child uses the potty by his or her own choice, doing something which the child knows pleases others. There is real satisfaction for the child in developing this kind of control. It is worth waiting for. With automatic washing machines and dryers and disposable diapers it is easier for mothers to wait.

Toilet training can be a step for the child in becoming more responsible and more grown-up and independent. Since being independent is an important step in development, we want to protect the child in this feeling.

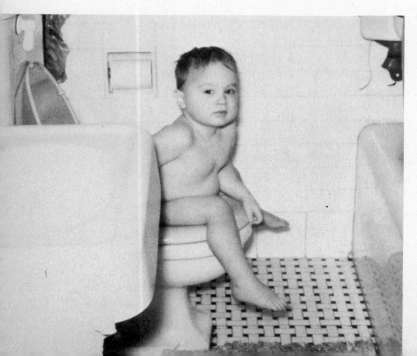

For a child at this age, learning to follow adult customs in the use of the toilet is a real accomplishment.

A child gives signs of readiness to learn control. One sign is that the intervals between wetting are longer. Another sign is the interest the child shows in the toilet habits of the people he or she lives with. The child may suddenly get interested in the bathroom, coming in to play or watch family members there.

Now is the time to have a potty chair or toilet seat available. Children who are afraid of a flushing toilet may find it easier to sit on a chair of their own. Other children like trying the regular toilet seat, especially if there is a solid place, such as a box or step, to rest their feet so they do not feel any danger of falling in. Children will often sit with no results at first, but in sitting on the toilet for even a minute or two they become familiar with the process. When they get the idea, they will be successful in imitating adults here as they do in so many other ways. If they resist, they should not be forced. Forcing children to sit on the seat may build up their resistance to the whole idea. It delays sound learning.

Some children seem to take on toilet habits easily and fairly early. Others are not ready for this learning until much later. The majority of children are ready to learn somewhere between 18 and 27 months, but the timetable is flexible. Some children take only a few days and some children take several months before they can be relied upon to be dry most of the time. Probably a good deal depends on the children's own development in motor control along with their confidence that they can do what others expect of them. Perhaps just as much depends on us and our confidence that they will learn when they are ready.

There are a few general procedures parents should follow in toilet training, but if they have been matter-of-fact about the child's elimination, have changed diapers with no fuss about the messes made, the child should have no special problem in learning to stay dry and clean when ready.

When the child is successful in urinating in the proper place, he or she needs plenty of approval. It *is* an achievement! We should show our pride and pleasure. But we can expect plenty of failures, too. When the child wets or soils, we should never scold or shame him or her. If we do, the child may completely lose confidence in his or her ability or come to dislike the whole process. It is enough to say hopefully, as we change the pants, "Next time you can use the toilet."

At first it is the adult who needs to be responsible for seeing that the child gets to the toilet. We can say, "Time to go to the toilet. Let's run inside." Saying something such as "Which way shall we go?" or "You *are* a big person now," to make the idea attractive will help. It is up to us to be responsible and to use all the skill we have in helping the child be successful. We should approve every success.

We need to be careful about praise, however. Praise that is out of proportion to the effort may make a child anxious. Failure may seem too serious to accept comfortably. The child is almost sure to fail many times.

It is better to take off diapers and use training pants when the child seems ready to learn. His or her clothes should be easy to slip off—for the child's sake and ours. Children may come running to us in a hurry and we need to be able to hurry. We must help children keep dry if they are to learn. By taking off diapers and putting on pants we are showing confidence in children's ability to learn. Diapers are a symbol of babyhood. When clothes are easy to manage children are likely soon to use the toilet without adult help and to enjoy being independent and feeling grown-up.

If children come and tell us they have already wet, we can take that as a sign that they are at least getting the point. We should take them to the toilet and see if they can "finish" in the right place and be pleased about it if they do. In time they will learn to come and tell us *before* they have wet.

Accidents are likely to happen when children are under the strain of a new experience like starting Sunday school or nursery school, or if they are excited by having visitors or sick or even afraid. But these lapses will get fewer with time. Successful toilet training is an important milestone in development. But we should not be in a hurry to reach it. The child should set the timetable and we should be content to help him or her.

Successful learning here helps the child with the feeling that she or he is really "somebody" in this world.

A child cannot learn everything at once. A very young child is finding out what he or she is like, what other people are like, and what the world is like. But a child cannot learn everything at once.

Children feel more confidence if we try to help them learn those things which are understandable to them, and which they

Children gain confidence when we help them learn those things that they are able to understand and learn most easily at their stage of development.

are able to learn most easily at their stage of development. They need to find the world manageable. We need to trust their capacity to learn the necessary lessons with time.

For example, we do not expect a two-year-old to remember to say "please" and "thank you." Two-year-olds are only vaguely aware of relationships among people. They are mostly concerned about themselves. We can help children by using the words ourselves, by saying them for children at appropriate times, and much later by letting them know when these words are expected of them. We can give them approval when they do use them properly. In this way we help children with successful learning. They feel competent. Insisting on the child's using these words when they are meaningless to him or her may confuse the child. A child may say, "I said 'please' so you *must* give it to me." These words seem to have magic powers to this small child.

Proper table manners is another example of behavior that is learned step by step.

Learning table manners is another example of behavior which is learned step by step. At first children are concentrating on getting food into their mouths. This is an achievement. They use their fingers instead of spoons or forks when it is too hard to use the implements. They can feel quite discouraged if we expect good manners from them at this stage. Expecting too much may make them less likely to be successful later.

There are many lessons to be learned about property rights and sharing, too. The two-year-old girl or boy is finding out that some things are hers or his and some things are not. They belong to others. The child is learning to possess. "Mine! Mine!" he or she cries. It is difficult and often confusing to master the concepts of property rights.

The two-year-old must learn something about possessing before being ready to learn about sharing. A neighbor comes in with a child, and the parent takes the child's toy and gives it to the visitor. The child snatches it back, not because of being selfish, but because it seems part of him or her. It is *his* or *hers,* which means the child can have it. A wise parent proceeds with care here. The parent does not insist on the child sharing at this age. The parent may help the child give a less treasured toy to the visitor. This is a good compromise and represents progress. When the child enjoys playing with other children, he or she really may want to share toys with them.

There are many lessons to be learned about property rights and sharing.

The child is not ready to do much sharing, not only because of learning that things belong to him or her, but also because the child has not reached the stage of being concerned about the needs of others. He or she is still pretty much wrapped up in himself or herself and in the business of asserting himself or herself. Gradually the child will discover other people and be interested in a relationship with them. The child will *want* to give to them, and this feeling is the basis for sharing. Until the child has this feeling, she or he may learn the wrong things if we push the child into giving up toys when she or he is unwilling.

There are other situations in which we build the child's confidence and self-respect or weaken them. The child faces another big lesson in dealing with frustration and angry feelings. The toddler is little and often feels helpless and hopeless in trying to make things happen as she or he wants them to happen. Frustration leads to anger or even depression. The child must live with these difficult feelings and not feel too overwhelmed by them. All of us know this is not an easy task even for an older person. The little child is helped in this task if we are calm and reassuring, and give him or her the confidence that even these feelings can be managed. The child must have confidence that he or she will be accepted as is, with all the less lovable parts of him or her, accepted as a person who at times feels angry or resentful or afraid. The child must have some assurance that we can and will help manage these kinds of feelings.

Taking Care of a Toddler

When we are taking care of the one- or two-year-old, we usually feel ready for a rest ourselves when she or he falls asleep. Fortunately the toddler takes naps. But when awake, the toddler is likely to be into things constantly so that if he or she is quiet we know that we had better find out what's up. The child may be into the soap powder or pulling towels off the shelf or putting the latest magazine into the toilet. It is useless to scold or punish for the toddler usually is not sure what the scolding is about. We have to be the person responsible for keeping her or him within safe and acceptable limits. In doing this we are helping the child learn what the limits are.

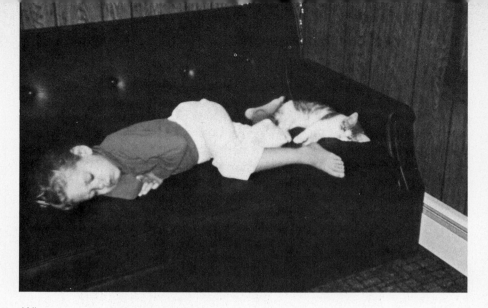

When we are taking care of the one- or two-year-old,
we usually feel ready for a rest ourselves after she or he falls asleep.

We must watch the child if there is no fence to keep him or her out of the street. We must put away the things that should not be touched or be there to say "No" and give the toddler something he or she *can* touch. The child's strongest urges are to touch and explore. By touching the toddler finds out what things are like and what one can do with them. We have to learn to work *with* these urges, not to disapprove of them.

Toddlers learn from every experience. They may run down a slope and fall. We comfort them if they want to be comforted. Sometimes comfort isn't necessary for they get right up and go on. When we do comfort them, we don't act as though a fall was a "major calamity," something to be frightened about. We just give them some extra loving, take care of the scratches, and send them on their way. Next time, we may take their hands and walk down the slope with them saying, "Walk slowly."

Taking a child's hand and *walking* down the slope with her or him, then letting the child go as fast as she or he likes up the slope will help the child learn how to manage on hills. Much later, the toddler will learn more things about inclines and forces. Now the child is learning how to manage on a slope with *confidence*. Beginnings are always important and especially those in the development of a personality.

Personality traits develop in these simple, early experiences. Self-confidence for the toddler grows out of being able to manage on a slope which seems steep to her or him. It grows out of success in exploring something new or climbing over an obstacle or even in saying "No." The toddler does not develop confidence if he or she experiences more failure than success. In the way we care for the child, we are helping him or her build healthy personality traits, as well as keeping the child physically safe.

The toddler is fortunate if there are a lot of things to touch and to feel and to find out about, simple things that can be grasped both with the hands and the mind. The child likes playing with the pans from the kitchen cupboard, for example, fitting lids on over and over again. The toddler practices skills. Sizes, shapes, and form relationships are explored. The child squeezes things. He or she crumples and tears things like paper. The child is learning about materials—the soft, the hard—about differences in texture. Some things tear and some things don't. The toddler often puts things into her or his mouth. We have to watch to see that harmful things are not popped in. The child is testing things out in all kinds of ways, not only by touch but also by taste and sound. What is this world really like?

This child is learning how to manage on a slope with confidence.

A child likes to play with pans from the kitchen cupboard.

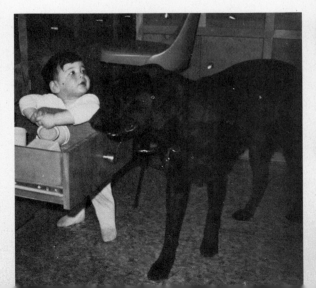

Never threaten to leave a child. Because young children are really dependent on adults, children need to feel sure that they can find them or reach them whenever they need to. There is no worse panic for children than to feel that they are lost, that their parents or other persons caring for them have abandoned them. It terrifies them because children know they are helpless without adults. It is cruel to say, "I'll go away and leave you," as a threat to get children to do what we want them to do. We hear thoughtless people say this, but it does real damage to the children even though it may get results for the adults.

A parent can say, "It's time to go now," (or whatever the parent intends to have the child do) and take steps to see that the toddler does what is asked, but a thoughtful parent never threatens to leave a child. The threat may make the child stop trying to be independent. The toddler may become very anxious and this is unfortunate for the child.

Let the child know when you must leave. A child is usually content as long as he or she is sure a parent is near. Wise parents never go away without telling the child they are leaving. The toddler may cry. He or she may not like having the parents leave, but the child will recover and will come to trust the parents. If the parents slip away without letting the child know, she or he is likely to grow anxious even when parents are around for fear they might leave, not knowing when they might. The child doesn't trust and may grow more dependent.

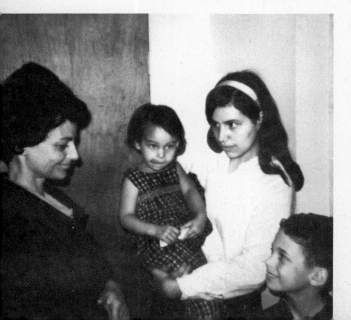

Wise parents never go away without telling a child they are leaving.

The child who has been left many times by his or her parents is often a child who finds it difficult to have them leave. The child has had too many of these experiences, too early, before enough trust in himself or herself was built up. Or, a child who has been left many times may become almost too eager to make friends and to reassure himself or herself about being safe. The child is *too* dependent on pleasing others and ignores his or her own wishes. The child goes from one person to another without the depth and closeness of feeling which are good for all of us to have with the most important people in our lives.

What about discipline? Our approach to discipline should be consistent. The steps we take to remedy any situation should occur every time that situation or a similar one arises. There are beginning steps which we should use to help a child learn to control her or his actions and make them acceptable to us. What approach should be used and what steps should be taken to establish sound discipline?

When a toddler hits another child, for example, what should we do? The first thing is to stop the hitting, of course. We don't permit a child to keep on hitting. We don't punish them, however, for they won't understand why at this stage. They may think we don't like *them*, which will only make them feel more like hitting other children!

We may help by trying to show them how to touch the other child gently. Hitting is often a way of making social contact and toddlers may be fascinated by the noise they can evoke by hitting another child—like a live music box which responds to a punch. They can learn to make a contact less roughly and therefore more acceptably.

We may help them say the other child's name so they can learn to use words instead of blows as a way of being social.

We stop children firmly and then we show them what to do—patting or speaking or offering something or just turning back to their own business. When they use the acceptable method of managing themselves, we approve, "Fine." We have helped them with the right kind of learning and shown our approval of their success in learning. The process will need to be repeated many times before it is fully learned.

If we ourselves are really good at forestalling things, we may be able to stop the child *before* she or he hits, saying "No" as we do it. This is the effective time to say "No," before, and not after the deed. We want her or him to learn to stop *before* hitting, not afterwards.

Now look at another kind of situation. Suppose the child starts to run into the street. We bring him or her back with a firm, "No," and show the child something to do which may be interesting to him or her. But suppose the child heads for the street again. We must *do* something about the matter.

A good thing to do is to take the child into the house and close the door, telling him or her to play inside because he or she has not stayed in the play yard or on the sidewalk. The child is likely to be very mad at us. A toddler may lie on the floor and kick and cry. We don't get mad in return. We remain pleasantly neutral, but we may state the problem clearly for the child, again, "When you are outside, you *must* stay on the sidewalk or in the yard." It is the child's problem, and the child has to face it and suffer the consequences. It does not hurt a child to cry. We can bear his or her anger. We do not need to be upset about it.

When the toddler calms down, we should be friendly and make her or him comfortable. We want the child to *accept* the limit, not resent it. If the child is quite young, there is no need to keep her or him inside for a long time since a short time seems long to a child, but we *make sure that the child stays in for a time.*

When the child goes outside again we keep a close watch. He or she may go toward the street again. If he or she does, it does not mean that the discipline is no good. It only means that the child is testing out conclusions as any scientist would do! It's important that the *same* result happen, a firm "No" and immediate removal to the house in spite of protest. You are big enough to carry a two-year-old even if he or she is kicking and screaming.

If you are firm and sure in what you do, the lesson is clear and the child should learn it quickly. You can leave the learning to the child. Threats or attempts to frighten may only make the child confused. A toddler may learn all kinds of things that are not true—that streets are always dangerous or that cars are sure to hurt him or her—which may give the child nightmares but may not keep him or her out of the street.

C. Glassman

Aukema

Derfus

Varied activities, including riding a tricycle, cutting out cookies, and dressing up in costumes, help children learn about the world in which they live.

Derfus

Playground equipment should be simple, sturdy, and safe for young children.

This toddler enjoys splashing in the water, but needs to be watched very carefully, even though the water is not deep.

Lee

Sometimes spanking works, but we know that often a child learns the wrong things from it, things we didn't intend, like "people hurt you" or "I'm bad," and is less clear about the real lesson which is simply, "You must stay on the sidewalk."

We want to be effective in discipline. To be effective we must say and do what will be clear and make sense to the child. The trouble with using spanking in such a case is that being spanked really has nothing to do with the problem. If we spank the child, he or she may feel quite right in being mad at *us*. The child thus avoids facing the real problem and the responsibility for managing his or her impulses. Spanking only muddles the learning. The child learns from facing reasonable consequences of an act rather than from punishment.

Growing Intellectually

There is a great deal of evidence today that even two-year-olds need a variety of experiences in order to grow intellectually. Learning to use words helps them grow in this way, but they also need experiences to talk about. They need to become familiar with a variety of objects and to watch a variety of events if their mental capacities are to develop. Experiences nourish their minds. They give children the raw material for thinking, wondering, talking, and thus growing intellectually. Taking them on walks or for rides where there are new things to see, giving them time to watch, talking in simple language about the object or about what is happening are important for children.

Two-year-olds are also ready to be introduced to the world of books. Select picture books with bright colors and only a sentence or two of text on a page. The pictures and text should be about things with which they are familiar, such as animals, everyday objects, everyday experiences, and children. A book will help them learn by reinforcing their discoveries about the world. An enjoyment of books opens the door to many kinds of learning.

If they are interested in sounds and rhythm, they may especially enjoy the language of poetry. Not only nursery rhymes but also simple, lovely poems which they may not understand but which they can enjoy because of the sound and the rhythmic language will open doors for future satisfying experiences.

Two-year-olds are ready
to be introduced to the
world of books.

Music offers another experience in hearing sounds. A child of this age enjoys listening to singing and instrumental music. He or she enjoys making sounds, high ones, low ones, soft or loud ones. A child enjoys songs we make up about what he or she is doing just as a child does such stories. Children need to hear a variety of good, simple music. When music accompanies rhythmic activities, they respond with special pleasure. Try singing to a child as you swing her or him. Notice how often a child's movements as she or he plays are in tune with the music which is being played at the time. All these experiences increase the child's awareness of sounds and his or her feeling for the rhythm of language itself. They develop the child's capacities.

A sense of humor is a help to everyone. There are already individual differences in two-year-olds. More things are funny to one two-year-old than to another. We can encourage them all, however, to laugh at some things, to play games that have an element of humor. Almost every two-year-old enjoys hiding and having someone find him or her—quite quickly—or finding the adult quickly. They all have enough experience to know that putting a hat over one's face instead of on one's head is funny.

We need to be sure that a child is not puzzled and bewildered or even frightened by something we see as funny. If it isn't funny to the *child*, it isn't funny. We should help the child understand what really happened. The big job for the child is to get things straight, understand them clearly, and not feel confused. It is not fun when people laugh at things that one doesn't understand. It only makes one feel little and helpless rather than independent and adequate. Part of growing is to understand better and to see things in a better perspective. It is good when we can laugh about some things.

The most significant thing that happens to the child one and two years old is to find that she or he is a person, that she or he is respected, and that she or he can feel good about being independent, and about exploring and discovering more and more about the world and the people in it, including, most important of all, herself or himself.

The most significant thing that happens to a one- or two-year-old is to discover that she or he is a person, that she or he is respected.

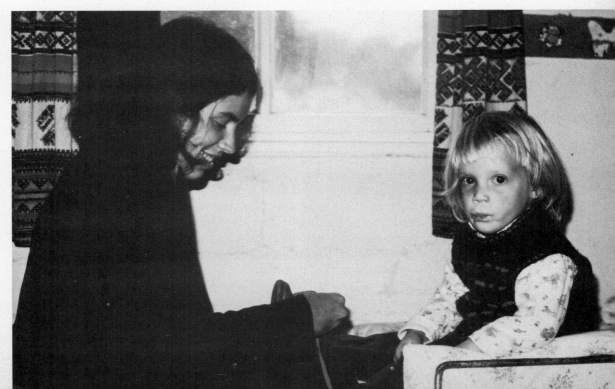

What We Know About Toddlers

We can summarize what we know about toddlers in this way:

1. *Physical development:* At two years of age some children are steady on their feet. They walk well, and enjoy walking. Others are unsteady and likely to fall. Their walking skills are less well developed.

The second and third years are still a period of rapid physical growth. The child's body is changing and she or he needs—and wants—plenty of chance for exercise. The child needs space to run and play both indoors and out.

Coordination of large muscles is developed through *climbing, pushing,* and *pulling* things, *riding* kiddy cars or a small tricycle, and *carrying* objects which are large (for him or her) and lightweight.

The finer muscles develop through activities such as these:

doing part of her or his *dressing,* putting on socks, shoes, pushing an arm into a sweater as we hold it for her or him.

hanging a jacket or coat on a low hook.

feeding himself or herself with fingers or with a spoon.

playing with blocks of different sizes and shapes.

manipulating toys, as wooden rings on a stand and simple puzzles.

2. *Social development:* The toddler is finding out that he or she is an *individual,* and it is essential for the child to feel valued, loved, and respected by the important people in his or her world.

Although the child urgently desires to be independent in some ways, adults are still needed for emotional support, encouragement, and care.

The child is learning to feed herself or himself, to like more foods, to control her or his elimination, and to talk. In accomplishing these things, the child is growing into the society in which she or he will live.

A toddler is learning about the world and his or her place in it as he or she begins to respond to people and their expectations for him or her.

3. *Play:* At this age, when play is so important to the child, a variety of experiences provides the foundation for future learnings. Play remains important to the child as a three- or four-year-old, but at two he or she has begun all the significant approaches to learning. The child is curious and tries to find out. We make sure she or he is safe and let the child go ahead and discover. We help with words, the tools for thought and communication. We see that the child has opportunities for many different play and exploration experiences.

Here are some things to remember when selecting play materials for a child of this age. Choose:

Things that *feel* different.

Things that can be used *many ways*.

Things that a child can manipulate successfully *by herself or himself*.

Things that are *raw materials* such as water, sand, and mud.

Avoid:

Things with sharp edges or points.

Things that splinter.

Things that get broken easily.

Things that have only *one* use, such as mechanical toys.

ACTIVITIES

TO DO AND DISCUSS

1 Observe a toddler at home for 30 minutes.
   a. See if you can keep a record of the objects touched or looked at, the things that the child notices and seems interested in.
   b. What kinds of responses does the child make toward people?
   his or her parent   other grown-ups
   you   other children
   c. Describe what the child does in one ten-minute period at play. What do you think was learned in this time?

2 Plan one day's meals for a preschool child after you have read the section on food in *Your Child from One to Six,* Children's Bureau Publication No. 30, 1962, pages 66 to 71.

3 If you know a family with a preschool child, ask the parents to tell you what the child had to eat yesterday. Write it down and check the foods with the list on page 67 in *Your Child from One to Six.*

4 Prepare to discuss in class: What are children of one and two years like? How do they differ? Compare descriptions with other members of the class.

TO THINK AND WRITE ABOUT

1 How do parents help a one-year-old develop his or her intelligence?

2 Why is the parent of a two-year-old busier than might be the case with a child of any other age?

3 List some of the experiences which help a two-year-old develop self-confidence.

4 How may the parents of a two-year-old provide opportunities for learning?

5 Why is play the important work of little children?

6 Why is it important for children of all ages to have limits set for them? What kinds of limits should there be? What is the importance of enforcing these rules consistently? Do you think there should ever be exceptions to the limits or their enforcement?

7 What is the difference between discipline and punishment?

8 Why is it important that mealtimes be pleasant times?

REFERENCES

Food for the Preschool Child—Ages 13 Months to 6 Years
Leaflet for Parents
New York: Child Study Association of America (5 cents)

Keister, Mary Elizabeth
The "Good Life" for Infants and Toddlers
Washington, D. C.: National Association for the Education of Young Children, 1970

Lane, Mary B.
"An Infant Center"
Children Today, Vol. 2, No. 3, May–June, 1973

Spock, Benjamin
Baby and Child Care, Revised Edition
New York: Pocket Books, Inc.

Your Child from One to Six, Revised Edition
Children's Bureau Publication
Washington, D. C.: U. S. Superintendent of Documents

Children Who Are Three and Four Years Old

4

After studying this chapter, you will be able to

1. State the growth changes to expect in three- and four-year-olds.
2. Adjust a child's schedule to changing patterns of eating, sleeping, and eliminating.
3. Help a child develop a favorable ratio of dependence and independence.
4. Encourage a child to develop initiative.
5. Guide a child's growing sense of responsibility.

Children three and four years of age like to explore, to investigate, and to imagine. They like to pretend that they are mothers or daddies or doctors or cowboys or anyone else. They are now playing together in more purposeful ways. Their speech is more equal to the expression of their needs. Their feelings of anger or fear or joy are strong and are often strongly expressed, although they struggle to fit themselves into civilized patterns. When they misbehave, they feel uncomfortable and guilty, for they have the beginnings of a conscience. They are very much in need of firm but loving discipline. They are eager for attention and approval from adults and for contact with other children. We can see more clearly the unique personality patterns of each individual. Each one has begun the task of discovering what kind of place he or she may expect to have in the big world. Growth is taking place in all areas—physical, social, emotional, intellectual, and ethical.

Differences Among Children

Children of three or four look very different from one another. They behave differently and these differences are easy for us to observe.

Some of these differences are the result of all the things which have been part of living for each child through her or his prenatal months and the months since she or he was born. Each one has been surrounded by different sights and sounds. More important still, each has been surrounded by people who have behaved toward him in different ways and set different patterns for her or him as the child perceives and responds to the world. The child may speak English or Italian, for example, depending upon the people with whom she or he has lived. The child may be friendly or unfriendly, afraid of dogs or fond of them, depending on her or his experiences. The child is developing patterns of behavior for coping with difficulties. She or he is developing characteristic ways of reacting to situations.

Growth Changes in Three- and Four-Year-Olds

Let us look at some of the growth changes which have taken place in children of three or four. They look different from the toddler. They have changed in appearance from chubby babies to pre-school children. Their individual patterns of growth, whether they are slow growers or fast growers, for example, are pretty well established. In most cases, they will stay fairly constant throughout their childhood.

Children need a great deal of active play to exercise their growing muscles.

Children of three or four can dress themselves with very little help if they have the proper clothes.

Their legs are getting longer and straighter. They tend to be knock-kneed rather than bowlegged as they were at first. They still have potbellies. By the time they are four or five their feet are not growing as fast as they were earlier. A lot of muscle growth is taking place throughout their bodies. This means they need a great deal of active play to exercise these growing muscles. They tire quickly and recover quickly. Their bones are still soft and flexible. They get tired sitting in one position. They often do a lot of wiggling.

They need loose-fitting clothes which let them move freely. They need shoes which fit well. They need firm mattresses for sleeping and, when they sit down, chairs in which they can put their feet comfortably on the floor if they are to develop good postures.

They have gained skill and balance in walking and running even though they are not very graceful yet. By the time they are four they are usually walking up and down stairs in the grown-up way. They climb a great deal and try jumping from boxes and planks. Most children do not skip easily until they are five or six. Roller skating is also a five-year-old activity for most children.

Children of three or four can dress themselves with only a little help if they have the proper clothes. They cannot tie a bow knot yet. They will not be ready to learn to do it easily until they are six or seven. They can cut with scissors after a fashion, and they love to draw with a pencil or a crayon. They use their right or left hands consistently.

The preference for one hand over the other is usually established around twelve to eighteen months, although sometimes it is not established until the child is much older. We think now that it is wise to encourage the use of the right hand in ways such as passing an object so the child finds it easy to reach for it with the right hand. But we think it is *not* wise to force a child to use the right hand if the child persists in using the left. In some children changing hand preference leads to difficulties in learning and in speech.

The child of this age talks a lot and is adding words to his or her vocabulary rapidly. The muscles involved in speech do not always work together smoothly. The words tumble over each other and the child may stutter. The child just needs more practice and this is what he or she is getting. Our part is to listen and not to comment on his or her lack of skill.

We think it is not wise to force a child to use the right hand if the child persists in using the left.

The child of this age has learned to manage a spoon and fork pretty well but does not find it easy yet to use a knife for cutting. The child can pour from a pitcher if the pitcher is not too heavy.

The young child is far-sighted at this age, but may hold an object close to her or his eyes in order to make it look bigger. Spending much time looking at small things or doing close work at this age is undesirable. It may result in nearsightedness. Binocular vision (use of both eyes to focus on an object and perceive depth correctly) is not fully developed until the child is six or eight years old. A child younger than this will often misjudge distance in jumping. Reading puts more of a strain on her or him than on an older child. Print in books for even seven- or eight-year-old children should be large.

The child of three or four usually has all of the baby (deciduous) teeth, and the permanent teeth are developing in his or her jaw. The child should start visits to the dentist. Some tooth decay (dental caries) occurs with most children. Cavities in the baby teeth should be filled in order to keep the mouth in good condition and protect the permanent teeth.

Research has shown that tooth decay is less frequent where (1) the child's diet is well balanced with plenty of protective foods, (2) the sugar intake is reduced, and (3) there is a small amount of fluoride in the water.

Changes in Patterns of Eating, Sleeping, and Eliminating

Three- or four-year-olds follow the family meal schedule. They often need a snack between meals to restore their energy but they should not "piece" constantly or have a snack just before meals. Their appetites may be less than when they were toddlers. They are often unpredictable. They may eat a lot of one food and very little of another. They thrive best if nourishing food is put before them with little comment about the food, and they are free to eat what they want of it. They develop poor eating habits if their food whims are constantly catered to or they are urged to eat more than they wish. Plenty of active play will take care of their appetites. (See *Your Child from One to Six*, Children's Bureau Publication, No. 30, 1962, on foods and snacks, pp. 67–68.)

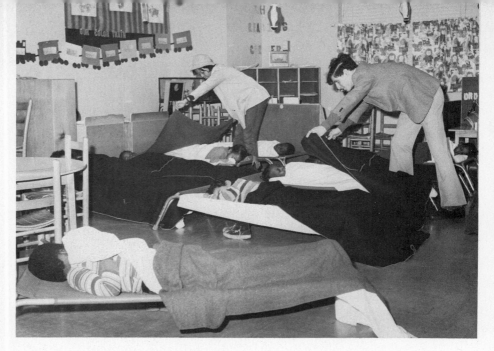

Most children take a nap, sometimes sleeping an hour or two.

Three- and four-year-olds continue to sleep about twelve hours a night and to need a rest during the day. Most children take a nap at least part of the time, sometimes sleeping an hour or two. Some do not take a nap, but only rest. Bedtime is usually accepted with less protest at this age. Each child will have his or her own routine and may still depend on a favorite toy or blanket at bedtime.

"Bad dreams" are common at this age and go along with the fears and the active imagination of the child at this stage. They may be connected with the struggle the child is having to control her or his "bad" impulses and become a civilized person. The child needs comfort and sympathy but not indulgence. The child should stay in his or her own bed.

Most children of this age have a reasonably good mastery of toilet habits. They are dry in the daytime most of the time, although they still may have toilet "accidents" when upset or excited. They are pretty dependable at night, too. The timetable for completing this learning varies with individual children. Unless circumstances are quite unfavorable, children learn these habits of control. We continue to be matter-of-fact in our attitude toward "mistakes" and try to build up their confidence in succeeding.

Tasks in Personality Growth

By three or four years of age the foundations for the child's personality are laid even though many changes may take place in the years ahead. Let us look at some of the personality characteristics which appear in children by this age.

Developing a feeling of trust. We have talked about the importance of helping the infant develop a sense of trust in the world. Developing trust is the first basic task in the development of a healthy personality. Infants learn to trust as they find that they will be fed when they are hungry, kept safe, and given attention when they want it. Through these experiences they begin to trust the world and its people and themselves. With a foundation of basic trust they are helped in meeting the disappointments and frustrations which are sure to come as they go on in life. Trust is the basis on which their religious faith will grow later.

If the infants' early experiences have satisfied them, their feelings of trust in others will be greater than their feelings of mistrust. If this kind of balance is not achieved, they may find the world a frightening place. We all know people who are suspicious of everyone, who always expect the worst and get very depressed over what would seem a trifle to someone else. They are the people who have not succeeded in developing a sufficient amount of trust over mistrust. We all may have moments of feeling like this, and we know how hard it is to live with these feelings.

Developing trust is the first basic task in the development of a healthy personality.

With a healthy personality the feelings of trust which were built up in the first year or two keep on growing. The child develops more trust in himself or herself through being able to cope with the experiences which come with living. Under favorable circumstances the three- or four-year-old child continues to strengthen and extend his or her feelings of trust in the world while also perceiving the world more realistically than he or she did as an infant.

Developing a feeling of independence. A child of three or four also continues to work on the task which was most important when she or he was in the toddler stage. The child was discovering then what it was like to be independent and no longer entirely dependent and helpless. Achieving a favorable ratio of independence and dependence is the second basic task in healthy personality growth. It is not simple to develop feelings of independence when one continues to be dependent on others, and the child must learn to balance the wish to be independent and the desire to be dependent. How well he or she succeeds in achieving this balance will influence the kind of adult he or she will become.

The changes which are part of the physical growth of children help them cope with this task. They are now able to use their bodies in ways which make it easier for them to be independent such as in walking, reaching, and climbing. They really can do things for themselves. We help them by seeing that they have clothes that they can manage themselves, for example, so that they can begin to dress themselves and use the toilet without help. We help them by

Achieving a good balance of independence and dependence is the second basic task in healthy personality growth.

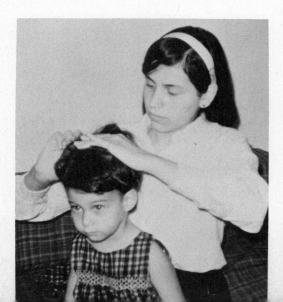

Three- and four-year-old children really can do things for themselves.

seeing that they have play materials that they can make into whatever they want without having to ask for help. We help them by keeping their things where they can get them and can also put them away easily.

Watch for signs of this urge to be independent in the children you observe or care for. Listen for words like, "Let me do it," or, "I can do it myself." Words like these show that there is a healthy balance of independent feelings in the child. If you often hear words such as, "I can't," or, "You do it for me," you may wonder whether this child has had enough chance to be independent in his or her own way and at his or her own rate. You will know that the child needs help in feeling that he or she *can* do things and that you value the child's being independent.

None of us can be entirely independent. In fact we wouldn't really want to be entirely independent. But it is often hard to have to depend on others when one wants to be independent, just as it is hard to have to be on our own when we would like to have someone to depend on. Things seldom work out for us in this respect just as we would like. The little child is really up against it here. A healthy amount of independence is hard for her or him to achieve because the child is little and there is much that cannot be managed on her or his own. It takes a large measure of trust on the child's part if healthy growth toward independence is to be achieved.

One child may seem to find it easy to move along the road toward being independent. Another child will have more difficulty and may keep retreating to the much easier stage of being like a baby and needing more help. This child may need encouragement if he or she is to become independent in a healthy way. There are individual differences in development here.

We sometimes fail to give a child the help that we might because of the way we feel ourselves. It may seem pleasant to have a child prefer sitting on our lap to playing with others. Of course it is nice to know that the child prefers us. But we may be making it easy for the child to remain a dependent person. He or she may even feel that it is good to please people by dependence.

Of course there are times when it may be all right to hold a child on our lap. The child may need, at the moment, the reassurance of feeling safe and loved. Being held in someone's lap replenishes his or her store of secure feelings. But it is a sign that all is not well with the child if he or she keeps retreating to a too-inviting lap. It is a good thing to show a young child that we like him or her and enjoy having him or her sit on our lap. But it is also a good thing and very necessary for the child to get down from our lap and go about the business of play, the business of reaching out toward new and sometimes difficult experiences, the business of finding his or her place among children. A child needs to know that we really *want* to see her or him grow in independence.

The third task in personality growth has been called the development of a sense of initiative.

Developing initiative. While children of three or four years continue to work on the "unfinished business" of the earlier stages in developing a healthy amount of trust and independence over mistrust and dependency, they are also spending a lot of energy on the next developmental task in personality development. They are working on the task of finding out more about themselves and the place they may expect in the world. They are ready for this task to the extent that (1) they have learned to feel safe with people and (2) they have found that they can assert themselves in independent ways and still be accepted. They are now ready to discover what their place in the world may be.

This third task in personality growth has been called the development of a sense of initiative. The child is working on it when she or he wonders, "What will I become?" It takes a good deal of initiative to explore the possibilities of what one can become. What will it be like to be a mother or a daddy? Or a fireman or a soldier or a nurse or a doctor? What will it be like to be big and powerful? In her or his play the child acts "as if," pretending to be all these things. The child exercises her or his initiative in play.

Children can ask questions even if they do not understand all the answers.

If one is to explore and learn in creative, imaginative ways, one needs to have a sense of initiative—a desire to go ahead and discover. We all need this feeling of daring to try out new ways and take on new responsibilities. We are hampered in this if we are afraid of being blamed or of being held responsible and found guilty. Guilt and the part it plays in healthy growth will be discussed later. A sense of guilt usually interferes with the development of initiative. It is important for the child of three or four to develop a sense of initiative in greater amounts than a sense of being to blame for things. We need to make sure we give support to the behavior which represents initiative whenever we can. Encouraging his or her initiative helps the child in healthy personality growth. Initiative means daring to do, to imagine, and to learn.

Many things help children with this third personality task. They now should have fairly good control of their bodies. They can walk, run, climb, and jump. They can ask questions even if they do not understand all the answers. They can imagine and pretend. They have had a variety of experiences to draw on to help them with their thinking about things. They now enjoy some experiences away from home for short periods of time, especially with other children. They are ready to test things out on their own. They explore and experiment. As they use their initiative, they move toward making a place for themselves in the world.

Characteristics: A Growing Person

The child is a growing person. What kind of person? What kind of world will she or he live in? What kind of "world" will the child create for herself or himself?

It is important to be clear about what is in the outside world. This world is observable to others as well as oneself. It is also important to be aware of the inner world, which is not observable by others, but which can be shared with those who understand. Both worlds are part of a whole, and life is enriched when they both can be experienced fully.

A child's feelings are strong. This age is a time when *feelings are very strong*. A child this age gets very upset. He or she gets angry and anxious and very discouraged and very excited and delighted. The child is often difficult and is also often a delight.

This age is a time when feelings are very strong. A child this age gets very upset.

The child responds with all of his or her being. The world is fresh and new, and the child has a feeling of wonder at the things around him or her. At times a child may feel overwhelmed at the multitude of things and "dos" and "don'ts."

What does the child expect of himself or herself? What does the world expect of the child?

We can appreciate something of how a child feels because these questions are never completely answered. We can understand how overwhelming they must seem to the child who is just becoming aware of them and has had so little experience with the world and the people in it.

A child has an active imagination. The child's imagination is so active at this age that she or he may develop many fears. The child is likely to see bears in every corner of the bedroom at night! The child is often confused about what really happened, for his or her stories seem so vivid. Truth and fantasy get mixed.

Children of this age have many fears because they often misunderstand what they do see and hear going on around them. A child may be afraid of real things. A child may be afraid of imagined things which seem real to him or her. When a child tries to tell us about his or her fears, the stories may sound pretty wild to us. The child often tries to hide fears and thus gets more confused.

Slowly we try to help children distinguish between the real and the pretend kinds of things. We are careful not to make fun of their stories for they are serious to them and for them. We don't confuse children by passing judgment on what they say as though they were adults. That is, we do not label their stories "lies" before they know what the truth is. We try to help them get clear what is pretend and what is real. It is fun to pretend, and imagination is a precious quality to be guarded carefully.

A child needs playmates. A child three or four years of age seeks other children and needs them. Playing with others, a child finds a new kind of relationship. He or she is an *equal,* not just a little person with a lot of big people and perhaps a new baby in addition at home. When with other children, a child finds out much more about what he or she is like, the kind of person he or she is, and what it takes to build a place for himself or herself in the world.

Most three- and four-year-olds actively seek out other children.

Most three- and four-year-olds actively seek out other children. They may watch or they may take part in play with groups. They like and need to be around others, to have experiences in giving and taking, in finding friends, in standing up for their rights or their ideas in situations where they are among equals or near equals. They like and need experiences in sharing and cooperating with friends or even in arguing and fighting with them.

Some children have an imaginary playmate during this period. We do not encourage this fantasy, but there is no need to deny it. We can remain neutral. Real playmates have more to offer. The best course of action is to satisfy the child by treating the imaginary playmate with respect and to wait until "it" fades out of the picture.

At this age nursery schools or play groups become important for children. Experience with other children is essential for the healthy growth of most children.

While relations with other children are very important to the development of a healthy personality, relations with grown-ups are also important so that the child can discover what he or she may be like in relationships with people different from his or her parents, such as nursery school teachers or Sunday school teachers.

A child begins to understand the role of a man and of a woman. In wondering what his or her place in the world will be, each child explores ideas about the roles of men and women. What is it like to be a man? What is it like to be a woman? In dramatic play as they

All children can play homemaking roles with which they are familiar.

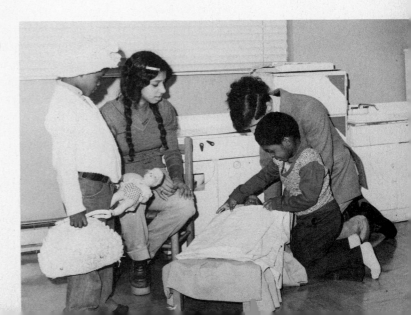

Fathers need to spend some time with their children, both girls and boys.

play house, children enjoy dressing up like adults, putting on a long skirt, or a hat or a belt. Girls usually dress up as women and boys as cowboys, but sometimes they try out reversing roles. They all can play homemaking roles with which they are familiar. It is harder to play out roles filled by parents working outside the home, for many children have had little contact with those work roles of their fathers or their mothers.

Children need contacts with a man. Boys need to have experiences with men so that they have an idea of what men are like and can identify themselves imaginatively with masculine roles. Girls, too, need contacts with a man to become clearer about their feminine role. It is especially important for children growing up in homes without fathers to have these contacts. Some nursery schools are using boys as assistants or volunteer aides when possible. The group seems to become more stable with fewer conflicts when there is a man teacher at least *part* of the time. The children respond differently.

Accepting one's own sex is essential for future adjustment in adolescence and maturity. A three- and four-year-old, or even a two-year-old, is working on identification with his or her sex. We need to give children all the help we can at this age. Fathers have a very important role to play here. They need to spend some time with their children, both girls and boys. They need to take opportunities to do things with them—errands, jobs around the home, walks, trips. In recalling events from their childhood, many people report that special experiences with their fathers stand out in their memories. Both mothers and fathers are important, of course, for they are both needed if the child is to understand the roles of the sexes, the part they each play in making a home as mothers and fathers, and as contributors to the life of the community. In different families the roles men and women play may differ. We know these roles are changing and should change, but the child needs to understand and to feel good about these roles. If his father is harsh and unreasonable in his discipline, for example, it is hard for a four-year-old boy to identify with the male role If a mother is demanding and exacting, it is hard for the girl to identify with the feminine role.

Each of us as a parent or as an adult whom the child knows well is giving him or her experiences in learning what it is like to be a man or a woman in an adult world.

A child learns more about his or her body. Just as during the first year the child learned about fingers and toes by touching and examining them, he or she now learns about other parts of the body.

A three- and four-year-old child
learns more about his or her body.

The child of three or four has special problems because she or he still is not clear about which things are right and wrong.

All children discover the different parts of their bodies and do some touching of their genitals. It is nothing to be distressed about. If this is done often, it may mean they need more things to play with or more activities to interest them. One should use correct terms with a child from the beginning, such as penis, bowel movement, urine. The child needs them in his or her vocabulary now and will not have to relearn them later.

Children of this age will be interested in what other children look like, too. In nursery school boys and girls use the toilets together. This gives them a chance to watch others going to the toilet, to make comments and ask questions as they wish. They are learning about some of the physical differences between the sexes.

A child is interested in where babies come from. Questions about where babies come from may keep coming up. It is a hard matter to get straight. Simple, truthful explanations will need to be repeated.

The baby grows in a special place inside the mother. This is where you grew. The father starts the baby growing. When the baby is big enough he or she comes out through a special place. This is being born.

We shall have more to say about these questions in a later chapter.

Acquiring Inner Controls

The development of inner controls is a necessary part of being civilized. This involves recognizing that there is a right and a wrong way to act. It means facing the reality that each of us has impulses that are bad as well as impulses that are good. It means facing the fact that we sometimes behave in undesirable ways.

A child develops a conscience. It is at this age that the child's *conscience* begins to develop. Children now feel guilty for things that they do that they feel they should not do. They begin to feel responsibility. Insofar as they are independent persons and can act on their own they must begin to take responsibility for what they do. Being responsible means feeling guilt for wrongdoing. The child at this age has special problems because she or he still is not clear about which things are wrong. It is not easy to be clear even when we are much older. The child is not even clear about the part she or he plays in making things happen. The child feels responsible for an event with which, in reality, she or he had no connection.

We take an important step when we begin to accept our responsibility for managing our actions. We would all prefer to deny the anger, the cruelty, the resentments that we harbor inside us, but denial does not help us deal with these feelings. It is probably confusing to children to be told that we love them but we don't like what they do. It suggests the primitive notion of a demon which makes us behave in ways for which we cannot be held responsible. We are responsible for our acts. What we do is an expression of ourselves. It is better to help children feel that, although we may disapprove of their behavior and thus of them at the moment, our love is strong enough to stand this strain. We love them for better or for worse. We love them because they are themselves, and we are here to help them strengthen the good part in them. It may be frightening to a child to feel loved only as a good boy or girl. Because the child knows he or she is also a bad boy or girl, the child may fear that he or she will lose love if the bad shows.

Conscience is a tremendous force and should be treated with respect. We do not ask a child to be responsible until she or he is really ready. The child may become inhibited and fearful or just give up being responsible because she or he is too afraid of being wrong. The child may feel too much guilt or guilt for the wrong things.

Guiding a child's conscience. It is possible to take advantage of a child's growing conscience in a way that is really harmful. If we try to *make* the child feel guilty when doing something wrong, impressing on her or him how bad it is to act like this, we may make the child feel *too* guilty. Children often feel more guilt than they can bear. They may become depressed. They may feel confused as to just what they did that made us angry. As a result, the guilty feelings spill over into other acts which they think are connected, and they become afraid to do these things, too. They feel less confidence in themselves. They may also feel resentful toward us for making them suffer. These are not good feelings to have.

We may think it is fine when a child is very good and never gets into trouble, but it sometimes means that the child has lost his or her capacity to dare to do things. This is very undesirable. A child may be unable to act freely in desirable ways. Because he or she is afraid to be considered naughty, a child may become afraid to explore and use initiative. This is not what we intended when we scolded the child, but it may be the result. At this age consciences tend to "run wild" and pile up a heavy burden of guilt. Instead of being too good, on the other hand, the child may become defiant and "mean" because of feeling hopeless about keeping out of trouble.

Most of us have had the experience of *feeling* guilty because of what someone did or said to us even though we knew we had no reason to feel this way. Conscience is a necessary and fine thing but it can get on the wrong track or spill over where it doesn't belong. Many of us suffer at times because of a conscience that got out of bounds and made us needlessly afraid of being wrong.

We should tell children what they can do and what they can't do and what the consequences will be if they do.

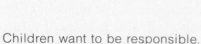

Children want to be responsible.

We should be very careful to avoid blaming a young child or shaming her or him or trying to *make* the child feel guilty. We just tell children what they can do or what they can't do and what the consequences are if they do. We see that these consequences happen. We are firm without getting angry. We may show them that we are displeased and that they are responsible, but we let them struggle with their own consciences and senses of guilt. We don't add to the burden of guilt by trying to increase it, or by *making* children feel ashamed, "You naughty child, shame on you."

Guilty feelings can do a lot of damage to a personality in its early stages of growth when it is very important to develop a sense of respect for oneself. But feeling guilty and accepting one's guilt is a necessary part of character development as one grows older. Then one's understanding and inner strength become better able to bear the burden guilt imposes. We can take responsibility and we can maintain principles of morality.

A child may feel confused about responsibility. We help a child by giving only the responsibility the child is ready to assume. A four-year-old who is told he must be responsible for keeping an active two-year-old off the street is pretty sure to get interested in play and forget. If the two-year-old goes into the street and gets hurt, the older child has an impossible load of guilt to manage, a load that he never should have had.

Adults should not place these kinds of responsibilities on a child. Children should be responsible for things that they can understand and have a good chance to be successful in doing and where their failures are not serious. They *want* to be responsible and big. They are trying to build this kind of "image" for themselves and they need success, not failure.

The child sometimes feels responsible for things that happen even when there is no real connection, as mentioned earlier. As a toddler, a child pulls on a cloth hanging over the edge of the table. A whole shower of dishes and things spills onto the floor. A parent says, "Look what you did!" and is very angry. The toddler is startled and thoroughly bewildered. It must feel like magic to the child. One little tug and all this happened! The toddler tugs other things with no such results. Or the child may push a button on one wall and a light flashes on in an entirely different spot. No wonder the child often thinks he or she has caused something when not really responsible for it.

Circumstances may occur which confuse a child. A child may have played with a baby sister a bit roughly and the next day the baby becomes seriously ill with the flu. The child feels responsible and guilty. He or she does not understand that he or she had no connection with the germ which caused the illness. No one realizes that the child feels this way and the child suffers real misery.

Children have feelings of guilt often enough so that it is always wise to reassure a child when an accident happens. "Nothing we did made it happen." One mother reported that when her car skidded off the road, the four-year-old sobbed, "I didn't do anything." This mother could reassure her child in this case, but children often don't put it into words like this.

Guiding the sense of responsibility. It is important, too, that when children *are* responsible we make it clear just what they did that led to the happening (so they do not imagine other things). We share the burden with them if it is in truth part of our responsibility. We may say, "I'm responsible, too. I should have been watching."

We don't use, "It's only an accident" as an excuse for not being careful. While accidents happen to all of us, accidents happen to us sometimes because we are not doing much to prevent them. A child pushed another child off a box and climbed on, answering the other child's protest by saying, "It was an accident." The child did not feel a sense of guilt for the action. Undue guilt feelings may make a child passive and obedient but they may also make the child unhappy and sometimes cruel and unable to grow in healthy ways. The child may fail to develop the amount of initiative needed to

As we help children learn, we should use ways that help them increase their confidence and feelings of self-respect.

be a creatively functioning person. As we help children learn, we can help in ways that increase their confidence and feelings of self-respect. We can help them develop a conscience which promotes responsible behavior without inhibiting initiative. This kind of conscience belongs to the mature, creative person.

Discipline at This Age

If we discipline in a firm, kindly way, depending on the child's conscience but not provoking unnecessary guilt, we teach the child what is reasonable while allowing her or him to feel that she or he is a person of worth as the child learns. The child will not be afraid to try things. The child will not be too hard on herself or himself.

At this age children are ready to learn quickly and with eagerness, to become "big" in the sense of sharing in responsibility and discipline and achievement.

By the time children are four, they do not respond to "distraction" as they did when they were toddlers. Children are able to bear unpleasant situations and to accept responsibility for their behavior. They understand more about reasons for things. When they fuss or sulk they are often *not* helped by our attempts to turn their attention to something else or distract them. It may be better to let them face the situation, work through their feelings, and then recover. It shows more respect for them and their capacities than if we coax or offer substitutes or indulge them in order to make up for some unpleasant reality.

When it is time to stop play outdoors and come in to get ready to go to bed, for example, the fact need not be sugarcoated by trying to take the child's mind off it. It can be made more acceptable by a statement about a story to be read as soon as he or she is ready for bed, but the child must face the necessity of stopping play and getting ready for bed. If we feel uncertain ourselves or dislike dealing with a child's fussing or sulking, we may be tempted to try to distract or bribe him or her. But we should be friendly and firm. This child is no longer a baby. He or she can face difficulty if it does not come in "doses" that are overwhelming. We can bear the child's fussing without getting upset by it.

If we discipline in a firm, kindly way, depending on the child's conscience but not provoking unnecessary guilt, we teach what is reasonable while allowing the child to feel that she or he is a person of worth.

From what has been said, we can see that punishment does not have much place in the guidance of children of this age. We should be firm and friendly and help children learn to act in acceptable ways. By this age many rules have become a matter of mutual regulation, with responsibility shared by child and parents. When this happens, the child and parents have a better chance of discovering real pleasure and companionship in being together. They can enjoy sharing experiences. Punishment interferes with this kind of growth.

Through these first years the child has learned and grown a great deal, and many personality patterns have been laid. A child remains absorbed with the task of discovering who he or she is, what the world is like, and what the child's place in it may be. As a child enters school he or she will begin to feel more satisfaction in accomplishments and achievements. What the child does and makes will become as important as the processes of doing and making were earlier. The child will find enjoyment in accomplishing things with other people. If earlier experiences have prepared the child well, he or she will be able to cooperate with others while keeping a sense of his or her own identity as a person. The child will be ready to take his or her place among others.

ACTIVITIES

TO DO AND DISCUSS

1 Observe a three- or four-year-old for half an hour.
  a. Describe the child's appearance.
  b. Describe what you observed about the child's physical development. (How active was the child? What did he or she do which showed you something about motor coordination, large muscle coordination, and small muscle coordination?
  c. Describe what you observed about the child's social development.
   (1) Did you observe her or him learning something? Describe it.
   (2) Did you see an example of reasoning? Describe it.
   (3) Give some examples of the child's speech.
   (4) What did the child do that told you something about her or his imagination?
   (5) What did the child's interests seem to be?
   (6) What else did you notice about this child?

    d. What comments would you make about each of the following?
        (1) The child's sense of trust.
        (2) The child's amounts of independence and dependence.
        (3) The child's sense of initiative or confidence in exploring.
    e. What kind of person does the child seem to be at this stage? What do you think this child would be like with other children? Why?

2 Observe a three- or four-year-old child and try to write down exactly what happened for five minutes. This will give you some practice in becoming an accurate and objective observer.

    An objective observer is one who records what takes place without passing personal judgment on it or coloring the report with his or her individual way of looking at a particular bit of behavior.

    "She was selfish when she played in the sand with Jane." This is a subjective statement. "She took a spoon from Jane and used it in filling her pan with sand." This is an objective record.

TO THINK AND WRITE ABOUT

1 A child falls, and you feel sure that he or she has not been hurt, but the child begins to cry loudly.
    a. What would you do
        (1) if the child is at home and you are the regular baby-sitter?
        (2) if the child is at Sunday school or nursery school and it is his or her first day there without a parent?
        (3) if the child is with a group of children whom she or he knows, but the child has just had a fight with one of her or his best friends?
    b. Be prepared to discuss in class your answers in each of these situations and the reasons for each answer.

2 How do the parents of a three- or four-year-old help the child to develop good habits in regard to cleanliness, eating, and sleeping?

3 How do the parents of a three- or four-year-old help the child become independent in such matters as dressing, eating, and taking care of his or her things?

4 Why are games like playing house and playing store important to a child's development?

5 Why is it important for parents to use good speech and the correct words when speaking to children?

6 What is the parents' role in helping a child develop a feeling of trust?

7 Why is it important for a child to develop a sense of initiative?

8 Think back to your own childhood at the time when you were developing a conscience. Describe an incident in which you wanted very much to do something, but your conscience prevented you.

REFERENCES

Beck, Helen
"Pressures in the Nursery"
Children Today, September–October, 1972

Burgess, Helen
How to Choose a Nursery School
Public Affairs Pamphlet No. 310
New York: Public Affairs Committee, Inc.

Kellogg, Elizabeth with Dorothy Hill
Following Through with Children
Washington, D. C.: National Association for the Education of Young Children, 1969

Law, Norma
"The Strengths of the Young Child"
Young Children, Vol. 22, No. 3, pp. 176–180, January, 1967

Murphy, Lois B.
"Foundations for Good Beginnings"
Young Children, Vol. 25, No. 1, pp. 5–11, October, 1969

Your Child from Three to Four
Children's Bureau Publication No. 446
Washington, D. C.: U. S. Department of Health, Education, and Welfare, 1967

5

We Learn Through Experiences with Children

After studying this chapter, you will be able to

1. Participate in varied activities with young children.
2. Establish goals for working with young children individually and in groups.
3. Clarify personality qualities needed by a parent or teacher.
4. Analyze characteristics of preschool children.
5. Guide young children for health and safety.

We have studied some of the characteristics of infants and young children as they grow through stages in development. We have discussed some of the things young children may need for good development at each stage. Now we will turn our attention to having experiences with children and learning some of the skills needed if we are to guide them successfully.

Experiences With Children

Young children are everywhere. They may be members of your own family or live in the house next door or in the apartment above you — or in all these places. Have you ever thought about the ways in which these children may be alike and the ways in which they are different? What makes all these children "tick"? To understand any child we need to observe her or him in many situations and really come to know that child as a person. Every child is unique, different from anyone else.

Each of you should plan to have experiences with an individual child and also with children in groups. Both kinds of experiences are of value in learning about children. Your first observations should be of one child in his or her home, if possible, rather than of a group of children in one of the many types of day care facilities. Groups are composed of individuals. In working with young children we think in terms of individual needs even when children are in groups. To understand one child is the basis for understanding others.

For those of you who may be planning to prepare for a career in the field of child development, this course will be a step in such preparation. You will be particularly interested later in observing a variety of child care facilities to find out more about the earning

To understand any child, we need to observe her or him in many situations and really come to know that child as a person.

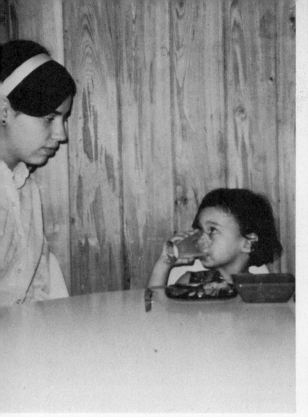

(Left) You may know a child in your neighborhood that you can arrange
to visit over a period of time and perhaps to care for.
(Right) You are a very important person to your sister or brother.

opportunities in the field. You and your teacher will want to find
out about the existing facilities in your community.

Observing an individual child. Selecting a child to observe and
with whom to have experiences should not be too difficult. Young
children usually enjoy attention from anyone who is interested in
them. You may know a child in your neighborhood and can arrange
with the parents to visit over a period of time and perhaps to care
for the child. The parents may welcome a free hour while you
"baby sit."

If you have a small brother or sister at home, you may wish to
observe him or her. Relations with siblings (brothers or sisters) are
different from relations with a child outside the family. They are
much closer. This may make it harder to see how the sibling really
behaves. You have already formed opinions about what your

brother or sister is like. You may find a younger sibling more irritating at times. You also like him or her in a deeper way. Because you are closer to your sister or brother and have strong feelings about her or him, you may find it difficult to observe objectively, that is, without letting your own feelings color what you observe. But it also may be more important to try to find out what your sibling is *really* like and what she or he is feeling. You are sure to be a very important person to your sister or brother.

When you have selected a child, you should arrange to observe him for 30 minutes at a time at weekly intervals for four weeks, longer if possible. You will have pencil and paper with you. Jot down as much as you can of what the child does and says and what the child's response is to you. You may add things about the situation, such as where the child is playing, with what materials the child is playing, or what interactions the child has with other people. Add, too, any comments or impressions you have. When you have finished your series of observations, read your notes over carefully and *summarize* them. What did the child play with? What different kinds of things did the child do? How long was spent at one activity? What characteristics would you say the child had? On what evidence are you drawing these conclusions?

How does the child you observed seem to be different from the typical child of the same age. In what ways does the child you observed show the same characteristics?

Next review the material in the text describing children of this age and report on how the child you observed seems to be different from the typical child of this age and in what ways the child you observed shows the same characteristics. What do you think may explain these differences? Environmental causes? Inherited factors?

Finish your report with a statement about what you feel you have learned about this child. In addition, describe your attitude toward the child. Have your feelings about this child changed since you began your study?*

Observing and then working with children in groups. Most communities have a variety of child care facilities where you may be able to study children. You may be able to observe and assist in a church school, or in a play group run by parents in the neighborhood, or in a nursery school, or in a day care center for working mothers, or a parent-child center. You may find you can observe in a nearby kindergarten. Those of you who are interested in preparing for work in child care may wish to do some observations in several different types of centers.

*Refer to the case studies in the bibliography at the end of Chapter I and to references on observing.

Many communities have a variety of child care facilities where you may study children.

Your teacher will help to make the arrangements with the center you select. You will want to find out if there are any rules about observing (where to sit, what to do, what not to do) and also what rules are set for the children (what they may not do or how equipment should be used).

If you are to assist, you should make an observation first, so that you can fit into the program in a way that will be really helpful. Staff members usually appreciate help with the necessary housekeeping, such as putting blocks back on the shelf and wiping up spilled paint. These are ways you can show your appreciation for the help they are giving you in your learning. Above all, you can observe closely all that goes on, learning more about methods of managing children in groups.

Whatever you do you will find the opportunity to observe and assist with a group of young children is rewarding. You will discover how different each child is. You will see how children react to others of their own age, not just to older people. You will also discover how much skill is needed to care for children in groups if individual children are to benefit from the experience. You will develop your own resources as you are meeting their needs.

Setting up a play group. In some cases a class may arrange to have a play school in their own classroom for a certain number of class periods. It takes planning and a lot of preparation to run a play school successfully for even a limited time, but it can be very rewarding.

Before undertaking to have a play group in your own classroom, you will need to find some answers for questions like these:

How much space and what kind of space is available? Indoor space? Outdoor space?

How many children will make a satisfactory group in the space available?

What equipment is needed? How can it be arranged? Inside? Outside?*

*Refer to Gross, Dorothy, "Equipping a Classroom for Young Children" in *Young Children*, Vol. 24, No. 2, December 1968.

What supplies are essential? (Paper, paints, paste, puzzles, games, first aid kit, etc.)

What safety precautions and health precautions need to be taken in your set-up?

What about accident insurance?

What ages should be included?

What will be the most desirable length of time for one session? How many sessions should there be?

What is the best time in the day for the children? (This will mean talking with parents.)

What kind of schedule will you follow? How will the time be planned?

What familiar experiences will be included? What new experiences?

How will each class member participate? What talents do class members have as, for example, playing a musical instrument?

How will you divide responsibilities in supervising?

What records will you keep on each child?

What problems are likely to arise on the first day? Later on?

When will you do the day-to-day planning of activities?

How well can individual needs of children be met? (Until the children come you do not know much about their individual needs unless you are already acquainted.)

When will you plan to meet for regular discussions about what has happened and to evaluate the program?

What kind of final report will you prepare which will be most helpful for you and for another group?

Answers to these and other questions will depend in part on the circumstances in your school. You will find some published accounts of the different ways in which other schools have operated such play schools.*

If there is no suitable space available in your school for a regular play group, you and your teacher may decide to invite a small group of children to come to play in your classroom for one or more periods, so that you may observe and become acquainted with

*Refer to the bibliography at the end of Chapter I.

them. You may set up the room with blocks, housekeeping materials, art materials, picture books, and plan for some activities such as a story period or some singing and a snack time. Much of the time you will just want to become acquainted with the children and help them begin to feel at home with you.

If you are very fortunate, your school may have an ongoing "laboratory" group of children where you can observe and assist. Here you will have the advantage of watching a trained child development person at work and of having conferences with her about your own work.

How do we help young children to develop well as we work with them? There are some things to keep in mind as general principles when one begins participating with children, whether individually or in a group. We want every experience a child has to give her or him a greater sense of respect for herself or himself and more confidence in her or his capacity to cope with the world. We want the child to feel more sure that he or she is liked by others and that he or she is an important and trustworthy person. We want the child to feel more certain that he or she can be successful and that his or her efforts are worthwhile.

Each bit of guidance that we give children should be of the "building-up" kind.

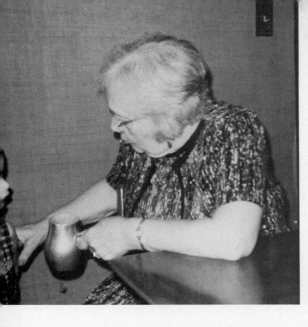

The child who has been given respect is the one most ready to respect others.

Each bit of guidance that we give should be of the "building-up" kind rather than of the "tearing-down" kind. These are significant feelings which will influence the child's future adjustments. The child who has been given respect is the one readiest to respect others. The confident child is most likely to succeed.

Some children hear words like these too many times: "Stop that," "That's no good," "You did it all wrong," "Get out of my way," "You are such a nuisance," "You are driving me crazy with your questions," "I'm ashamed of you," "Don't you know better."

Children who hear these words may come to feel that nobody likes them. They may not even like themselves. They often grow afraid of people and experiences, afraid of trying. They may withdraw into themselves or they may fight with everybody and never feel really satisfied with anything. They develop unhealthy personalities.

Of course it takes more than one or two poor experiences to have much effect on a child. Children are pretty well made to withstand the hazards they meet, both physically and psychologically. We will be sure to make some mistakes with them. But it is the mistakes in guidance that are repeated and repeated that damage a child and change the kind of person each may become. Repeated mistakes are like many small drops of water, dripping on a rock long enough to wear it away. We do not need to be afraid of mistakes if we are thoughtful and make an effort to grow in our understanding. We will not be repeating mistakes or making many significant ones.

Goals to Keep in Mind in Caring for Children

As we care for children, we should be clear about what we want to try to accomplish. We need to have goals. What are some important objectives to keep in mind as we care for young children? Discuss in class the following goals and add some of your own goals. We will consider some of these goals in more detail later.

Goals: What We Want to Accomplish for a Child

1. In caring for children it is important to keep the child *healthy*. This means maintaining good standards of cleanliness and hygiene, helping the child with good health habits like washing hands before eating or after toileting, adjusting clothes to weather conditions, ensuring a balance of rest and physical activity among other things.

2. It is important to keep a child *safe*. This means such things as preventing accidents by effective supervision, taking responsibility for foreseeing and avoiding danger, or limiting

It is important to build up the child's feelings of self-confidence.

In caring for children, it is important to keep the child healthy.

what the child does if there are hazards he or she cannot be expected to manage such as playing with sharp pointed scissors, and setting up other safety procedures.

3. It is important to build up the child's *feelings of respect* for *herself* or *himself,* the feeling that she or he is a person of worth, liked by others. We do this by giving the child attention when the child seems to want it, listening to the child when he or she speaks, and being courteous to the child. We do this by respecting the efforts the child makes and by looking for characteristics in the child we can like. We also refrain from shaming or blaming the child.

4. It is important to build up the child's *feelings of self-confidence and trust* in himself or herself and in other people, giving the child encouragement and approval whenever we can, and helping the child succeed in her or his purposes.

5. It is important to help the child *enjoy being with other people* and *gain the social skills* needed in adjusting to others, such as learning to use words to settle disputes, to work out compromises. The child who likes other people will be readier to perceive their needs and respect their rights. We want the child to make friends.

6. It is important to protect and encourage a child's efforts to be *independent.* We let children do all they can for themselves and give them a chance to make as many decisions as they can by themselves. Sometimes decisions we make for children are ones they could be allowed to make for themselves. We often regiment a child unnecessarily for our own convenience.

It is important to help the child enjoy being with other people.

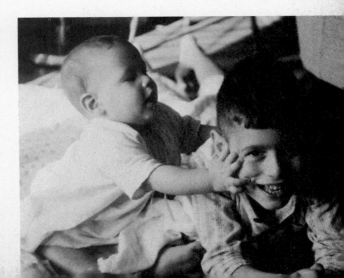

7. It is important to value and foster a great deal of *play* which is not teacher-directed play but which depends on the child's imagination and ingenuity. Play, especially dramatic play, is probably a very important factor in a child's healthy development.

8. It is important to value and foster all kinds of *creative expressions* on the part of the child, in art, in music, in dance, and in language. Expressing feelings through all these avenues is an important safety valve for children at this age when their feelings are strong and their controls are weak. Whenever you can, help children to understand the connection between what they do and what they feel.

9. It is important to give support and encouragement to the child's active *curiosity* and his or her drive to *explore* and *discover* and *question*. This means answering questions or helping the child find the answers. Children are avid learners at this age and are laying the foundation for later school achievement. It means providing children with a richly varied program of experiences; opportunities to see, feel, hear, smell; opportunities to see different people at work and par-

It is important to value and foster all kinds of a child's creative expressions.

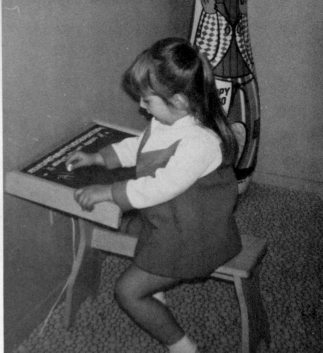

It is important to encourage and assist a child to master skills on higher and higher levels in as many areas as she or he can.

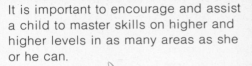

ticipate whenever possible; experiences with animals, experiences with doing and making. There should be orderly sequences in a child's day, but it should be full of variety, balancing the new with the familiar, and stimulation with relaxation and privacy.

10. It is important to encourage and assist the child to *master skills* on higher and higher levels in as many areas as she or he can. Some important skills are

(a) skills in the use of the child's own body — in dressing herself or himself, or in riding a tricycle, or in climbing.

(b) social skills in living and working with and enjoying other people as well as in spending time alone.

(c) language skills (language competence). Talk with children; listen to them; read to them and tell stories; encourage their verbal output!

(d) skills in classifying and organizing impressions and perceptions, and developing strategies for solving problems. Matching and sorting activities, recalling, associating, and planning are worth encouraging. Ask questions such as "What will you need to make the airplane?" "How are you going to make it?" "What did we see on the trip?" or "What shall we do about it?" in the case of a dispute.

Goals: personality qualities needed by a parent or teacher. There are other kinds of goals. They are personal ones. They refer to the personality qualities desirable in someone who is responsible for the care of young children.*

Our personalities play an important part in the relationships we have with children whether we are parents or teachers. Improving what we do means strengthening some characteristics or qualities in our personality. Young children deserve the best that we can give them. We are their "models." They imitate us more than we often realize. If we are cranky or impatient or thoughtless or rude, get angry easily or are indifferent, the child absorbs something of the attitudes we display. Growing may become a bit more difficult for the child.

We need to be ourselves, of course. We need to accept and be comfortable with ourselves as we are. But all of us keep growing and changing and adapting to circumstances. We are never fixed or finished. We keep modifying aspects of our personality. We can modify these in desirable directions.

A person caring for young children needs to have these qualities:

*Refer to the article by Gross, Dorothy, "Teachers of Young Children Need Basic Inner Qualities" in *Young Children*, Vol. 23, No. 2, November, 1967.

A person caring for young children should have sensitivity and an awareness of each child's needs, interests, and feelings.

When people are comfortable with themselves and self-accepting, they are better able to accept children, with all their differences, and better able to discipline sensibly.

A person should truly *care* about what happens to a child in his or her care.

1. *sensitivity* and *awareness* of the child's needs, interests, and feelings.

2. *interest* in *learning*. One should find satisfaction in adding to knowledge of a subject, in exploring, in discovering, and also in reflecting. One should feel that learning can be exciting. This makes a person able to share the child's excitement in discovering and achieving.

3. *self-respect* and thinking of herself or himself as a person of worth. When people are comfortable with themselves and self-accepting, they are better able to accept children with all their differences and also better able to discipline sensibly. Feelings of self-respect are essential in good guidance.

4. *generosity*—a "giving" kind of person, not a "withholding" person. One should be able to give attention freely and generously when a child wants it, for example. One should be generous in approval and encouragement, giving support to the child in his or her efforts.

5. *responsibility*. One should be free of a need to control and direct others, but should be able to step in with confidence to give directions when necessary. The type of person who is glad to hear a child say, "Let me do it," for example.

6. *understanding of herself or himself* and *able to manage her or his own feelings* so that they do not interfere with functioning. One should have learned to deal with one's own feelings as they arise, on the spot if possible. One should have learned to channel feelings into constructive avenues such as art, music, or purposeful activity where they become a source of energy and creativity. A person should be honest with herself or himself.

7. *flexibility* and *resourcefulness*, with wide interests and a zest for living. But one should also organize and plan and maintain a balance between thinking and activity. This kind of person creates an environment for the child that is orderly without making order an end in itself. Such a person welcomes new ideas.

8. *ability to work cooperatively* with other people, whether in the family or in a child care center. One should be able to communicate well with others, take responsibility, make suggestions, accept suggestions and directions, and stand up for what one believes is right.

None of us begins with these qualities all developed. But with experience and thoughtful effort it becomes easier to act in these ways. We are human. Being human we have the capacity to grow and change. There are sure to be times when we disappoint ourselves by what we do, but there is always another time. We will be rewarded by the children's responses as we approach our goal.

You may want to try rating yourself on each characteristic listed. Check your strengths and your weaknesses. Keep notes on your progress.

Analysis of a response: an example. We have stated the goals in general terms. How does one identify these qualities in action in particular situations?

Let us take situation 4, one of the situations given in the list of typical situations at the end of this chapter, as an example. What *may* be implied in each answer?

a. "Aren't you going to let the other children have some of the clay?" is likely to be said by someone who is unsure of himself or herself and lacks confidence. The person is probably also someone who does not have a clear idea of what expectations are reasonable for a three-year-old. Jane can hardly be expected to understand much about dividing the clay with others. She is in the stage of having little interest in or even awareness of the purposes of others.

A confident, better informed teacher would have accepted the responsibility himself or herself, protecting the rights of all the children. In doing this the teacher would have shown Jane that others have rights, without lessening Jane's joy in her own product and purpose. The important thing for a three-year-old is to enjoy being with others and to give sustained attention to achieving a purpose.

b. "You must not take any more clay, Jane. The other children want to use it too." This is a negative statement, and seems to have a controlling, directing sound. Is this spoken by a teacher who tends to emphasize what *not* to do? A reason has been given which would seem to have more meaning for the teacher than for Jane.

A confident, informed teacher accepts the responsibility for protecting the rights of all children.

We may wonder whether the words will help Jane learn the lesson of sharing and respecting the rights of others, although these words are probably more effective than those used in (a). We do not know what Jane's response was. Did she try to take more clay later? Did she leave the situation soon after this? How does she feel about playing with clay when others are around?

c. "Use the clay you have, Jane. The rest of the clay is for the other children to use."

This is likely to be spoken by a teacher who is sure of herself or himself and also free of the need to reprove. The teacher makes a positive statement, supporting Jane's use of clay, but setting limits for it as the teacher also supports the other children's right to use the clay. Jane can be expected to perceive and understand this much; it does not interfere with her purpose. It is a good step in learning more about sharing while she still enjoys herself.

Here is an exercise which will increase your skill in guiding children:

Analyze an experience you have had with a child. Write down exactly what took place. Think it over. What do you think your feelings were at the time? What were the child's possible feelings? What might the child have learned?

Think also about what other ways you might have spoken or acted in the situation? Decide which one might be best suited to the needs of that child at that particular time.

Below are a list of suggestions for developing skills in guidance. They are ways in which we can put our goals into practice or act on them. See how they work for you. Keep these suggestions in mind when you are with the individual child you have selected to observe as well as when you are with the group.

Suggestions for Guiding Children
Supervising for Health and Safety

1. Supervise for good health.

a. *Be sure that each child's clothing is adjusted to the weather.* Be sure that the coat or sweater is taken off if it begins to get hot or put on if it begins to get cold. See that the child has on rubbers if the ground is wet.

Be sure that children practice sanitary habits.

Be sure that each child's clothing is adjusted to the weather.

b. *Be sure that children practice sanitary habits.* See that the children do not use the same glass or bubble pipe, for example, until it has been thoroughly washed. Be sure that children wash their hands before eating at snack time and after going to the toilet.

c. *Protect the child's health.* In cool or damp weather be sure that children do not sit on the ground. Be sure that the children have some rest time. If children have been running about, you might have them sit quietly and read or tell a story to them or have them play in the sandbox for a time. Be sure to observe any special restrictions that a child might have—a child recovering from an illness, for example, may not be permitted to run and climb.

Assume responsibility for these things yourself.

2. Supervise for safety.

a. *Check equipment to be sure it is safe to use.* Be sure that ladders are firmly fixed, for example, or that boards are not likely to slip. If you see a loose nail, remove it or pound it in.

b. *Watch children closely when they are using play equipment which may present dangers.* Give special attention to the safe use of a swing or a teeter. Show children how a piece of equipment can be used safely. "Walk around the swing," or, "Get off the teeter slowly," or, "Put the wood in the vise before you start to saw it."

c. *Stand in a position to prevent trouble.* Stand so that you are in a position to prevent possible accidents. Stand close to a group of children who are using the teeter or climbing. If you are helping one child, stand facing the other children so that you can also keep your eye on them.

d. *Keep the playroom clean and in relative order.* Children will not be likely to trip over equipment if it is not left out of place after use. Encourage children to replace material or do it yourself. Show the children how to carry equipment safely such as how to pick up and carry a chair, how to walk carrying a pencil with the point down, and so on. Good housekeeping is important.

Keep the playroom clean and in relative order.

Give your suggestions or directions in a positive way.

Teaching Skills

1. *Give your suggestions or directions in a positive way.* This means telling the child *what to do* rather than what not to do. It is easier for a child to follow directions if you turn his or her attention to what he or she should be doing. The child is less apt to resist. Be sure to make your directions simple and specific. Use a *do* rather than a *don't,* as "Keep the sand in the sandbox," or, "Dig in the sand," when you wish to redirect a child who is throwing sand. Say, "As soon as you are quiet, I will read the story" when you are helping a noisy group settle down for the story period.

2. *Use a quiet, confident tone of voice.* When you speak quietly to children, they will pay more attention than when you raise your voice. When you speak in a confident tone, they feel more confidence that you mean what you say; they find it easier to comply. If you use a demanding, bossy tone, the children are more likely to resist. It makes them want *not* to do what you direct, just as you yourself might feel if you were in their place.

3. *Give your directions in as few words as possible and use simple words.* It will be clear to the child who is learning to use the toilet, for example, if you say, "Time to go to the toilet," as you hold out your hand to her or him. The child will not need any long explanation. Children often do not listen to involved reasons or explanations.

4. *Offer the child a choice only when you intend to leave the choice up to the child.* When we are unsure of ourselves, we often make a request in the form of a question because of our own uncertainty. Listen to yourself when you are with a child whom you do not know very well in a situation which is new to you. "Are you ready to go?" may be a request for information or it may be an attempt to suggest going to the child. If it really is time to go, it is better to state the fact, "It's time for us to go now," and then help the child bring his or her play to an end. You may ask, "Would you like to go outdoors?" if the child is free to choose whether to play inside or outside. Avoid putting a direction in the form of a question. If you want a child to close the door, say, "Please close the door." Be clear in your own mind whether you wish to give a direction, offer the child a choice, or ask for information.

5. *Give the child plenty of time to finish her or his play if it is possible.* A child may resist if she or he feels hurried. The child may want and need time to park her or his cars or to finish a job before changing to another activity. We need to respect the child's purposes just as we like to have our purposes respected.

We can respect the child's purposes without permitting "stalling." If we find a child thinking of one thing after another to delay matters, we can say firmly, "It really is time to stop now. You must come as soon as you have put that one car in its garage." Then, when the one car has been put away, we can quietly take the child's hand and see that he or she complies. Perhaps we will make it easier for the child if we start a conversation about something else as we do this.

6. *Make desirable behavior interesting.* Things like picking up play materials can be made more interesting by the use of a little imagination. A suggestion such as, "Let's pretend we're deliverymen taking these blocks back to the shelves," may help when children seem to feel that picking up is a chore.

7. *Encourage the child to be independent.* Give the child only as much help as needed and only when the child asks for help. Children can manage to put on their own coats or boots, for example. It may take them more time, but it gives them satisfaction to do it themselves. Give them opportunities to take responsibility. If they spill some water or paint, let them wipe it up themselves.

A child may be able to climb into the swing himself or herself if we steady it. This is better than lifting the child into the seat. If a child wants to reach something, we can show her or him how to make a step with a large block and get it herself or himself. When we can help a child in this way, we are teaching the child to solve his or her own problems and to be independent.

8. *Let children use all art media such as paints, clay, crayons, or collage materials, as avenues for self-expression, without models to copy.* Making a model for a child to copy in a drawing or in clay or in other art media provides the child with an activity, but it prevents the child from developing his or her own ideas or imagination. Copying may effectively block creativity in children. When children paint, draw, or use clay, they should use these art materials as avenues for *self*-expression.

Avoid drawing pictures for children. They are less likely to draw their own pictures then. When you play with clay, avoid *making* anything. Squeeze it or pound it or roll it. The process involved in using clay is important for the child rather than the product, although we may value what the child makes. We should make such comments as, ''That is a lovely color,'' or, ''Tell me about your picture,'' or, ''The clay feels good, doesn't it!''

9. *Depend on motivating the child by encouragement and approval.* When we give attention and approval, we give the best form of motivation for a young child. When we show our pleasure

When we give attention and approval, we give the best form of motivation for a young child.

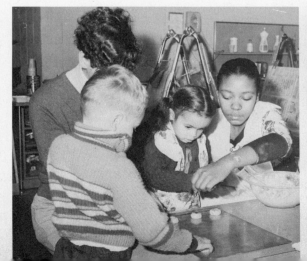

in what children do, we encourage them in their efforts. They feel respect for themselves and value what they have succeeded in doing. Doing something that wins the approval of the adults whom the children respect gives them satisfaction and also gives direction to their further efforts. They are motivated.

When we try to motivate children by making comparisons between one child and another or getting them to compete with each other, we only increase the feelings of rivalry and jealousy which are always present. These feelings are especially difficult for young children to manage. They interfere with the development of good social relations and make it harder for them to get along with others. Most young children have not yet built up enough confidence in themselves to face the failures which are inevitable in all competitive situations.

The best reasons for making an effort to do something well are because we get satisfaction from the doing and because the thing is worth doing. We should do something for these reasons rather than because we want to get ahead of someone else. Children are capable of making a tremendous effort when they are given encouragement and approval. They gain in confidence and self-respect. These are feelings which we all need if we are to be successful people.

A child is helped when we say, "You carried that glass of milk very carefully, without spilling a drop," or, "That's fine. You remembered to put all the blocks back in the box."

Children are capable of making tremendous efforts when they are given encouragement and approval.

Building Good Social Relations
Among Children

Our goal is to help children like each other more because of the guidance we give them in getting along together.

Children are individuals, and, as we watch them together, it is easy to see how different they are. In any group of young children we see children who are friendly and like to play with others. They are the secure, satisfied ones. We see children who usually play alone. They may be the timid ones. We see children who seem to want to play with others but are often not included. They are the frustrated ones. We see busy, purposeful children, children with few interests, imaginative children, unimaginative children, children who persist, children who give up easily, and many others. Children are people with the differences we all show.

Children need and want to play with other children. They learn some of their most important social lessons through play with other children. They often need help in understanding the behavior of others and their own feelings. They need help in understanding what behavior is acceptable.

If there are plenty of resources for play, plenty of space, and a minimum of interference from adults, most children can settle their differences most of the time. They learn from doing it. Others will need more help. Children who feel sure of their place in the group will need the least help.

Conflicts usually arise over possessions, over using equipment, or over carrying out purposes. Scolding children for their mistakes does not help them learn. It may only make them prefer to play alone. Telling them what they can or should do in a situation makes it possible for them to learn and to enjoy being with others.

A child may be having difficulty in being accepted by others. We may say, depending on the circumstances,

"Knock at the door and ask if you may come in."

"I think Mary and Jane don't want you in their house just now. Sometimes people want to play by themselves. You might build a house over here and ask Helen if she'd like to play."

A child may need help in working out a solution. We may say,

"If you want the truck he is using, get another truck and see if he will trade with you."

"Tell him why you want it."

"That tricycle belongs to Mary. You will have to use another one."

"Bill and Dick are using the shovel. You may have it after they finish digging their hole."

A child may need help in draining off anger so that he can have a better chance of getting along in the group. We may say,

"It's hard not to have the truck when you really want it, I know. It makes you feel pretty cross. Go ahead and bang the big can."

"No hitting people. It hurts. Bill doesn't like being hit. I know you are cross with him. You can go over and punch our dummy figure."

Sometimes it is important to encourage a child to stand up for himself or herself. Some children need help in learning that they do not have to do everything that other children ask but can carry out purposes of their own. "It is yours. You do not have to let her take it when you are using it." We need to help them stand up for themselves effectively in a friendly way, with words instead of by hitting.

Help the child learn to share by respecting the child's right to possess things of his or her own.

Let children handle their own conflicts whenever they can.

Help the child learn to share by respecting the child's right to possess things of his or her own. If possible, avoid insisting on children sharing things when they object strongly. As they come to enjoy and have fun with friends, they share because they want to.

A child is helped to accept "taking turns" if she or he doesn't have to wait too long and if the child has a chance to get the object back again in another "turn." He or she learns then that sharing does not mean just giving up an object. A child is also helped to accept "turns" if we show that we understand his or her feelings. *I know that you really want to keep it,* but you've had your turn. It is her turn now. I'll see that you have another turn." Words like these will really help a child.

Disciplining

Firmness with friendliness is the basis of good discipline.

State clearly what you expect of the child, what the rules or limits are, and the consequences, if there are any. An example of appropriate consequence is removing an object which was used to hit another child. Maintain these rules or limits consistently. A child will learn quickly if we are firm and matter-of-fact in maintaining *understood* limits or rules.

If children engage in play which is not safe for them or for others, *stop* the play, explaining the reasons to them; then show them what they can do.

A child may not like being kept from doing something. She or he may get angry. But if we are firm and do not get angry in return, the child will soon recover and will be helped in learning to control herself or himself.

Let children handle their own conflicts whenever they can. Sometimes it is enough merely to walk over closer to the children. Your presence is a steadying influence.

When you attempt to settle a conflict, speak quietly, getting the children's attention first and calling them by name. Help them look at the problem. If you understand the reasons for what happened, interpret the behavior of one child to the other. If you don't understand, tell them so. Trouble is often reduced by understanding or making an effort to talk matters over and understand circumstances better.

If conflicts are repeated, observe closely to see at what point the difficulty starts and help the children change what they are doing at that point. If a particular child seems to be causing most of the trouble, remove that child from the situation. Talk the matter over with him or her. That child may need to play alone for a while until better able to maintain his or her own controls. Be alert to what is happening and to particular combinations of children playing together. Some children often have trouble when they play together. They may play well with different children.

Forestalling (preventing) is the most effective way of managing problems. Learn to foresee and prevent rather than to "mop up" after troubles start. Make a suggestion to change the play *before* difficulties start whenever you can. As you come to know the children well, you will find you can often prevent trouble from arising. You will be a skillful teacher!

Remember that children learn from having conflicts and settling them constructively. Without conflicts there would be very little growing. We are concerned about giving good guidance to children in their struggle in growing.

ACTIVITIES

TO DO AND DISCUSS

EXAMPLES OF TYPICAL SITUATIONS IN GUIDING CHILDREN
On a separate sheet of paper, for each situation put the letter of the statement which describes most nearly what you think should be done. Then give the reasons you think it is the most desirable thing to do in the situation. In class discuss these reasons. See how much agreement there is as well as how many differences in points of view. Perhaps you will change your opinion in some cases as you talk it over.

A. *In a nursery school*

1. It is the first day of school. Mary's mother has just brought her to the nursery school. At the teacher's approach, Mary, who is three, clings to her mother. She is an only child and has not had much experience with children or been away from her mother. The teacher:
_____a. suggests to Mary's mother that she say goodbye and leave, assuring her that Mary will soon be all right.
_____b. takes Mary's hand and invites her to join the children in their play.
_____c. smiles at Mary and asks Mary's mother to sit in a chair near where the children are playing.

2. Three children are walking up a steeply inclined board and climbing onto the jungle gym. Three other children are playing in the sandbox nearby. The teacher who is supervising the play yard stands:
_____a. close to the children on the inclined board.
_____b. close to the sandbox.
_____c. halfway between the two groups.

3. Some three-year-old children are playing together in the sandbox at nursery school. Jane, a shy, quiet child, stands for some time watching them. The teacher:
_____a. asks Jane if she wants to play in the sand.
_____b. puts a spoon and truck near Jane.
_____c. asks the children to invite Jane to play.

4. Three-year-old Mark, who has taken almost half of the available clay, starts to reach for some more. Several other children are using the clay. The teacher says:

___a. "Aren't you going to let the other children have some of the clay?"

___b. "You must not take any more clay, Mark. The other children want to use it, too."

___c. "Use the clay you have, Mark. The rest of the clay is for the other children to use."

5. Jane is playing in the housekeeping corner when she notices a teacher sitting nearby. She looks at the teacher a minute and then says, "I don't like you." The teacher replies:

___a. "Oh, I'm sure that you do. You like everyone in school."

___b. "I like you. Maybe you'll like me when you know me better."

___c. "You should not say that. It's not nice."

6. John is angry because there isn't time left for painting. He shouts at the teacher, "You old stink pot." The teacher says:

___a. "I know how you feel. It makes you pretty cross not to be able to paint when you want to."

___b. "Let's talk about something pleasant, John."

___c. "You mustn't talk to people that way, John. They won't like you."

7. Mary, who has a new baby brother at home, is at the table using crayons with several other children. She has ten crayons in her lap protecting them from the others. The teacher:

___a. makes sure that there are enough crayons for the other children so they do not need the ones Mary has.

___b. says, "It's selfish to take so many crayons, Mary. You'll have to leave the table if you can't share."

___c. says, "You need to use only one crayon at a time, Mary. Put them on the table. We share them with all the children."

8. The teacher finds three-year-old Janet in the toilet room watching Joe as he urinates. Janet looks a little uncomfortable when she sees the teacher. The teacher:

___a. says, "You mustn't stay in here watching the boys. Come, we'll go out and play now."

___b. takes her out of the toilet room saying, "You are through. You are ready to go out and play."

___c. says, "It's all right. You want to see how Joe goes to the toilet. Boys stand up. Girls sit down," and the teacher talks with Joe as they both stand watching.

9. John is an active, aggressive three-year-old. For no apparent reason he hits Jane as she walks past him on her way to the sandbox. Jane runs to the teacher, crying, "John hit me. He's a naughty boy." The teacher says:

_____a. "John, you mustn't hit children. We don't do that at nursery school."

_____b. "That's too bad. I hope it didn't hurt much," and then adds, "Were you going to play in the sandbox?"

_____c. "You can hit him when he does that. You needn't come to me."

B. At home or school

1. John takes a big bite of mashed potato, spilling some of it in his lap. Father says:

_____a. "Don't take such a big bite, John, and then you won't spill."

_____b. "Take little bites, John. See what nice little bites Janet is taking."

_____c. "Take little bites, John. Then it will all go in your mouth."

2. Bill, who is nearly four, comes in from his play outdoors, pulls off his hat and coat, drops them on the floor. His mother:

_____a. picks up his hat and coat, goes after Bill and gives them to him saying, "Your hat and coat were on the floor. They belong on the hook in the closet. Take them back and hang them up before you play."

_____b. goes after Bill, saying, "Your coat and hat are on the floor. They need to be hung on the hook in the closet; then you'll be ready to play." She returns with him while he picks up his wraps.

_____c. picks up his hat and coat and hangs them in the closet for Bill, realizing that he is already busy with play and might object to coming back to hang up his wraps.

3. A father sees four-year-old Bob hitting his playmate, Mary, because he wants the tricycle she is using and she won't give it to him. The father stops Bob, saying:

_____a. "You are a naughty boy to hit like that. You go into the house and play until you can behave."

_____b. "You should hit him right back, Mary. That will teach him not to act that way."

_____c. "Mary's using the tricycle, Bob. You can tell her you want it when she's through. I'll help you find something else to do while you're waiting."

4. One rainy day Betty and her friend Mary are making pictures, using paste and scraps of colored paper. They put lots of paste on both sides of the scraps of paper and they rub their fingers over the paste. Betty's mother sees them. She:

_____a. says, "Do it this way. Just a little paste on one side. And try to keep your hands clean."

_____b. smiles and says, "It's fun, isn't it!"

_____c. says, "What a mess you've made! That's enough! You are just wasting the paste."

5. Louise is helping pick up the toys scattered over the floor when she runs off to the other end of the room and starts playing. Her father says:

_____a. "Louise, if you'll come back and help, I'll tell you a story about what I saw this morning out the window."

_____b. "If you don't come back and help, you can't go out to play with your friends."

_____c. "Louise, you need to finish picking up. When the toys are all picked up, I'll tell you a story about what I saw out of the window this morning."

TO THINK AND WRITE ABOUT

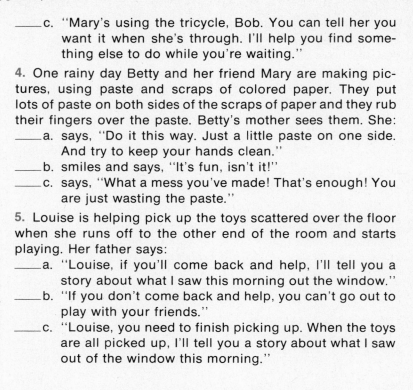

1 Try to describe some of the experiences you have had or things people have said to you which have increased your self-confidence.

2 Describe experiences you have had or things people have said to you which undermined your own self-confidence.

3 Why is it important to tell children what they should do rather than what they should not do?

4 Why is it better for a young child to do something because he or she has received encouragement and approval rather than through a spirit of competition?

5 How can a baby-sitter help a child who is too shy to play with other children?

6 Why are some conflicts between children a necessary and even desirable thing?

7 Describe some experiences you have had in which you used the "Suggestions for Guiding Children" in this chapter.

8 Describe a situation you faced which involved discipline.

REFERENCES

Biber, Barbara
"Group Methods in a Pre-School Program for Disadvantaged Children"
Children, pp. 15–20, January–February, 1970

Biber, Barbara, Edna Shapiro, David Wickens with Elizabeth Gilkeson
"Promoting Cognitive Growth—A Developmental-Interaction Point of View"
Analysis of Teaching Techniques, pp. 27–57
Washington, D. C.: National Association for the Education of Young Children, 1971

Cohen, Dorothy and Virginia Stern
Observing and Recording the Behavior of Young Children
New York: Bureau of Publications, Teachers College, Columbia University, 1958

Gross, Dorothy W.
"Equipping a Classroom for Young Children"
Young Children, Vol. 24, No. 2, December, 1968

Gross, Dorothy W.
"Teachers of Young Children Need Basic Inner Qualities"
Young Children, Vol. 23, No. 2, November, 1967

Horwitz, Elinor Lander
"Gifted Children"
Children Today, January–February, 1973

Kendall, Earline
"We Have Men on the Staff"
Young Children, Vol. 27, No. 6, August, 1972

Landreth, Catherine
Preschool Learning and Teaching, Chapter 4 "What Do They Learn" and Chapter 5 "Teaching: What Is It?"
New York: Harper & Row, 1972

Pfluger, Luther W. and Jessie Zola
"A Room Planned by Children"
Young Children, Vol. 24, No. 6, pp. 337–341, September, 1969

6

Children Learn
Through Activities

After studying this chapter, you will be able to

1. Analyze the way children learn.
2. Justify the value of play in children's development.
3. Select suitable books for children.
4. Provide activities that promote learning.
5. Encourage children's participation in art and music experiences.

In this chapter we shall discuss activities which promote children's learning about the world. Whether you care for one child at home or whether you have a group of children in a play group or a nursery school, you will be interested in activities which form a "curriculum" and promote learning.

If children are to have the best chance for well-rounded development they will need experiences in play which help them learn in all areas: language, literature, music, art, science, and social science—including psychology. We shall discuss each of these areas, beginning with the way children learn.

Learning

In the first months and years after birth individuals do more learning than they ever will again in a similar period of time. Watch a six-month-old baby as he studies an object in his hand, turning it, banging it, dropping it, or as he hears his mother's footsteps and greets her with smiles and gurgling. He is responding to the world around him very differently from a two-month-old infant. He has already learned a tremendous amount.

Watch a child who is just a year older, 18 months old. She is walking, doing some talking, turning her attention to many more things, solving simple problems, and drawing conclusions. She has interests and a range of relationships with other people. Young children are interesting to watch as they grow and change. If only we could learn as much in 12 months!

How does learning come about? Learning comes about, for one reason, because there is *an urge to grow and learn* inside everyone, a strong urge that overcomes many blocks or lacks in the environment. If the environment is a favorable one, if the child has the right kind of help, he or she will progress amazingly. Because the value of providing young children with favorable environments has been established, we are now accepting the need for more educational programs like Head Start, nursery schools, and parent-child-community centers where parents and children can learn to the benefit of both. At no time in life will the child be handicapped as much by an unfavorable environment as in these first years. At no time in life will he or she profit more from a favorable environment.

To meet their growing urge to learn, children should be nourished by a good diet of *different experiences suited to their levels of development*. Education for the infant, for example, means such things as having a variety of objects of different shapes and textures to grasp and handle, perhaps a mobile over the crib to watch, people who talk to the infant as they care for him or her, who change the baby's position so he or she can have new sights and sounds. It also means avoiding stimulating the baby too much, for an infant can get "fed-up" and close his or her ears and eyes to experiences just as we do sometimes. It means discovering the balance that suits this particular child between experiencing and relaxing.

The process of learning. Learning is an active process for the young child. A child learns by *doing things* to or with or about what she or he is experiencing—seeing, hearing, touching, tasting, experimenting, combining, testing out qualities of objects. We need to provide an environment for the child in which it is possible to act in these ways and *do* as much as possible.

To learn easily the young child depends, too, on our _interest and encouragement._ If we approve and are pleased with what the child is doing, it gives the boost that is needed for the child to go on with the adventures. A young child may not make much effort if those around her or him are indifferent, seldom even noticing her or his achievements. Later on a child will not need to depend as much on being noticed.

The young child *imitates* everything possible and this is one of the most important means of learning. We are the child's "models" and he or she tries to act as we act. Children are keen observers. No detail escapes them. Listen to the homemaking play of a group of three-year-olds. Notice how closely they imitate bits of daily life at home even to the voice inflections of telephone conversations overheard and the gestures of parents.

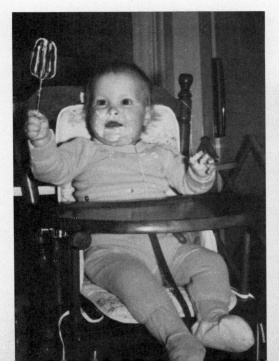

A child learns by doing—seeing, hearing, touching, tasting, experimenting, combining, testing.

In *learning language* the young child is very dependent on his or her family. If a child lives in a "verbal" family where a lot of speech is heard, where the grown-ups talk to the child and also are glad to listen, show interest in the child's efforts and are pleased with the child's attempts at speech, where they take time to look at books and enjoy them with the child, a child develops much more language competence than does a child whose home fails to supply him or her with this stimulation. Without the early environment encouraging language development no amount of speech teaching later can entirely make up for its lack.

Another thing that makes learning easier for a child is having *the right explanations* given at the right time. When children have new experiences they may need some matters explained to them in simple terms. They may need time to ponder these explanations and then ask further questions. Answers to children's questions should be in words they can understand, and we need to be as truthful and accurate as we can or they will be confused later. We will also try to clear up the many misconceptions children are sure to have, giving them more accurate ideas to use in their thinking.

Treating a child's questions with respect promotes learning. The three- and four-year-old is full of questions. Unfortunately a child is discouraged far too often by answers such as "You're too little to understand," or "Don't bother me," "Stop asking so many questions," or "Can't you leave things alone." The child is thus discouraged from making investigations.

The child should be encouraged to learn by having her or his questions treated with respect, by being given simple answers which are to the point and which don't offer more information than the child can grasp at the moment. Children should be encouraged by having many opportunities and materials to explore. Because they are eager and curious, they are ready to learn. We should try to answer their questions and give them more to explore. If we do not know the answers, we can try to find out. Investigating together is one way to treat a question with respect.

Value of Play for Learning in Many Areas

Play is the really important business of early childhood, just as school becomes the business of later childhood and adolescence, and a job is the business of adulthood. Some of our most important teaching is done when we are guiding the play of young children.

All healthy children play. They plan, build, organize. They make things and discover what materials are like and what they can do with materials. They imagine and wonder. They see themselves as part of the world of workers. A five-year-old who had been to the zoo drew a picture after the visit. The child drew some of the animals, but also added a truck and workmen whom the child imagined at work making the zoo. This seemed as important to the child as the animals seen at the zoo.

It takes a great deal of imagination to provide children with a rich variety of satisfying experiences for learning in some of the places where they may be growing up today. It takes planning on the part of citizens in every community.

What children may learn in play. In play children *practice skills*. They also *experiment* as the toddler does when fitting lids on pots and pans in the kitchen. Children *discover* as does the child picking up a leaf or a rock to examine it. Children *solve* problems as does the child building a structure with blocks, balancing pieces and planning. Children also imagine and *create* as they play, whether they are making sand pies, using art materials, or using words in making up stories.

In play, children practice skill. They also experiment, as the toddler does when fitting lids on pots and pans in the kitchen.

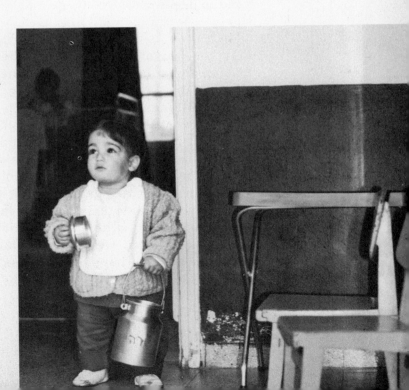

In play children lay the
foundations for intellectual
development.

In play children lay the *foundations* for *intellectual development*.
A child who has a rich variety of materials to use in play and a
breadth of play opportunities is getting preparation for formal
learning later on. These firsthand experiences in play equip the
child to deal with the concepts and symbols that will be met in later
stages of learning.

Play is a way of learning for children. As they play, children are
making all kinds of observations. They note details, and draw con-
clusions about the way things work, what things belong together,
and how things can be fitted. When playing with water, children
observe what floats and what doesn't, how water runs downhill,
and other properties of water or sand. They give close attention to
what is happening when another block is put on a pile of blocks.

We help children use words to describe the experiences by
giving them the names of objects, the "label" to stand for the
object. We ask questions and call their attention to qualities, to
similarities, and to differences. We help them organize and classify
information. When we are with children, we may comment, "I
wonder what will happen if we use the egg beater in the soapy
water?" Or we may answer a "why" question by saying, "Tell
me what you think."

As the child picks up a smooth stone, we can label its qualities. "It's a smooth stone. Have you found some stones that are different?" "Sort the stones you have into smooth ones and rough ones, and let's see which pile is bigger. Are there more smooth stones or more rough ones?" Comments such as these are needed to encourage the process of observing and questioning. The words "rough" and "smooth" begin to represent general characteristics, common to many objects. The child has begun to classify and generalize.

We can promote learning through play by the variety of materials and experiences we provide. A variety of things to touch and feel, to manipulate, to combine, and to make into other things can be found among discarded articles, such as an old clock, old pots and pans, lids, scraps of material, egg cartons, boxes, plastic bottles, lengths of hose, and boards.

Excursions to places such as a park, a zoo, a hatchery, a barn, a packing plant or warehouse, a fire station, a laundry, a railway or bus station, and an airport offer a variety of firsthand experiences.

Operation Headstart programs are designed to give children who have lacked a variety of play-learning experiences a chance to have these essential experiences, so that these children may have a better chance of success in school.

Excursions to places such as a park, a zoo, a hatchery, a barn, a packing plant or warehouse, a fire station, a laundry, a railway or bus station, and an airport offer a variety of firsthand experiences.

Make a list of some of the things a child can use in play which do not have to be purchased.

Make a list of places in your community which might provide learning experiences of interest to a preschool child.

Observe a child who seems to be absorbed in examining an object new to her or him. Describe what the child does with it.

List some of the concepts which are within the child's level of comprehension, such as up and down, above and below, light and heavy, loud and soft. What are possible play experiences in which the child can learn about these concepts and can put them into words?

Other Values of Play

Play is a way to deal with anxieties. The child uses play for this purpose. Children may be anxious about many things—about being little, about being helpless, about being left alone, about being left out or not liked, about failing to please. Many of these anxieties persist to some extent throughout life as we all know. Play is a way of reducing one's anxious feelings. A child can play at being big and strong, a cowboy or a soldier with two guns or a policeman or even a wicked witch. A child can make things happen in play as he or she wants. The child can be the one who does the spanking or the scolding or the one who goes off and leaves the little ones crying. He or she can comfort them and care for them. A child can do

Dramatic play is a great healer of fears.

Play is also a way of expressing and communicating ideas and feelings.

things to others or to dolls or even to materials instead of having things done to him or her. Dramatic play is a great healer of fears. Playing doctor makes having "shots" less upsetting. Escaping into roles such as these makes it easier to live in a real world where one is only a little boy or a little girl bossed around by almost everyone else.

Even when we are older, we continue to need to escape into fantasy sometimes. We imagine ourselves behaving with great bravery or being very beautiful, and we feel better able to live with the somewhat more limited selves we possess. Paul Bunyan legends grew out of just such feelings because people may need to imagine themselves more powerful than they are. They enjoy the thought, at least. We may imagine ourselves "telling off" a teacher or taking revenge on someone we don't like. We wouldn't really do these things, but imagining doing them relieves our feelings and leaves us with more energy to give to the actual, everyday situation we face. We are better able to sit in the class because we have drained off some of our irritation. It is a desirable thing as long as it helps us deal with reality more comfortably. It is not a desirable thing when we use it only to escape from facing real situations.

Play is also a way of expressing and communicating ideas and feelings. In many types of dramatic play children are expressing their feelings about the world around them and the people in it. Homemaking play is the most common expression of feelings in play, taking the role of father, mother, or baby, or perhaps doctor or nurse. In play the child expresses his or her feelings about all these roles. In block building, in play with clay, paints, sand, or any other material the child is expressing ideas, thoughts, and feelings. The child often thinks we understand far more than we do. Play may be broken off suddenly if the child finds this play-expression too disturbing for him or her at the time.

Watch a group of children playing house and see what they seem to be thinking about as shown in their play.

Children often use play quite openly as an avenue for communicating and thus relieving their feelings. A child may be upset because her mother has scolded her. She is angry with her mother and feels like doing something "bad" to her so the child goes out and digs a hole and buries her favorite toy, or throws all her sand toys into a big heap and then becomes interested in the tunnels she can make through the heap. The child's feelings have changed. Or she may get a toy gun and swagger around playing at shooting up the neighborhood. As she plays being a dangerous bandit, she can show her mother how angry she is without really hurting her. Play helps restore a child's emotional balance.

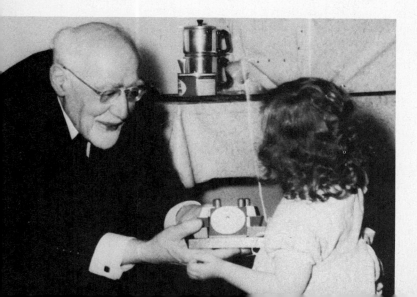

Children who are emotionally ill can often be helped through a process known as play therapy.

Children who are emotionally ill can often be helped through a process known as *play therapy*. Play therapy takes place under the guidance of a trained therapist. After the child has come to trust the therapist, the child is able to deal with fears and conflicts through playing them out in the presence of the therapist who can respond with understanding.

A very important value of *play* for children *is* that it is *a means of establishing social relations* with each other. Children come to know each other through playing together. At first children play side by side, often talking without listening, but enjoying the activity more because of the presence of another child. This is parallel play. Later, children will play in pairs. These pairs may shift frequently, so that in a few minutes a child is playing with a different companion. Next children form groups briefly around an activity or to accomplish a purpose. Group play gradually becomes more frequent by the time the child is four. By the time children are five they play in groups much of the time. Their language and social skills at this age are more nearly equal to the demands which group life makes. They have learned these skills through playing with others. In playing together children both lead and follow, cooperate and disagree. They use all types of techniques in getting along together. In play they have a chance to find the satisfactions which lie in companionship and in having friends. They have a chance to discover more about what they themselves are like. They can stand up for themselves. They give and take. Out of their successes and their failures they build patterns of living and working together. These experiences are part of the world of play and are an essential part of the process of socialization. Children need plenty of time for play.

Play Equipment

Many good types of play equipment can be made with soft wood and simple tools. A good piece of equipment should have most of these characteristics.

It should *have more than one use*, preferably many possible uses.

It should *be safe*, as with no sharp points or edges. It should *be sturdy* and able to stand up under all kinds of treatment.

A good piece of play equipment should be safe and sturdy, encourage imaginative types of play, offer possibilities for learning about the world, and invite use by more than one child at a time.

It should *encourage imaginative* types of *play.*

It should *offer possibilities for learning about the world* — such as learning about forces from using a pulley or about forms from fitting puzzles.

It should *invite use by more than one child at a time,* as a sandbox does.

Plan or make something a preschool child can use in play.

Language enables us to develop ideas and concepts, to communicate them, and to learn from other people.

Language and Books

Children are busy learning to talk. As we all know, talking is important! It is useful to be able to speak easily and comfortably, using correct grammar, and to understand a large number of words. Language enables us to develop ideas and concepts, to communicate them, and to learn from other people.

Babies cry and make sounds, all the sounds from which words are formed and many more, but babies need to hear speech if they are to learn to make words out of these sounds. Talk to a baby as you bathe or dress or feed the baby, not "baby talk," but the speech which you would use to anyone else. Give the baby good speech patterns to copy. Speak clearly and not too rapidly and you will make it easier for the baby to learn. Sing and repeat words and phrases. Rhythm and pitch differences are parts of speech. The baby needs to hear sounds that are rhythmic, that are high and low, loud and soft.

A toddler enjoys practicing speech. Children repeat words and phrases over and over. They chant them. They sing or talk to themselves as they play. Speech for them is not just a matter of communicating with someone. They think out loud. They enjoy expressing themselves through language without any thought of a listener. They also use speech for communicating with others.

A word may stand for a whole idea at first. "Me" may mean "I want it. Give it to me." It will help the toddler learn if we put in all the words, "You want it. I'll give it to you." This helps the child to realize that there is more to it than one sound. Sometimes it is better *not* to understand the child too easily. Not understanding the sounds encourages the child to make the effort to learn to use speech to get what he or she wants.

A toddler enjoys practicing speech.

Children need to have someone listen to them and show pleasure when they talk. A mother's delight at the "mamma" which the baby babbles by accident helps the baby remember and use that particular sound and associate it with mother. In this way a word is born for the baby! It has been there all the time. The attention she gives when the baby says the word makes the baby value and repeat that word.

As children get older, they need to find that there are people who take time to listen to them as they stumble and fumble to convey something that is important to them. They need to feel people are interested, too. We listen to children as part of helping them learn to talk.

Learning to talk. It takes time and plenty of practice to learn to talk. It takes time for speech muscles to function smoothly, just as it does for other muscles. The child stutters over a word, or the words may tumble over each other. The child misses the mark of easy flowing speech. But give him or her time. Don't tell the child to talk more slowly. Listen as though you had all the time in the world, so the child won't feel in such a hurry. Speak slowly yourself when you answer. When the child pronounces a sound or a word incorrectly, don't call attention to mistakes or correct the child. Repeat the word correctly yourself, so the child hears it pronounced properly. Do not make him or her repeat it.

Speaking serves complicated social and intellectual purposes and involves a whole system of muscles and nerve impulses. Learning to control them may take months and years of practice. There is effort involved. Most children go through periods of what we might call "stuttering" if we heard an adult talking this way. This is a normal part of speech development for a child and it is serious only if our comments make the child feel upset and afraid to try talking.

Many children have difficulty with some sounds. Try to say these sounds with special clarity when you speak to the child. There are exercises which make the tongue more flexible. These exercises are games which the child enjoys. They include a play on sounds which helps the child become aware of differences in sounds. Playing games which exercise the muscles used in speaking may improve a child's articulation without making the child self-conscious about his or her own speech. If a child has not learned to say a sound correctly by the time he or she reaches first grade, some help in school from a trained teacher should be sought.

Talk with a teacher of speech and get suggestions for speech-development games.

The important thing is to learn to use language freely, with pleasure in all its functions. Give a child plenty of experiences to talk about. Really listen to the child and encourage expression in words. Avoid correcting the child and making her or him afraid to try speaking.

Experimenting with words. As children learn to talk, they also go through periods of experimenting with words. They experiment with sounds, repeating new words that are appealing because of rhythmic qualities or repetition of syllables or associations. Children experiment also with the meaning of words and the responses they bring when they are used.

This kind of experimenting usually begins with toilet words such as "wee wee" or "poo-poo pants." By the age of three they may take delight in using such words at inappropriate times and

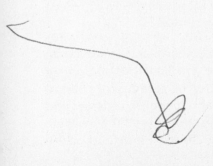

As children learn to talk, they also go through periods of experimenting with words.

places. When they are with other children, they often chant all sorts of nonsense words or phrases. These chants may include all the toilet words they know. Later children begin to add the swear words or the sex words which they have heard. They may call each other all kinds of names. They are finding they can be aggressive with words and can assert themselves verbally. They are just managing some control over hitting and physical aggression. Language is another way to be aggressive and is a step in growing.

This period in the child's growth presents a problem to adults. As a general rule, we deal with the problem best by ignoring most of this kind of language behavior. It is a phase which will pass. Children of this age use swear words because they find they get a response. When they are angry, they may use unacceptable words because they want to disturb us. If we object, we can tell them so, "I don't like that word. If you want to say it, go where I can't hear you."

It may be important to help a child who is four or five years old understand how other people may respond if he or she uses certain words. "Most people don't like hearing that word. Say it if you want to, but not when you are with grown-ups. They won't like it and may be cross with you for saying it." If he or she tries it out, the child will at least understand the reason for the response he or she may get, even though the child still may not understand why people feel as they do. A child is really confused if he or she feels that the word itself is naughty and that he or she is doing something bad in saying it, like creating some kind of black magic.

Most of the time it is better to change the subject. It is enough to say that you don't like to hear the word, and then introduce another activity, begin a story or a game. Usually the less attention that is paid to bad language at this age, the less attraction it has for the child. A child's judgment about which words to use in different circumstances improves with age and experience.

Creating with words. Children create with words just as they do with blocks or with paint. If we listen, we can hear the beginning of songs, poems, and stories. It is a matter of recognizing them. When you are with children, have a pad and pencil handy so you can jot down the song a child may be singing as he or she swings, or the story a child is telling while playing alone in the sand or the housekeeping corner.

Children create with words just as they do with blocks or with paint.

Children will enjoy hearing you read their own songs or stories back to them. Perhaps you can make a booklet of some of these songs or stories. Like keeping children's paintings and putting them up on the wall, this shows them you value their creative efforts and encourages them to keep on creating.

Children usually enjoy very much a story you make up about their own experiences. It may be about something they have done or something which has happened to them. Try making up a story when you are with a child. Give the child a chance to join in through repeating a phrase or answering a question or adding details. You are helping the child learn to create and express herself or himself through language.

Some of you may want to try to write a story for a certain child or for a group of children, keeping in mind the ages and experiences of the children. Stories for young children should be about familiar things: other boys and girls, families, animals, firefighters and police, or about childlike fantasies that are not frightening or confusing. Repetition, suspense, and brevity are important. Writing the story on colored paper and illustrating it will add to its interest. Try reading the story to the child or the group. Maybe you will revise it somewhat after you have tried it out. Making up a good story for children takes skill. Some of you may enjoy developing this skill. If you are doing some baby-sitting, you can try out your stories and discover what children enjoy and what stimulates their imaginations.

Telling stories to children is fun, too, especially if one learns to do it well. A good storyteller learns a story, practicing it until he or she can tell it with expression. It is a wonderful skill. Children make a wonderful audience.

> **Look up a book by Ruth Sawyer, *The Way of a Storyteller*, or Ruth Tooze's *Storytelling*. Learn a story and tell it to the class first, using a tape recorder so that you may listen later and criticize your own performance. If you have a chance, try telling the story to a child or a small group of children. What stories do you find hold the attention of the children? What are the differences between storytelling to two or three children and to larger groups? You will find that every audience is different.**

Books, especially picture books. There are places in the world where people have very few books, where there are no public libraries like ours from which one can borrow a book. There are places in which few people have had a chance to learn to read. It would change our world to live without books—cook books, song books, picture books, comic books, school books, mystery stories, adventure stories, history books, biographies, novels.

There is not time to discover everything for ourselves even if we could. We read to find out more about things in the world, to answer some of our questions, to learn about what other people have thought or discovered. Through books one can share in the thoughts and feelings of people who live in far-off places and of people who lived in other ages.

We want children to enjoy books, discover their magic, and be eager to learn to read and use books for all the purposes they can serve for us.

Being with people who, themselves, enjoy books sets a pattern for a child. If you like books, you can share your liking with the child. Read to her or him often. Read books that are attractive with good pictures and a text you can both enjoy.

We want children to enjoy books, discover their magic, and be eager to learn to read.

Suggestions for Selecting a Book

A book should have pictures. The pictures should be in color when possible, simple, easy to understand, but artistic and related to the story. They should be placed on the page with the part of the story they illustrate.

Books should be short, with only a few sentences or short paragraphs to a page. The language should be free of errors in grammar. Repetition of words, phrases, or ideas appeal to children.

The subject matter for two- and three-year-olds should be about things they know, such as children, animals, people. It is important that the facts be accurate. Older children like stories about familiar objects, but they are beginning to be able to distinguish fact and fantasy. They like fairy stories when they can tell what is real and what is pretend. The text in a good book for children does not distort the truth. It should help the child recall and understand better what he or she sees in the world rather than introducing the child to new and strange things.

Books with humor and with suspense hold children's attention. Children enjoy funny things. These things should be funny to the child—not adult humor. Children love the dramatic, but they must be able to understand the humor and drama. They can appreciate beauty in language just as they can appreciate illustrations that are beautiful.

There are wonderful books available for children today. Some are inexpensive as well as good, as for example, *some,* but not many, of the "supermarket-shelf" books. It is worthwhile to spend time selecting books for children.

Activities and Materials to Promote Learning

Water, sand, earth, and clay. Every child needs plenty of chance to play with *water.* Water play is satisfying, relaxing, and full of learning possibilities for children. Water fascinates children. They get absorbed in water play and are constantly finding new possibilities in it. Water pours; it spills. It runs downhill. It will not run uphill. It disappears in the sand. Some things float in it. Other things sink.

At home children play in the bathtub with bath toys, or they play bathing their dolls, washing doll clothes and hanging them up to dry, washing doll dishes, or cleaning and scrubbing with soap and water, perhaps wading in a puddle or playing under the hose on hot days. A big tub half full of water gives opportunities for play. Sponges, scrub brushes, funnels, pans, and all kinds of accessories enrich the water play.

A can of water and a broad paint brush keep a child or a group of children busy being painters, painting fences, walks, walls. The possibilities for exploring, for observing, for testing observations with water are endless. It is safe and not frightening when there is not too much of it!

Every child needs many opportunities to play with water.

If you are planning for a group of children, ask yourself what experiences you can provide for them with water. How can you arrange these experiences so children can be free in their play? Putting a piece of oilcloth, for example, under a tub of water means that spilling is not serious. Putting plastic aprons over the children's clothes keeps them dry when it is not bathing-suit weather.

You will need to decide what limits you will set to children's experiments such as rules about no throwing of water indoors.

Be clear about these rules and enforce them with confidence. Not all investigations should be carried out! Stop children immediately, for example, when they start to throw water. Point out what they *can* do with it. If they persist in throwing, remove the water for a while. Behavior has consequences.

> **List some of the objects that can be used with water.**
> **What are ways in which one can provide for indoor play with water for a group of children?**
> **What can a child learn from playing in water?**
> **Observe an informal situation in which children are playing in water. It may be on the street or in a park or playground, after a rain. What different activities did you observe?**

Combined with water, sand is fun for a child alone or for children in groups. The sand area should be large enough for several children to enjoy.

Sand is another material high on the list of desirable play materials for children.

Sand is another material high on the list of desirable play materials for children. It has endless possibilities. In playing with sand, children enjoy making things, planning, imagining, and cooperating. Combined with water it is fun for a child alone or for children in groups. The sand area should be large enough for several children to enjoy. Sand toys may be old cans with smooth rims, pans, funnels, small cars and trucks, and many other articles. Sand encourages sustained play. Rules are needed, such as, "No throwing of sand" or "Keep the sand in the box."

Earth is for digging, especially if it is soft and muddy. Small-sized shovels and spades are good exercise for muscles and balance. Feeling mud and watching it as it oozes, or as it dries, add to a child's experience. Messy play is possible in mud and children need messy play at times if they are to appreciate cleanliness at other times.

Soft clay gives some of the same sensory experiences as mud but clay has the advantage of being suited to indoor play and easier to contain on a table top. Children enjoy all the many things one can make with clay. Try playing with it yourself, without trying to make a product. See how it feels.

Boys and girls like building with blocks and learn many things from using them.

Blocks and construction. Next to water, sand, and mud, the most valuable play material for young children is likely to be *blocks.* Boys and girls like building with blocks and learn many things from using them. They learn about sizes, shapes, forms, numbers, and designs. They get creative satisfaction from making things from blocks. They often have fun in working out plans with one another. They give themselves lessons in cooperating with each other.

Blocks teach the child about forms and shapes and relationships and numbers. From blocks the child learns mathematical concepts. How many blocks will it take? Two short ones may equal one longer one. Understanding physics and mathematics is very important. The child needs many firsthand experiences in these fields — experiences which will serve as the basis for theoretical understanding later.

Children's building has more variety if they can combine things, such as small cars, airplanes, farm animals, or dolls, with blocks. These materials suggest roads, airports, farms, homes, and towns.

> **Watch individual children of various ages playing with blocks. Watch groups of children who are playing with blocks. What age children did you watch? How was their age related to what they built and to how they built it?**

The buildings of older children are often complex, extensive structures with interesting designs. Children are fortunate if they have *plenty* of building materials for construction play. They are fortunate if they have space for their building. And they are fortunate if they are left to their own devices concerning what to do or how to do it.

Imaginative children use many other things for construction. Cardboard cartons, wooden boxes, sturdy chairs on their sides, a card table with a blanket or sheet over it — all these things serve building purposes. We see individual differences here as in everything else. Some children spend a good deal of time in construction; other children spend only a little time.

Preschool children who have the chance usually enjoy a lightweight hammer (not a toy one), nails with large heads, and pieces of soft wood. It gives them a chance to gain motor skill and a sense of real accomplishment to make an airplane, for example, by nailing two boards together.

Sawing a piece of soft wood, held firmly in a vise on a low bench or table, is an achievement. It is exciting to a child to make two pieces where there was only one! When children use tools, they need responsible supervision. At home or at school children need a chance to learn how to use tools properly.

Before you can supervise children's use of tools, you must know how to use tools yourself. Make a simple wooden toy. This helps you appreciate the effort it takes. It helps you recall the frustration of bent nails, pounded fingers, and pieces that won't stay where you want them.

Homemaking play and play equipment. Dolls have always been an important part of children's play through the ages. Both boys and girls enjoy family play of mother, father, and baby, plus all the supplementary roles they see around them. At home children are almost sure to have a doll and in group play boys and girls together spend time in the space where the homemaking play equipment is — a family of dolls, doll beds, a stove and table, doll dishes, chairs, perhaps a chest of drawers with plenty of dress-up clothes, and some telephones. Here is where most of the dramatic play begins.

At home or at school children need a chance to learn how to use tools properly.

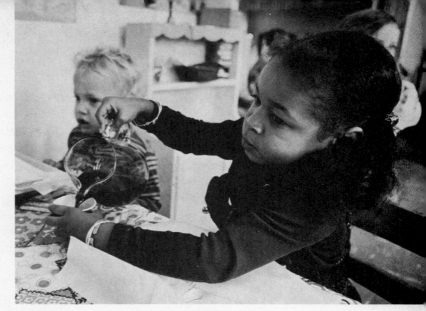

In group play boys and girls spend time where the homemaking equipment is.

When a new child enters the group, he or she is likely to feel at home first in this area where there are familiar things with which to play. Lessons in sharing are practiced here and social conflicts worked through. The child playing with friends at home or in school finds he or she must let friends share possessions if he or she is to enjoy their company.

Supply children with plenty of homemaking equipment and observe the way they use it. You will gain insight into the way they are looking at the world around them and how they feel about it.

There are other possibilities for dramatic play such as playing store, playing school, playing being a firefighter or a member of the police department or a letter carrier or a doctor. It is desirable to have materials available which can be used in acting these roles or the work roles of the parents when possible. Allow uninterrupted periods of time for dramatic play of all kinds when you care for young children.

The World of Nature

Gardens. Experiences with plant life are important for a child. For example, when digging outdoors the child may come across a root in the ground. He or she tries to pull it up. Help the child examine it and ask questions. "Do you know what it is?" "What do you think roots are for?" "Do you suppose we can find which shrub or tree this root comes from?" See if the children can discover the shrub or tree to which the roots belong.

Sprouting some beans and discovering how the first roots start will now have meaning to these children. This experience is based on interest which grew from their discovery of a root system. Its meaning can be broadened by other experiences to see how roots develop. All children will not be equally interested, but if some children are extremely interested, you have a good project.

The children may discover seed pods. Then you can extend their interest in this area. Bring in seeds of different sizes. (There are many sizes!) Help children find answers to questions such as "How are seeds scattered?" "What different kinds of seed pods are there?"

From the children's point of view, seeds are slow in sprouting, even radish seeds. As scientists, the children may want to see what is happening to the seeds. You do not want them to take your word for things that they can investigate. Let them dig and discover. Limit the number of seeds to be dug up, if you can, and explain why, so the children can be aware of what the results will be if they dig up *every* seed. You might get some radish plants along with the seeds, so that the children can water and care for something visible from the start. They can perceive more of the cycle of growth.

A garden is fun because of the digging.

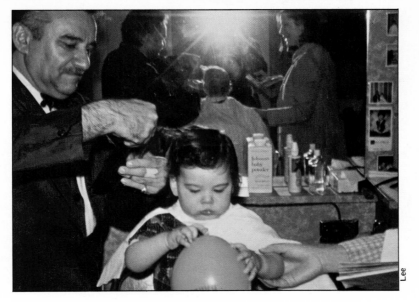

Lee

Playing with a balloon helps this young child accept
the new experience of having his hair cut.

Boxer

Three- and four-year-olds can
learn to do many things for
themselves.

Derfus

Derfus

A birthday party for a small child should be well planned, not last too long, and include only a few guests.

Derfus

Brothers and sisters enjoy each other's company most of the time.

Children enjoy going on outings with their friends. Frequent rest times are needed when the children are young.

Aukema

A garden is fun because of the digging. Digging leads to the discovery of earthworms. Here is another area you can explore. What are worms doing in the garden? How do they live? You may need to become informed yourself.

Weather provides all kinds of opportunities for science experiences — for finding out, verifying, reasoning, and drawing conclusions. "You need your boots on. The grass is wet with dew this morning," said the teacher. The little boy who had come to school in a car and was sure that it hadn't rained looked at her with disbelief. He turned and ran out and felt the grass. Yes, it was wet all right. He went back inside and got on his boots. He was testing a statement in a scientific manner.

The sun dries dew. There is a difference between shady and sunny places on the grass. Objects cast shadows in sunlight. Ask questions such as, "Why is there shade?" "What makes shadows?" Notice the difference between shadows in the morning and around noon. Try marking out where the shadows fall at different times of day. Play with making shadows.

If it is cold enough, water in the puddle freezes to ice. Bring it inside and let it melt. Other things change in other ways. Gelatin gets firm. Clay hardens as it dries and changes color, too. Water changes to steam when it boils. Boil some water and collect some steam. Observe the operation at all stages.

Observe, test, find out. Questions precede answers. We can help children by asking questions of them as well as by helping them find answers to the questions they ask.

Animal life. Most children love animals and we can enlarge their experience by introducing them to a variety of animals. How animals eat and what they eat, how they eliminate, where they sleep, how they behave and the kind of care they need, how they care for their babies, how they differ — these are all points of interest to a child.

The more experiences children have with a variety of animals, the more learning for them, even if the experience is limited to a visit to a zoo or barns in the country. Sometimes animals can be brought to the group for a visit. A goat or a lamb may spend time on the playground, or there may be animals for pets such as fish, a bird, chickens, pollywogs, salamanders, guinea pigs, or white rats, in addition to a dog or cat. When children have animal pets, it is very important that they learn how to handle them properly. They will need careful supervision at first and demonstrations of how the animal should be cared for, so that the experience may be a good one for both child and animal.

If children are able to keep a pet, such as a rabbit, they have many chances to observe animal life. If the rabbit is a female, she can be bred, so that in time there will be baby bunnies to care for. This adds to knowledge in an area in which children are keenly interested, that is, where babies come from and how mothers care for babies. You may find yourself learning some things about rabbits as you answer the children's questions and try to clear up some of their misconceptions. Children will talk about the rabbit. They may make up stories about it and about fanciful bunnies. You can bring out books about rabbits and read stories. Books verify experience and extend it.

Most children love animals and we can enlarge their experience by introducing them to a variety of animals.

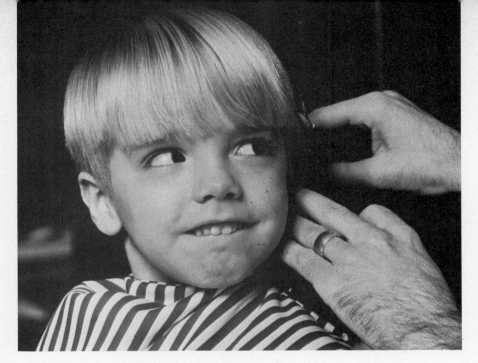

You will find yourself learning, too, as you look at things
through a child's eyes.

Excursions. Another way in which you can help children learn
about the world in which they live is through taking them on
walks. A tractor may be at work in the street, or in digging the foun-
dation for a new house. The nearest fire hydrant may be getting
flushed out, or the street may be getting swept. Children learn from
watching these things.

The grocery store, the feed store, the fire station are full of
learning experiences. The children will be interested in some and
not in others. Listen to their comments when they are there and
try to clear up their confusions and enlarge their understanding of
what they see. You will find yourself learning much as you look at
things through children's eyes. The world will look new to you. You
will see things you never noticed before and you will be teaching
in a very good sense of the word.

Plan a walk with a particular child or with a group of children.
Be sure to go first yourself so that you are thoroughly familiar
with what the children may see or do on the walk. What is the
purpose of the walk? What will you do to ensure a good experi-
ence for the child or the group of children?

Numbers, mathematics, and physics. A child has many experiences with *numbers* long before learning to count. The child finds he or she has *one* mouth and *two* hands. There are *two* chairs when a child sits looking at a book with someone. There are a *few* blocks or *many* blocks. The child is building up concepts of quantity from all these experiences. We can give him or her help by using the words, the labels for the concept, by saying, "Two hands" or "Two chairs." It takes many repetitions for a child to appreciate that two always refers to the same quantity of objects, two hands, two feet, two eyes, two people.

The average preschool child probably does not think in terms of more than about four or five objects, although she or he can learn to count more than that number. We help children best by keeping things simple in what we expect. We want them to "know" the concept of two or three or four. They should be able to say "We need two chairs" because they really know what two stands for. We can also help them by making sure that we use the number in what we say. We say, "Bring me the two books on the table, please," instead of "Bring me those books on the table, please."

All first-hand experiences which make mathematical concepts part of a child's own thinking will help him or her in later learning in school.

The child learns about *measurement*, too—what long and short mean and wide and narrow. Children enjoy measuring. A foot rule, a yard stick, a measuring tape, even a surveyor's chain are good additions to supplies for play. "Which is the longest?" "How can you tell?" and "How do you find out for sure?" are questions that will start them off on a new activity.

The child learns about *division* in many ways. There are enough cookies for everyone on the plate. The apple or orange is divided into two pieces or halves, or into four pieces or quarters. A set of measuring cups and measuring spoons are useful and these can be used in playing in water or sand. Blocks which are in units, some half as long as others and some in thirds or fourths, add to the child's opportunity to learn about mathematics.

All these firsthand experiences which make mathematical concepts part of the child's own thinking will help him or her in later learning in school. The child will be better able to deal with more complex symbols. Children whose play opportunities have been limited in their homes are in special need of this kind of help. Children in day care programs and Head Start need this kind of guidance. We should be careful to use the right words and ask the right kind of questions to make the most of these experiences for understanding.

Children do apply scientific methods in their play. They are curious and want to find out about the world around them. They try to test out their discoveries. They ask questions. These are desirable patterns of behavior and the sign of budding scientists. We can give them help by good guidance.

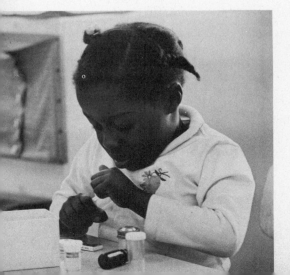

Children do apply scientific methods in their play. They are curious and want to find out about the world around them.

A child rolling a ball or building with blocks is discovering principles of *physics*. The ball rolls down. When it is thrown up, it comes down. Blocks piled too high or stacked unevenly will fall. A hammer and nails or a saw offer lessons relating to force and energy. Watch a child working with them. The child has already learned a lot about physics from his or her own body, balancing and using it.

A magnet, a vise, a pulley, wheels of all kinds belong among children's play materials. They are among the best toys for them. Many toys are a waste of money and precious time. They indicate little respect for the tasks of children in their growing. These real things will be more fun and give more satisfaction.

A child learns a lot in a kitchen. First, it may be how a lid fits on a pan, how to stack bowls, pans, cans. The toddler with access to cupboards opening at floor level arranges and rearranges, tests out sounds, sizes, shapes, qualities of things. Later, the child plays in water at the sink—warm water, cold water, sudsy water. Time is spent pouring water, filling pans, maybe dissolving something in water as the child helps with the cooking. He or she stirs and mixes, or plays with dough, making cookies.

List possible science experiences for preschool children. Make sure that you have covered a *range* of experiences—in biology (plant and animal), chemistry, and physics. Carry out some science experiences yourself which might be suitable to try with children.

Planning a Science Experience

Remember the following as you plan for science experiences with a child:

1. Begin with something familiar and interesting to the child.

2. Let the *child* do the discovering. Let the child approach it in her or his own way, do what she or he likes with it. Try asking a question which will direct the child's attention to something she or he may have overlooked. Give the child a chance *to discover for herself or himself rather than to be told.* You know how you feel when you get a lot of directions!

3. Make comments and explanations simple. Use few words. Listen to the *child's* comments. Let children discuss among themselves. Quietly call their attention to something they may be missing, try to correct their misconceptions, but let them develop their ideas.

4. A child learns by using his or her senses—sight, touch, taste, smell, hearing. Provide experiences which let the child use as many of these senses as possible.

5. You are helping the child learn to use the scientific method. Every one of us needs to make use of this method. Every one of us needs some understanding of scientific principles and some scientific knowledge in all the possible fields. We will add to our own knowledge as we prepare to help children learn.

Music and Dance

All children love to use their bodies in rhythmic ways. They march, swing, ride tricycles, run. In some places in the world, adults of all ages do a great deal of dancing. Children who watch adults dance begin to dance in more intricate ways early in their lives. For children music and body movements go together. They sing as they swing, or they make movements as they listen to music.

A child's sense of rhythm develops as a result of maturation. Children differ in their feeling for rhythm. Differences come more from inherent capacities in the child than from training. One child will beat on a drum and keep good time to music at three years. Another child just beats! It is little use trying to teach the second child. Just give that child time. His or her capacity for feeling rhythm may be maturing at a slower rate than that of the first child. Correcting that child may only be discouraging and prevent his or her enjoying rhythmic play.

Singing with children. A child's sense of pitch, on the other hand, is helped by practice. Singing with children, helping them hear the difference between high and low sounds, playing tone games will help them develop their "musical ear" and give flexibility and better pitch to their singing.

Most children like to pitch their singing lower than many people think, for children's voices *sound* high to us because they are light. An autoharp or an accordion is a fine instrument to play to accompany singing.

Sing with children around the piano. Sing with them when they are outdoors doing things like swinging or teetering. There are many good swinging songs, for example. You can also use songs the children themselves make up, singing with them. There are songs about rocking, walking, running through autumn leaves, which are short and easy to learn. Use them when the children are doing these activities.

Children often sing as they play, when they are happy. Music is an avenue for expression of feelings. In the beginning, it is used without any formal teaching.

Teaching children songs is done by *letting them learn* through hearing the song, using it, and, perhaps, polishing off the learning by repeating phrases the child has trouble with. Much effort spent in memorizing songs or rhymes may interfere with the child's interest in creating his own songs. If you enjoy a song and sing it frequently, you will find the child singing it, too.

Music is an avenue for expression of feelings.

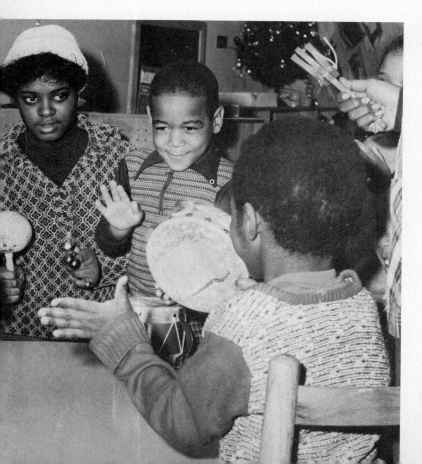

Songs with finger plays have action which a child enjoys. They are useful if you are baby-sitting and find there is little for the child to do.

Learn some finger plays to use as a resource when you may want them.

Creating songs or poems which express their own thoughts and feelings is worthwhile for all children. Parents can encourage children in expression of this kind by showing interest. If parents listen as the children sing, jot down the notes and words, and sing them later, saying, "This is your song," the parents help the children value their own creative impulses. They are more likely to continue producing music on their own just as children continue creating when we show our appreciation for their pictures, stories and poems. Our interest will encourage them to use music as an avenue of expression and to be more aware of the music they hear.

If you have a play group, be sure to plan many experiences with music for the children. They can use sound-making instruments, such as bells, tambourines, cymbals, triangles, and drums of all kinds. For reasons of hygiene, it is better to avoid an instrument that goes into the mouth. You can make or devise many sound-making instruments yourself—drums from cans, wooden bowls, or nail kegs; cymbals from two lids of pans; bells on sticks or elastic wrist bands; rattles from small boxes with rice or dried peas inside; or tambourines from bottle caps on embroidery hoops.

Moving to music. Music and movement are closely related. Music experiences for children should include a great deal of body movement and action. Children are likely to express their feelings in rhythmic ways. They may do this as individuals or in a group.

Give young children plenty of chance to move to music but avoid teaching them *how* to move. Let them move in their own ways. Here again avoid "patterns." Play fast music or slow and see what they do. Maybe you have a song about an elephant. See how many different kinds of elephants you will have! If you dance yourself, do it because you like it but not because you want the children to do what you do. Let them discover dancing in their own ways. Leave children free to create their own patterns in music and dancing—patterns which express the ways they are thinking and feeling at the moment.

A group experience with children may involve imagination and dramatic play. Such dramatic play may be pretending to be various animals or people—soldiers, policemen, or Indians. The children may "become" different animals or persons with each change in music. Marching to the sound of a trumpet or while using instruments themselves is also a wonderful experience for groups of children.

Listening to music. Listening is part of enjoying music. Children should have a chance to listen when they wish to do so. Some enjoy listening for only short periods. Remember that we want children to learn to *enjoy* music and to keep their spontaneous pleasure in sounds and rhythm. Children are not helped to do this if they are forced to sit quietly listening when they would much rather be doing something else.

When music is being played, you may notice that the child playing with dolls or running a truck will often move in response to the rhythm. That child is listening while playing. A child who may get tired of listening can play quietly without disturbing the

Children are especially interested if they can handle and try an instrument, listen to a note they have played, and explore how the sound was produced.

other listeners. That child learns about being considerate of others' wishes. His or her wishes have been respected, so it is easier for the child to understand what consideration means.

A valuable listening experience for children is to listen while watching music being produced by different instruments. Most children have heard music on the radio or a record player, but they have not seen the instruments which make the different sounds. They do not know about the great variety of ways in which music is made.

There are the stringed instruments used to accompany folk singing. A ballad singer accompanying himself or herself on an instrument will bring delight to children who enjoy music. There are violins. Invite a friend who plays a violin to visit, bring the violin, and play familiar songs. This gives the child a chance to become acquainted with a stringed instrument which is very different from the piano. Wind instruments, such as the flute, the saxophone, or the trumpet, offer another experience. Percussion instruments are different still.

A good listening experience may be one where the child can watch and listen to a school band as it practices or a drill in which drums accompany the marching. People who are studying music and practicing are usually glad to take time to play their instruments for a child who has come to visit. They appreciate her or his interest.

Children are especially interested if they have the chance to touch and to try the instrument, to listen to a note they have played, and to explore how the sound is produced. A person who understands children as well as music can help the children gain much from these kinds of experiences. Children enjoy listening to records. There are good records for children—with music and with stories. You will find individual preferences for selections. When you select records for children you can take into account these individual preferences. But remember that you are helping the child build an appreciation for music at its best. Select the records thoughtfully. Buy only those records that are well performed and well recorded.

All children profit from a rich variety of experiences in listening and learning more about music and the ways in which it is made. These experiences are good for an individual child or for children in groups. They help develop interest in music.

Group games with music. Games at this age should be very simple. It is hard for children to wait for turns, so groups should be small. "Ring around the Rosy," "London Bridge," or a simple choosing game are suitable for the fives and older fours. They will enjoy games for only short periods of time.

Simple finger plays are fun for groups as well as individuals at this age. Finger plays have a place at the end of the day when children are tired and need a quiet activity. Finger plays are useful with an individual child when he or she may have to wait somewhere and has nothing to play with.

Art

Just as children love to move to music, children love to draw and paint. Have plenty of paper, crayons, chalk, and paint around. But *don't* make things for the children to copy. Throw out coloring books! We want children to develop their artistic capacities with all the satisfaction it brings. Art is too important to turn it into "busy work."

Eddie. Here is a description of a child in nursery school who turned to the easel to paint after watching the group dancing to some very rhythmic music. It shows a child expressing his feelings about music and rhythm through his painting. It helps us see the relation between art and music. Eddie had not joined the group but had stood watching. Suddenly he turned and went directly to the easel. He was the only child there. He picked up two brushes, one in each hand, and began making sweeping lines and short staccato-like movements across the paper. He painted very rapidly. As he painted, Eddie's eyes sparkled, and there was a smile on his face. He attempted to remove the first painting when he finished but could not unclip it. A teacher stepped over and helped him with no comment. He continued with a second painting immediately. The second was similar to the first. Eddie made no attempt to control the drips. He was quickly finished with the second. It was removed, and Eddie began the third immediately. This time he took two brushes in each hand. He gaily blotched the colors on in a vigorous manner, dipping the brushes four at a time. He moved his whole body as he painted; it was delightful to watch. He

The child's art work should be an honest expression of what she or he is feeling and thinking.

painted intently, seemingly unaware of people around him. After the fifth picture he replaced the brushes and experimented for a second or two with mixing colors, perhaps as a result of placing the brushes in the wrong containers. His sixth and seventh paintings were done with two brushes. Now he made sweeping movements with great speed, covering the entire paper with paint. Before beginning his seventh picture he made a delightful musical sound. It was his only verbal sound during the experience. This seventh painting was like a grand finale. His movements became very intense. He gave a tremendous sigh as he finally placed the brushes back in the jars. As the teacher removed the painting from the easel, she asked, "Would you like to paint any more?" "No, I am finished," Eddie said and strolled away quietly.

Art as expression of thoughts and feelings. The child's art work should be an honest expression of what she or he is feeling and thinking. The child may never be a great artist, but should be able to express thoughts and feelings through art as Eddie did in the paintings. For some children art seems especially important as an avenue of expression.

Drawing techniques or skills in drawing are not important at this age.

Art may be important to children as an avenue for expression because they lack the skill to express themselves as adequately in words or in music. It is not difficult to pick up a crayon or paintbrush and make a drawing, either a simple one or a complex creation. Finger paints offer a medium which requires little skill and brings satisfying results.

Children delight in expression and in representing the way things look to them. They paint what is important to them. If they represent a person, the face gets the biggest place in the picture. A door may be almost as large as the house. A bee may be larger than a flower. Perhaps the child has just discovered bees or been stung by a bee. Children use the colors which please them. These colors may bear little relation to the actual colors of the objects they paint.

Children enjoy using their imaginations with freedom. We block their imaginations if we tell them what to draw or how it should be done. We take away the joy of creating and of self-expression when we give them something to copy. Copying changes the whole experience for them. Children who have had coloring books tend to lose the capacity to perceive in individual ways and with spontaneity. When children are free to use art materials as they wish, they have very individual ways of making use of the materials. One child covers the paper, making large sweeping strokes with the brush. One uses several colors in parallel lines or in adjacent masses. One child's strokes may be light and delicate. Another child may press heavily on the paper and cover only a small area. We see these same individual characteristics repeated as these children play. One may use the whole playground while another restricts play to one small corner. Each child is unique, a person different from all others.

Techniques or skills in drawing at this age are not important. We do not show the child how to represent an object. The process is far more important than the product. What counts is the expression of feelings and of seeing things and the satisfaction and release which this expression brings. Eddie might not have painted his symphony if he had had a diet of coloring books or a well-meaning teacher who kept showing him how to hold a brush and how to draw "correctly."

There are things we can do to encourage a child's interest and pleasure in art experiences. We can see that art materials are readily available for one to use. We can see that there is a place where one can work without interruption. We can express our appreciation for what a child does, "That is a lovely picture. I like it." We can also show our appreciation by putting the picture away carefully or by having a place where the picture can be displayed. Children need to feel that what they communicate through art is valued by others.

Some art materials have especially satisfying qualities for children because of the sensory experiences they offer.

Sensory experiences, "messy" play. Some art materials have especially satisfying qualities for children because of the sensory experiences they offer. Finger paint is an example of such material. There is no brush between the child and the medium. The child is touching it directly as well as seeing it. With one sweep of a hand the child can destroy the picture, and then can create another. Clay is another example. A child can put his or her hands in it, squeeze it, and pound it. A child makes something, then can smash it. The child is the creator and destroyer. Clay is a good medium for releasing tensions. It should be soft so that it can be easily worked by small fingers. When children use paste they may want to use a lot. There may be more paste than paper in their product because they like the feel of the paste itself. Collages with materials in a variety of textures give children opportunities to enjoy the feel as well as the sight of what they create. Paper hangers' paste (the *non*poisonous kind) can be combined with sawdust, corn meal, even sand, to give additional sensory experiences.

You will find some children who are unable to enjoy a sensory experience such as these we have suggested. These children are afraid of getting dirty because getting dirty is associated with being naughty. They are unable to enjoy "messy" types of experiences. It makes them uncomfortable to touch a gooey mass of color as in finger painting. Usually they do overcome this attitude as they watch other children who feel free to explore sensory experiences. Many children who are not able to enjoy messy play are confused as to when messiness is appropriate and when it is not. They have overrestricted themselves in the process of learning what is acceptable and thus limited their experiences.

What Help Do We Give With Art Experiences?

To help children experience art media with greater freedom and enjoyment there are certain *things we do.*

1. We provide materials for children—large sheets of paper (newsprint or unused backs of sheets of paper), crayons, washable paint in strong colors, including black, paint brushes, a smooth wet surface for finger painting, soft clay, paste, sheets of colored paper, bits of colored paper, scrap material for collages, blocks in different sizes and shapes, sand, and mud.

2. We provide a place and suitable conditions—plastic apron or old shirt to wear, protection for floor and table. A child shouldn't have to give too much attention to the job of keeping clean.

3. We give children uninterrupted time.

4. We give children help as they ask for it as in mixing paint, or when they're puzzled over something and need some explanation.

5. We see that children have plenty of the kind of experiences which they will want to think about and express in an art form.

6. We provide art as part of a child's familiar, everyday world. A good reproduction of a fine painting on the wall will appeal to a child. A lovely piece of pottery, flowers arranged artistically, or a piece of driftwood, fall foliage, color in the dishes the child uses at the table, and an attractive place mat for the child's use help him or her appreciate beauty.

Patterns, cutouts, duplicated outlines, and coloring books have no place in creative art expression. If we draw for children to "help" them, we actually stifle the development of creativity and make them dissatisfied with what they do produce. In helping children with art experiences, there are certain *things we never do.*

1. We never give them a model or pattern to copy.

2. We never draw pictures for them.

3. We never criticize or show them how we think it should be done, as "This is the way to draw a man," or "That's not right."

4. We do not say "What is it?" (How stupid we are not to know!)

5. We never say, "You've painted enough." Instead, we may say, "It's time to stop painting. We need to get ready to go."

Use art materials yourself. If you are going to help children with art experiences, you will need first to explore art media yourself. One of the most satisfying is finger paint.

In finger painting you can create and destroy with one sweep.

In finger painting you can create and destroy with one sweep. You can forget about the product and about being critical of what you make. You can enjoy the *process*. You can come closer to understanding what a child feels. You may find it difficult to overcome your feelings against the "messiness" of finger painting.

Try to use finger paints yourself. You can spread a sheet of plastic over the kitchen tabletop and paint on the plastic. Mix poster paint with wheat paste or starch so that it can be spooned on to a wet surface (wet butcher paper, a plastic sheet, or the tabletop itself). While you finger paint have plenty of paint, also have some music playing. Music with a strongly accented beat and then soothing, restful music. You will discover what it is like to paint with rhythm and to enjoy with more of your senses.

After you have tried finger painting, try playing with clay yourself, without making any special object. What does it feel like to you? Clay is a good medium for making and then destroying what one has made, getting out in an acceptable way the feeling all of us have at times of wanting to smash things.

Lots of paste (mix up paper hangers' paste, being sure to avoid the poisonous kind) and things to make collages with are fun. Try these things yourself before you give them to children. At first children are likely to be most interested in just using the materials, especially the paste. Later they pay more attention to design. Let them discover for themselves what they can do with the materials you provide. Is it different from what you did?

Modeling dough is made of flour, water, and salt. Food coloring or poster paint powder can be added to it. Paper hangers' paste mixed with other materials which give it different textures offers other experiences. Try using as many of these materials as you can. See if you can recall using similar materials when you were a child.

ACTIVITIES

TO DO AND DISCUSS

1 Try making up a story when you are with a child, giving the child a chance to join in by adding details, repeating phrases, or giving replies to questions. The subject of the story may be an experience the child has had. It may be an imaginative experience. Which does the child seem to enjoy more? Is there a difference depending on the age of the child?

2 Select three books which you consider to be good books for a child whom you know. Make the selection in the light of what you know about that child's individual experiences and interests. Test out your selection by reading them to the child and see whether your choices seem to be good ones.

3 Observe the story hour in your local library if there is an opportunity to do this. How does the children's librarian present the books to the group? What is the response of the children? How are problems of behavior managed?

4 Learn some simple songs which will be suitable for singing with children when they are swinging, marching, and carrying on other activities as they play. If you play an instrument, you might try accompanying the singing.

5 Use soft clay without trying to make any recognizable object. What are some of the feelings or sensations a child might get from handling clay?

TO THINK AND WRITE ABOUT

1 Why is the learning which comes from play a necessary foundation for later mental growth? Discuss at least five examples.

2 How does dramatic play, where a child acts out the parts of adults, help a child to grow into an adult? Give examples.

3 Prepare a list of toys which can be made at home out of low-cost materials which are on hand.

4 Discuss some of the ways in which adults help little children develop good speech habits.

5 What are the reasons little children like to use bad words? How should adults cope with this problem?

6 Why should children be introduced to simple story books at an early age?

7 Why are coloring books considered a poor art experience for children?

8 In what ways can parents create an environment in their home in which children will best develop their interests in art and music as avenues of self-expression?

REFERENCES

GENERAL

Baker, Katherine
Ideas that Work with Young Children
Washington, D. C.: National Association for the Education of Young Children, 1972

Green, Marjorie and Elizabeth Woods
Nursery School Handbook for Teachers and Parents, Revised Edition
Sierra Madre, California: Sierra Madre Community Nursery School

Holt, John
How Children Learn
New York: Pitman, 1969

Landreth, Catherine
Preschool Learning and Teaching
New York: Harper & Row, 1972

Murphy, B. and Ethel Leeper
Caring for Children Series (5 leaflets)
Office of Child Development
Washington, D. C.: U. S. Department of Health, Education, and Welfare, 1970

Tarney, Elizabeth Doak
What Does the Nursery School Teacher Teach?
Washington, D. C.: National Association for the Education of Young Children,
    1965

PLAY

Almy, Millie
Early Childhood Play—Selected Articles
New York: Selected Academic Readings, 1968

Baker, Katherine
Let's Play Outdoors
Washington, D. C.: National Association for the Education of Young Children,
    1966

Engstrom, Georgianna, Editor
Play: The Child Strives Toward Self-Realization
Proceedings of a Conference
Washington, D. C.: National Association for the Education of Young Children,
    1971
    Especially these articles:
    Brown, Nancy, Nancy Curry, and Ethel Tittnich, "How Groups of Children Deal
        with Common Stress Through Play," pp. 26–38
    Smilansky, Sara, "Can Adults Facilitate Play in Children? Theoretical and Prac-
        tical Considerations," pp. 39–50
    Sutton-Smith, Brian, "The Playful Modes of Knowing," pp. 13–25
Stone, Jeanette Galambos and Nancy Rudolph
Play and Playgrounds
Washington, D. C.: National Association for the Education of Young Children,
    1970

ART

Lindstrom, Miriam
Children's Art
Berkeley, California: University of California Press, 1963

BOOKS

Griffin, Louise
Multi-Ethnic Books for Young Children: Annotated Bibliography for Parents and Teachers
Washington, D. C.: National Association for the Education of Young Children

Larrick, Nancy
A Parent's Guide to Children's Reading
New York: Simon & Schuster, 1964

Lewis, Claudia and Miriam McPhee
"Books for Young Children"
Young Children, Vol. 26, No. 1, pp. 329–332, August, 1971

Stern, Virginia
"The Story Reader as Teacher"
Young Children, Vol. 22, No. 1, pp. 31–43, October, 1966

Wickens, Elaine
"Please Don't Tell the Children"
Young Children, Vol. 23, No. 1, pp. 15–18, October, 1967

LANGUAGE

McAfee, Oralie
"The Right Words"
Young Children, Vol. 23, No. 2, pp. 74–78, November, 1967

Mattick, Ilse
"The Teacher's Role in Helping Young Children Develop Language Competence"
Young Children, Vol. 27, No. 3, February, 1972

MATERIALS AND ACTIVITIES

Bender, Judith
"Have You Ever Thought of a Prop Box?"
Young Children, pp. 164–169, January, 1971

Buschhoff, Lotte
"Going on a Trip"
Young Children, pp. 224–232, March, 1971

Dittmann, Lora, Editor
Curriculum Is What Happens, Chapters 1–5
Washington, D. C.: National Association for the Education of Young Children, 1970

Hammerman, Ann and Susan Morse
"Open Teaching: Piaget in the Classroom"
Young Children, October, 1972

Johnson, Harriet
The Art of Block Building
New York: Bank Street College of Education

Ovitt, Jean
"What About the School Bus?"
Young Children, Vol. 25, No. 5, pp. 293–296, 1970

Seefeldt, Carol
"Boxes Are to Build—A Curriculum"
Young Children, Vol. 28, No. 1, October, 1972

Sunderlin, Sylvia, Editor
Bits and Pieces—Imaginative Uses for Children's Learning
Bulletin 20-A
Washington, D. C.: Association for Childhood Education, 1967

NUTRITION

"Nutrition Education for Young Children"
Adventures in Learning: A Guide for Teachers and Aides
Nutrition Publication E. F.—Office of Child Development
Washington, D. C.: U. S. Department of Health, Education, and Welfare, 64 pp., 1969

Discipline, Punishment, Spoiling

After studying this chapter, you will be able to

1. Analyze good discipline for infants and toddlers.
2. Differentiate between discipline and punishment.
3. Clarify the concept of spoiling a child.

Good discipline is important to everyone. As grown people we take responsibility for our own discipline. By discipline we mean maintaining standards for our behavior, for controlling and directing our impulses into satisfying and acceptable ways of behaving.

It is not always easy to live up to our standards. None of us can have everything we may wish or do just anything we may wish. We all must submit to some rules and regulations for the good of the group in which we live. When regulations and demands are unreasonable, we have a responsibility for helping to change them. We make decisions but we accept the fact that some limitations and restrictions are necessary because we are part of a society.

Young children are not ready to be responsible group members. They are lacking in experience and the judgment it brings. They have not yet learned to control their impulsive behavior. They have to depend on us to keep their behavior within safe and acceptable limits while we help them learn what is possible and how they may control themselves.

The ultimate goal for the child is self-discipline, as it is for us. Discipline from the outside will *gradually* turn into self-discipline for the child if our methods are good.

Sensible Discipline for the Infant and Toddler

Let us take a look at what discipline is like for the infant and the toddler. In infancy children are helpless and at the mercy of grown-ups. They do not know any of the rules or anything about what may be expected of them. A child only senses her or his own needs. The child has strong feelings when hungry or in pain or without comforting.

Crying is the child's way of telling us. Cries get stronger and more demanding until the child begins yelling. How is a child to learn the lessons that must be learned if the child is to be a happy, successful member of society?

At first a good mother and father will try to *satisfy* the baby's demands. They give freely to their baby—love, care, and attention —as their baby seems to need these. The baby wants only what is needed. When parents can satisfy those needs, the baby feels good and so do they. This way babies begin to build up trust that they will get what they need and want. They also learn something about giving and receiving, so that later they, in their turn, can give freely to meet the needs of other people. The roots of trust and generosity lie in these early experiences.

At first a good mother and father will try to satisfy a baby's demands.

We do the "giving" at first, trying to satisfy the infant's demands if we can. But gradually in a matter of weeks, we begin to expect the baby to do some adapting. And the wonderful thing is that the infant can. The baby has begun to be aware, for example, that he or she *will* be fed. When hearing mother's footstep, baby stops crying. Baby waits for her to come. Maybe when she comes she talks or plays with her baby for a few minutes. The infant isn't too hungry for that. Baby and mother are building a relationship together in which the baby is becoming aware of her as a person just as she has been aware of her baby from the first. The foundations for discipline have been laid.

Mutual regulation is part of good discipline. Good discipline is based on trusting relationships, each respecting the other. It is a matter of mutual regulation in adapting, each giving up something for the sake of the other. Parents will ask more of their baby as they come to know what is possible for her or him. Parents try to be sure that what they expect is within their baby's capacity to do. If parents are busy, they know the baby may be able to wait if they prop him or her up so baby can see something new, perhaps watch a mobile over the crib, until the parents are ready to come. Parents learn how to regulate wisely in meeting their infant's demands, increasing what is expected without demanding too much of the baby. The baby has come to feel trust in the parents. They help their baby understand that things can be all right even when they do not go just as the baby might wish.

A baby may have to wait for a feeding while the parents finish cooking the family meal. The parents may go out shopping and leave a friendly neighbor in charge. The baby is angry at first, but is quite comfortable in the neighbor's arms and may find something to watch which is distracting. The baby is able to tolerate these times if there has been a good balance of satisfying experiences to draw on. Gradually the baby becomes comfortable about waiting for longer periods. It is easier to accept substitutes when the baby cannot have what he or she wants. The baby begins to regulate desires to the needs of the family without necessarily giving up his or her wishes.

The mother and father adjust their demands and expectations to the baby's growing capacity to cope with these demands. The parents try to make sure that the baby does not feel that one *never*

The baby soon begins to regulate desires to the needs of the family without necessarily giving up his or her wishes.

can get what one wants. A baby's sense of time is not like ours. Five minutes without parents when the baby wants them seems like ages. The infant may be in a panic. Later it will come to seem like the short time that it is.

As one writer has said, babies need to have the world presented to them in small enough doses so that they can get a feeling of being able to master the experiences. They should not feel anxious, afraid, deprived, helpless, lonely. If the "doses" of experience of not getting what they need are regulated well for them, babies get the feeling that they can cope with such things. They enjoy the things that they have, or they find other ways of getting what they want—ways that fit in with the needs of their families and later with other people.

Babies need to have the world presented to them in small enough doses so that they can get a feeling of being able to master their experiences.

Building Any New Relationship

Mutual regulation is needed in building any new relationship. When you baby-sit with a little child for the first time, you do more of the "giving" in the process of getting acquainted. This may mean that you give your attention to all the things that the child wants to show you. You play the games the child wants. If he or she is a shy child, you may offer some of your most interesting songs or stories or folding paper tricks or just wait quietly until the child indicates that he or she is ready for action. You regulate what you do with the child. You establish a good relationship in which the child can trust you and feel safe with you.

Then you are in a position to begin to expect some things of the child. You try to be sensitive to this balance, sensitive to what will be enough — but not too much — to expect. After you have been with the child a good many times, you can expect that he or she will be able to look at what you want, too. You will be firm. You may refuse to do some things. The child may get angry with you, but won't feel fear and panic as might have been the case before the child learned to trust you. You and the child are friends.

Sensible Discipline for the Preschool Child

A preschool child is better able to accept the demands made on her or him if the child has had this kind of favorable start as an infant and toddler. The child's demands become more "reasonable," from the adult standpoint, because of secure feelings built up through infancy. The child begins to fit into the family group. Things are better understood at this age. The child can do more "giving up" without feeling less of a person in her or his own right. The child may not like some of the demands but has faith in herself or himself as a person who can meet expectations. Discipline has not made the child feel resentful. If there has been sensible disciplining, the child has begun to learn from it about controlling her or his own behavior without having to be *too* good at all times. The child is not unduly anxious.

We set a good example. In addition to wise mutual regulation in getting and not getting all that one wants, a young child is helped by the guidance we can give in other ways. Much is learned from our example, for children are great imitators of patterns of behavior. If we are thoughtful and considerate of them and of others, they will find it easier to act this way. If we obey rules, if we are polite, if we share willingly, if we are patient and try to settle arguments by discussion, they will tend to follow these patterns. Children imitate the behavior patterns of the important people around them.

Our expectations for children are within their capacities. We help young children, too, when we expect behavior of them which is within their capacities at the age and stage of development where they are. To do this it is essential for us to be well informed about age characteristics of children.

What does one expect of a two-year-old, for example? We know that a two-year-old's coordination is not yet good. A child of this age will be clumsy in using a spoon or fork. He or she will spill food. If we expect neatness in eating, we run into trouble and so does the child. The child may begin to see himself or herself as "bad" and may refuse to eat. Discipline problems develop.

We help children when we expect the kind of behavior of them that they are capable of giving at the age and stage of development where they are.

We avoid using threats. In good discipline we avoid using threats at all times. Children may not really understand what a threat means but they will realize that we think that they are likely to do wrong—and they may. Some children grow anxious under threats. Neither anxiety nor defiance is a basis for good self-control. We do not shame children or blame them after they have done something unacceptable. Doing this only lessens their self-confidence and makes them less reasonable in the end.

We let children learn from their mistakes when possible. We will find, too, that children learn from making mistakes just as we do. When they misbehave we may talk things over with them to be sure they understand what they did, the part they may have played, and the consequences. We do this without attempting to shame them or to increase their guilt. They will feel guilty and we only want them to understand, so that they will not be likely to act this way another time. We trust them. We expect them to be trustworthy.

We explain in simple words. To explain, to put things into words, is a very important step in good discipline. The child needs to understand and face her or his own behavior. To do this the child needs our help and support. Bringing things out into the open in words, without passing judgment, is a good way to give the child this support.

Here is an example. A mother was taking her daughter to nursery school when she suddenly remembered that a toy she wanted had been left behind. She demanded that her mother return to get it. The mother refused as she had other things to do. The daughter cried loudly, finally shouting, "You are mean. You won't do what I want." The mother replied calmly, "No, I won't because I haven't the time. I'd like to but I can't this time. I know you are very angry with me. I'm sorry." The crying stopped and a minute later the daughter was giving her mother a warm kiss of good-bye and greeting her teacher pleasantly. She had recovered her balance.

What is good discipline? It is discipline based on mutual respect and understanding. It is discipline based on reasonable expectations of what the child is like as an individual, at this stage of development. It is discipline carried out firmly and calmly without

If a young child starts to do something dangerous, or destructive, or harmful, we need to step in quickly and firmly and stop her or him.

an attempt to increase the child's feelings of guilt. It is discipline that helps the child face and understand better her or his own behavior. Good discipline is good guidance.

We will need to use discipline as we guide children. If a young child starts to do something dangerous or destructive or harmful, we need to step in quickly and firmly and stop her or him. We tell the child why we must stop her or him and we may enforce some logical consequence, such as taking away the stick she or he was using to hit with. "No playing with a stick if it is used for hitting."

If there is no logical consequence for the act, we may talk things over with the child and ask some questions. "Why do you think you did this?" "What do you think should happen now?" "What can we do about it?" The child may have some good ideas and we may get a better understanding of what it all means to her or him. It also gives the child a pattern for dealing with problems by discussion and decision making rather than by acting on impulse.

What are some reasons why a young child may misbehave? We ourselves should always try to understand *why* the child is misbehaving. Discuss this question in class.

D. Funt

An older child can often reassure a younger one when something seems strange or threatening.

A child needs time to think about the things he or she has seen and done each day.

Toddlers enjoy imitating the role of a parent.

Fane

Derfus

Mattel

A favorite toy and her thumb help this little girl go to sleep.

Every child should have the opportunity to enjoy the wonders of nature.

D. Funt

Punishment

Punishment plays little part in good discipline. Punishment is a word often associated with discipline, but sensible discipline makes little use of punishment as a method of changing behavior. Punishment refers to methods involving the use of force or fear or pain or humiliation of the child. There is evidence that these methods are not much help to the child and may hinder the child in learning to direct and control his or her own behavior.

The lessons learned through punishment are often not those we intended to teach. Being made to sit on a chair after one misbehaves may do little to improve behavior. Many children punished in this way have little idea of why they are there. Their thoughts while sitting are not likely to be very constructive thoughts. They are not finding out more about how they should behave, only being impressed with what they should *not* do. It takes help to learn how one should behave.

A parent may bite a young child who has bitten in order to teach him or her not to bite others. Doing this may only teach the child that it is better to be the one who bites than to be the one who is bitten. This kind of punishment is hard for the child to reconcile with loving relationships. Or, a child may be beaten because of disobeying. As a result of the punishment the child may learn to be more clever in concealing what he or she does or to be more

Often, the lessons learned through punishment are not those we intended to teach.

Spanking, scolding, blaming, or threatening children may make adults feel they are doing something, but these methods do not give the children the direction they need.

deceitful. It is also likely to provoke impulses that are hard for the child to manage. He or she may become a bully, taking out feelings on other children.

Some children have had a lot of punishing but very little disciplining. They cannot control their impulses in socially responsible ways or direct their energies responsibly. When children behave unacceptably they need to learn how others feel about their behavior, but punishment like being beaten or bitten almost never teaches them.

Spanking, scolding, blaming or threatening children may make adults feel they are doing something, but these methods do not give the children the direction they need. A cartoon once showed a big man with a little boy over his knee. As the man administers a spanking, he is saying to the child, "I'll teach you not to hit other people." Confusing, isn't it! Punishment like this is not good discipline. It probably relieves the adult much more than it helps the child. In some cases it may be better to spank than to do nothing, but we can tackle the problem of discipline in more effective, more reasonable ways than by force.

What Does "Spoiling" a Child Mean?

Some people defend their methods of discipline by saying that they do not want to "spoil" the child. No one likes a "spoiled" child. But what is "spoiling"? The word means different things to different people.

How would you describe a spoiled child? Your description will probably include all the kinds of behavior that you dislike. We often lump many of the things we dislike about people under the label "spoiled." Then we conclude that these people needed more discipline. All of us are just a bit spoiled. We want our own way. We are thoughtless and selfish at times. We are human beings. But what does "spoiling" really mean? How does it happen that these ways of behaving become usual ways for a person? How does one recover from "spoiling?"

Being Spoiled

A good many people are afraid of spoiling children. Because they are afraid, they may not give the child what he or she needs. They do not enjoy the child as much as they might and their relationships are not as satisfying. Other people say, "He's only a baby," and then go ahead and do what pleases them, but not always the child, at the moment. The next moment, they are cross with the child because he or she is not being the good baby they want. These are some of the ways of spoiling children.

We know that "spoiled" children have not been disciplined in a good way. They may have been indulged. They may have been denied a chance to be responsible and to learn from experience. They may have been given things that their mothers and fathers felt like giving them, but they usually have not had the things that they themselves want most. They want love and understanding, not just toys and gifts. Getting these things may seem like getting a candy bar when you are thirsty and wishing for a nice cool drink of milk.

Because they get the wrong things, these children keep asking for more and more. They are never quite satisfied and often become discontented and disagreeable. Their parents don't bother to stop their doing unpleasant or naughty things. Other people get cross with them. Nobody seems to like them very much. Spoiled people are unhappy.

No wonder people are afraid of spoiling their children. It is worth understanding something about how *not* to spoil children. There is no foolproof recipe. Each child is different, and each parent is different. But we can learn something about how these things may work out.

In the beginning of a child's life we can forget about spoiling. No baby a month old cries because of being spoiled. An infant cries because something is wrong. It is his or her only way of communicating.

Good parents will try to give the baby what he or she needs and make him or her comfortable, but they do not keep on giving their baby everything he or she happens to want as he or she grows older. Mothers and fathers help prepare their babies for life with other people by setting limits for them and by expecting things from them. They regulate what they expect according to their growing capacities to live up to expectations. The babies begin to do some self-regulation. They get a sense of satisfaction in living up to demands. Children can be very unhappy if no one expects much of them. They can stand failures if they have had enough successes. They need parents who care enough about them to expect them to behave well and who take responsibility for sound discipline.

Babies need loving attention. Underlying all the seeking and demanding of a so-called spoiled child, as of every child, lies the deep craving for love and attention from someone who cares. When children fail to get this kind of care, they may turn to objects to satisfy the need they feel. They become greedy. They take from others. They want what others have. These children are often the hardest ones to love in the end. We have to call on our understanding of their basic loneliness and lack of loving attention in order to feel respect for them and guide them wisely at this point.

All kinds of things may prevent a parent from satisfying the child's need for loving attention and for failing to work out a good basis for trust and mutual regulation of needs. The mother may have had a severe illness which made her unable to care for the child when she or he needed her. The parents may have been faced with a family crisis which absorbed their energies at the time. They may have faced more problems than they themselves could deal with and there was no one else who could give the baby the love and care needed to help her or him with adjustments at a critical point. The child may have had an illness and required a lot of care and the parents were unable to adjust to the child's lessening need for attention as she or he recovered. They may have failed to expect enough of their baby.

Conflict between a husband and wife is another thing which complicates the process of adjustment for the child. The child may not feel sure of his or her relationship with either parent. There are plenty of things the child has to struggle with at first—the change from prenatal living to living on his or her own, temperature changes, new food, gas pains, new sights and sounds—and if loving care is lacking, the baby really is overwhelmed.

A child is not "spoiled" by too much loving. It is the child who has not had enough satisfying love who continues to be demanding and "spoiled." This child may get all kinds of material things or indulgences but if she or he feels helpless in efforts to get what she or he needs most, *loving* care, the child goes on seeking and demanding and usually gets less and less of what she or he really wants.

A child is not spoiled
by too much loving

Some children are "spoiled," meaning that they want all kinds of impossible things and show little consideration for others, but this spoiling is not the result of being given too much. It results from having received too little of what they really need. Without enough loving care they have had too much of what they could not "digest." They have not been protected by adults willing and able to deny children what they should not have or should not experience. This child may defend herself or himself by acting in ways that we call "spoiled."

Helping Spoiled Children

How do we help a "spoiled" child? It's not easy and it may be impossible for any one of us to do. The trouble may go too deep. It began very early. But we can try.

We can begin by being a *giving* person with the child. We do not always give a child what he or she may be demanding at the moment. But if it is all right to give the child what is asked for, we give it to him or her freely, not grudgingly. We want to give the child the feeling that we are *glad* to give it. A child needs to feel that giving comes freely, not as a result of demanding. Children need to find that people give because they want to give. This kind of giving is important to all children, not just the ones we may consider spoiled. It is important to have this feeling when you give children what they want, for there are also times when you must deny children what they ask for or refuse to allow them to do what they wish. They will understand better the meaning of these denials and refusals if they know that you are glad to give or allow when you can properly do it.

It is hard for a child when the giving is done reluctantly, the "Oh well, I guess you can have it. I think it would be better if you didn't," kind of attitude. The child is not clear about what is really meant. It does not help to give in after you have refused and the child has cried or coaxed. He or she gets the feeling that, "Nobody really wants to give to me. I have to push and demand before I get anything," or "The way to get what I want is to cry and coax enough." This feeling makes it harder for the child to take over control of himself or herself in the future.

Firmness

Try to give freely and willingly when you give to any child or when you do something for a child. Then she or he won't have to push so hard. If you can't give what the child wants, say "No" firmly and immediately and be sure that you mean it.

Suppose you are taking care of a child and she or he demands large sharp-pointed scissors. You are right to say "No," and you say it quietly and firmly. The child may fuss. The child may get angry and storm around or call you names. She or he may even have a temper tantrum. Of course, the child is upset. From her or his standpoint, the child has a right to be upset, but you have enough experience to know that she or he has no right to the scissors. You try not to get upset because the child is upset. You are patient with her or his anger. You try to help the child master it by saying, "When you get through fussing, I'll show you a way to fold a paper hat," or "When you get through fussing, we'll go out and build those roads we were talking about." You don't bribe him by putting it this way, "If you'll stop, I'll fold a hat or build roads with you." There is a difference between the words "when" and "if."

The child may be so angry that she or he starts throwing things. Again, you stop the child firmly (holding her or him if necessary to show the child you mean it), saying, "You must stop doing that. I know you are angry. I get angry, too." Here you may find that the child will suddenly listen with great interest while you can tell about some of your childish temper outbursts. It always helps to share these things.

More vigorous action may be needed. Maybe there is a pillow to pummel, or the child can hammer if the equipment is available. Perhaps the child can go outdoors and really throw something against a target. You make suggestions, but you do not get drawn into an argument. You do not have to justify your "No" at this point. Just remain firm. It is all part of good guidance or discipline.

Summary—What Is Good Discipline?

1. If we are to discipline well, *we* must *care about the child*. We must like and respect and want to help the child. This kind of attitude is

very different from one in which we really think the child is a nuisance and "ought to be taught a lesson" or "be made to suffer for his or her sins." Nothing we do will change the child's behavior, except for the worse, if we feel like this.

Of course, we all get angry and impatient with children at times. We get tired. We have our problems. We do not like all they do. We act hastily and are sorry afterwards. But they can survive times like these as long as there is a feeling of respect underneath. Children are remarkably hardy. We say we are sorry and go on from there. We are human and children can appreciate this. We are sharing our humanness with them.

When we feel that children do not amount to much and need to be put in their place, they will resent whatever we do. They resist changing or feel hopeless about being able to change. The result is that any disciplining we do will not help much.

2. If we are to discipline well, *we* must *feel confidence in and respect for ourselves.* A rather surprising thing is that the more we feel respect for ourselves, the more we can respect other people.

Self-respect is a good trait to have if you are going to be effective in your discipline. It enables you to feel more confidence when you say "No" to the child. You are sure of your right to set limits as a responsible person. You trust your judgment. You are not afraid of being wrong. You can afford to make mistakes. You know everyone makes mistakes. Making mistakes is one way to learn.

When you respect yourself, you give the child confidence by the way you act. It is easier for him or her to accept your "No." In addition the child is learning something important about ways people can feel about themselves. You have set a good pattern for the child.

We are better able to act in a firm, friendly way if we respect both the child and ourselves.

3. In good discipline *we take the responsibility* for seeing that children do what they are supposed to do. We don't leave it all up to them. It's a matter of mutual regulation again. With a toddler you take most of the responsibility. With a four-year-old who has had good experiences you can leave quite a bit of the responsibility for managing himself or herself up to the child. You have to estimate when the temptations may be too great and regulate yourself accordingly. For example, if children are playing ball near the street,

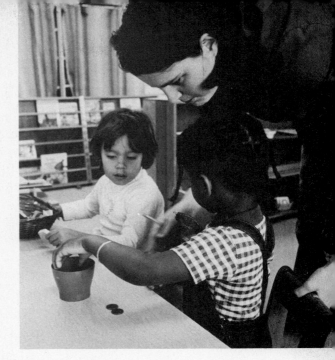

In good discipline we are clear about what we expect. We try to make it clear to the child. Then we stand our ground with sympathy for the child's feelings but no weakness.

they may be tempted to run into the street to get the ball. They had better play ball in the back yard, although at other times you can trust them not to go into the street.

4. In good discipline, *we let children learn from experience* and suffer consequences from which they have chances of learning cause and effect, or act and result, without any real harm. They learn what we mean when we say, "No, it's hot," if they touch the stove. We can say then, "I'm sorry, but now you know about hot things." If we can, we prevent their touching the hot stove by removing them, for the pain may leave them afraid of stoves. We do not want children to learn by being injured or by becoming afraid.

A child learns most when the consequence follows immediately, occurs every time, and is directly connected with the act. A child blows up a balloon and keeps on blowing. The balloon pops and is gone.

5. In good discipline, *we are consistent* in what we do and say.

Sometimes people feel that a method of discipline is no good because the child repeats the same behavior later. It may only mean that the child is testing things out and asking "Does it always happen? Or does it depend on how the adult feels?" Children really test out and probe for any loopholes. We have to see that things happen the same way if we really expect them to learn.

6. *We are firm* and follow through with what we say. Sometimes people feel uncertain about discipline because children get upset. We have a right to expect them to act in certain ways but we can't always expect them to like it. They have a right to their feelings. We are not trying to regulate feelings, only behavior.

Usually our uncertainty comes from feeling unsure about whether or not we should have asked this of the child. That is a question we had better ask ourselves *first* whenever we can.

7. In good discipline *we are clear about what we expect.* We try to make it clear to the child. Then we stand our ground with sympathy for the child's feelings but no weakness.

8. *We leave the matter behind when it is over* without trying to rub it in. Rubbing things in may spoil the learning.

Discussions about the toddler and the three- and four-year-old child included other things which have to do with discipline. It is part of toilet training in the case of the toddler, for example. It is related to the development of the conscience in the case of the three- and four-year-old.

Understanding about discipline is an important matter. We all have a good deal to learn about it as we take over more and more of the management of our own lives. Self-discipline is necessary for this. With self-discipline we have a better chance to accomplish our goals. Because of self-discipline we are freer to enjoy experiences and to find satisfactions.

We continue to learn about discipline and authority all our lives. We want the children we care for to get off to a good start as they begin learning.

ACTIVITIES

TO DO AND DISCUSS

1 In your notebook, list ten examples of behavior which you would consider signs of a spoiled child. Beside each example, write the probable reason why that type of behavior developed. Can you draw any generalizations by analyzing your list?

2 Plan a role-playing session showing a parent and a spoiled child. Have the parent vary reactions to the child's nagging by being strict, permissive, and attentive. See how the child might react to each of the parent's attitudes. Why might the child react in each of these ways?

3 Try to remember back to a temper tantrum you had as a child. Write an essay describing the cause and how you felt about it. What was the result of your tantrum?

4 Arrange a panel discussion on parents and their methods of punishing young children. Base the discussion on your own experiences or incidents which you have seen.

TO THINK AND WRITE ABOUT

1 In what ways is an overindulged child really a deprived child? Explain.

2 In what ways does giving a child attention prevent the child from becoming spoiled?

3 How does self-discipline grow out of parental training? Why do you think some people lack self-control?

4 Think back to your own childhood. Can you recall ever having a feeling of resentment after being punished? Describe the incident.

5 How may a parent punish a child without having the child develop resentful feelings? Give examples.

REFERENCES

Fraiberg, Selma
The Magic Years, Chapter 8 "Education of Conscience"
New York: Charles Scribner's Sons, 1959

Galambos, Jeannette
A Guide to Discipline
Washington, D. C.: National Association for the Education of Young Children, 1969

Henricks, Joanne
"Aggression: What to Do About It!"
Young Children, Vol. 23, No. 5, pp. 298–305, May, 1968

Read, Katherine
The Nursery School, Chapter 8 "Using Discipline"
Philadelphia, Pa.: W. B. Saunders Co., 1971

Children Are Members of Families

8

After studying this chapter, you will be able to

1. Compare advantages to a young child of family care and group day care.
2. Examine the importance of relationships within the family and with friends.
3. Accept a child's need to have all kinds of feelings and emotions.

The children we meet come from many different kinds of families. They have been influenced by their family experiences.

Children's first understandings about what they are like, about what other people are like, about what it means to be a man or a woman, and about giving and receiving love grow out of their family experiences. From such experiences they learn, also, something about managing feelings of jealousy and rivalry. Children experience their first close relationships with people within their families.

Family experience tends to be favorable for a child if he or she has parents who are happy together. When there are strong bonds of affection between the parents, they serve as good models for the child. They give the child the freedom and the discipline needed. They answer questions and give the child opportunities to learn.

A favorable family experience means that the child is freer of needless fears and anxieties than one in a less fortunate family situation. Such a child can move more easily toward independence and a life on his or her own as a man or a woman, and is better able to take responsibility and to enjoy the experiences life brings.

As we care for and observe children, we learn to understand more about families and what they offer.

There Are Many Kinds of Families

Each one of us grew up in a family of some kind. We all know something about family life. We have all been influenced by our family experiences.

Families are very different, as we know. Some are large; some are small; some are made up only of boys or only of girls; some have children close together in age while others have children spaced well apart. Present-day knowledge about contraception makes it more possible to plan the number and spacing of children in a family. Parents can make the decision. The average family in the United States today has two children in contrast to the family of 100 years ago when the number was five. Some families are large because they include relatives such as grandparents or aunts or uncles. Each family offers a child different experiences.

Patterns of family life are different. The family living in the country may live in a somewhat different way from one in the city or one in a suburban area. Everywhere the kind of jobs members of the family hold, the hours of work, the income, all have an effect on patterns of family living. Self-employed people, factory workers, professional people, will lead somewhat different lives, and these differences influence their children.

People from different cultures differ in the manners and customs they follow. A Japanese family, a Mexican family, an Italian family will each live in a somewhat different way even when they are living in the same country. Their food and their ways of life will differ.

Families Change

Families do not stay the same. They change with changing circumstances, and these changes affect the children. Some families move often. A member of the family has a long illness or dies. The family becomes a different family. There are changes through the life cycle of every family, from the time the children are young, through the adolescent years, and later when they have left home. Sometimes it is hard for parents to adjust to these changes.

A country at war will present the family with very different problems than will a country at peace. There are so many ways in which families vary that even if we all started out the same at birth we would grow up as very different people.

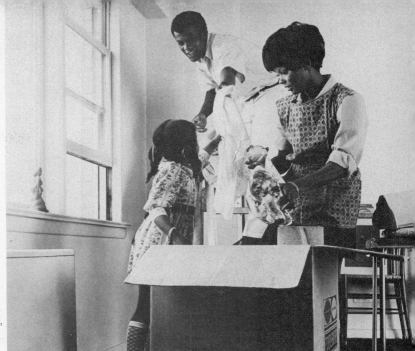

Families change with changing circumstances, such as moving, and these changes affect the children.

Social Patterns and Attitudes Change

Social patterns and attitudes change with the generations. There is much more sharing of homemaking tasks between husband and wife today than was common formerly. There is more equality between men and women. More jobs are open to either a man or a woman. There is more individual decision making by members of a family. Parents are less likely to decide what occupation the child will follow than they once were.

There is more acceptance today of differences among people in color, in race, and in cultural patterns. We have more chance to meet all kinds of people as equals. We may find friends among people because we enjoy them as individuals with interests similar to ours or because they help us broaden our horizons and bring us new interests.

There is more acceptance, too, of differences in the way families live. Life in small houses or apartments leads to a family different from the extended family that was typical years ago when all the members lived in a group. Some people are exploring other ways of having family experiences. Young families may share life in a "commune," or they may work out ways of sharing and participating in the community. One way might be setting up a "play group" and sharing the care of young children. All of these changes have an influence on the growing child.

Today people are more accepting of differences in color, race, and cultural patterns.

Changes in Education

Another change is that education is now being thought of as something that takes place outside the school as well as in school. It may be of many types, and it gives consideration to family needs as well as to the needs of children. The family is a whole. Today parents and teachers are working together more and consulting each other on many more questions.

Parents have always been the child's first teachers and, in the area of personality development, probably the most important teachers. But parents also help lay the foundations upon which later school achievement is based. There are "Home Start" experimental programs in which a trained teacher makes regular visits to the

Today parents and teachers of young children are working together and consulting with each other on many questions. This is happening in this Japanese nursery school.

home to show the mother and father there what they may do to promote good intellectual growth in their child before he or she enters school. "Education for Parenthood" programs, offered in the schools, reflect the change toward greater appreciation for the important role of parents and the influence family experience has on child development. The aim of the "Education for Parenthood" courses is to provide young people with the knowledge and skills that will enable them to become *effective* parents.

As a future parent you will expect to work with the teacher and the schools to ensure the best possible education for your child. As a future teacher you will expect to work with parents for the good of the child in the family.

Family Experiences Teach the Child About Loving

One of the most important things that a child learns from her or his early experiences in the family is about love and loving.

The ties between a husband and a wife in a good marriage are strong. It is the strength of these ties that helps the children feel secure, whatever the type of family. A man and woman who are happy and satisfied in their own relationship create a healthy climate for children to grow in. They are showing their children how a man and a woman can live together, enjoying each other and enjoying being parents.

The aim of "Education for Parenthood" courses is to provide people with the knowledge and skills that will help them become effective parents.

Walt Whitman wrote about parents in his poem, "There Was a Child Went Forth," which appears in his collection of poetry, *Leaves of Grass.* He wrote this about the parents of a child:

> . . . he that had father'd him and she that had conceiv'd him in her womb and birth'd him,
> They gave this child more of themselves than that
> They gave him afterward every day, they became part of him. . . .

From the parents who become "part of us," we build our ideas about what we are like and our ideas about the relationships of husband and wife and parent and child. The standards and values of our parents become part of us just as much as the "family usages" and the language we speak.

Learning from a loving family. If a child's family loves and values her or him, the child feels herself or himself to be a valuable person. The child builds confidence and self-respect. If the parents are pleased with what she or he does, the child feels good and wants to accomplish more. If, on the other hand, the members of the family are continually scolding or reproaching her or him, the child comes to think of herself or himself as a troublesome person and may continue to develop that way. The child tends to become the kind of person the family expects her or him to become. It helps us to understand the child if we know something about the way in which the family regards the child.

If a child's family loves and values her or him, the child feels valuable, too.

The basic learning about love begins for each of us when, as infants, we are cared for lovingly.

The basic learning about love begins for each of us when, as infants, we are cared for lovingly. Babies are easy to love — at least most of the time! Mothers want to care for them, love them, feed them, protect them, and give them what they need. Getting what one needs, feeling loved, feeling wanted and safe are good experiences for anyone to have. They lay a good foundation for relationships with people and make it possible to grow in healthy ways.

Having the experience of being loved by a mother and a father and perhaps by brothers and sisters makes it possible for a child to be loving also. The child can give love in return. There are things we learn from experience better than we can be taught about them.

The roles of mother and father. The ordinary healthy baby starts with a strong attachment to the mother who cares for him or her. The baby is completely dependent on her and is concerned with only his or her own needs. The infant soon discovers and enjoys father and others but continues to depend on mother. The baby turns to her when hungry, tired, or hurt. At times, as they grow and develop, children feel some conflict in their relations with their fathers and their mothers.

A boy wants his mother all to himself. How many little boys have said that they are going to marry their mothers when they grow up! But in the end they must accept the fact that they are little boys, not yet men. They must move on to want to be like their fathers, not to take the place of their fathers. A boy is helped toward this resolution of the conflict in his feelings if his mother is not too possessive and does not try to keep him too close to her for too long. He is also helped if his father is not too strict or harsh with him during this period. It is especially helpful if his father spends time with him. In a good family situation the boy will be able to move away from his dependence on his mother and move toward his future role as a man.

When the family situation is not favorable and the father is indifferent or harsh or the mother overly possessive, the boy may have great difficulty in managing his feelings. He may become difficult, overly aggressive, and cruel toward other children. He may, on the other hand, become overly passive and dependent, finding it hard to lessen the attachment to his mother.

The girl, too, needs and wants to have her father approve of her as a girl. She is likely to feel a sense of rivalry with her mother for his attention. If her father is harsh or indifferent, the girl may find it difficult to feel confidence in her own attractiveness. She may grow afraid of men. For the girl, as for the boy, there are fewer difficulties in adjustment if the parents are secure in their love for each other and in their roles as parents. The girl can enjoy doing the things her mother does and can look forward to her future as a woman.

The infant soon discovers and enjoys his or her father.

The Question of Work Outside the Home for a Mother

One decision which a mother may face today has a bearing on our study of children. It is the decision about taking a job outside the home.

There are many reasons for a woman to decide to go out to work. The commonest reason is that of economic necessity. She may be the sole support of the family. Or, it may be that money is needed for a new car or a better home or for the education of older children. Or, it may be because she wants to use her training in a useful way and she likes the work. She may have spent several years training to be a teacher, for example, and teachers are needed.

In making this decision, a mother with young children must think through the question of what it may mean to her to lose the close relationship that comes in caring for her child at the start when "mothering" is so important.

If she wishes to work or if she must work outside the home while the children are young, a mother then needs to consider possible arrangements for the care of the child. She may have a willing relative or neighbor who can come in to take care of the child. If not, she will look at the community facilities for child care — a day care center, or home day care, or a combination of the two, part-time group day care and part-time home day care. In every case she should be sure that these meet *good* standards for care and are adapted to the needs of her child because these early years are important ones for his or her development.

For the child under two years old home day care is usually preferable in almost every case. For the child between two and four a combination of the two types of care may be preferable, with the two-year-old spending much more time in home care than in group care. It may be better for even the four-year-old to have some time in home care away from the group, unless the group is well adapted to the needs of children in all-day care.

In thinking about arrangements for care of a young child a mother needs to be aware of some of the possible differences between good group care and good home care.

In all-day care a young child is almost certain to receive less attention from the caretaking adults than would be received at home from parents and other members of the family. The child's personal relationships will be, of necessity, more superficial and less full of deep, intimate feeling. The child must control himself or herself more, give up more of what he or she may want, such as the chance to follow one's own interests, suit one's own schedule for rest and play, and have time alone. The child may have to be more independent than he or she may really be ready to be. The child has less chance to learn about family life. In other words, the child may learn less about loving and more about conforming.

A recent study of children in all-day group care concluded that it "seems likely to reduce rather than enhance a child's sense of his own importance and to offer relatively limited experiences which foster a sense of self identify."[*]

Since, as we pointed out earlier, the basic first task in personality development for the young child is to gain the sense of being a person of worth as a foundation for later loving and achieving, we can see that mothers will want to take a careful look at the question of full-time work outside the home while children are below school age, provided they have the choice.

For mothers of young children, working outside the home should be a matter of *choice*. Society may be sacrificing the welfare of its children if it sets up a policy which forces a woman to place her young children in group care so she can work to support them.

When good group day care is available and can be used to *supplement* home care rather than to substitute for it, it has advantages for most children. Care for half a day or less in a good nursery school offers the child a chance to have a wider variety of experience than home is likely to offer, a wider range of contacts with people, and a broader base for later learning. When parents feel they can provide their young children with both a good home and a good school experience and when the mother enjoys being at work as well as at home she may decide to go to work, possibly on a part-time basis at first. There is now a growing body of opinion that some school experience should be made available for *all* children by the time they are four.

---

[*]Prescott, Elizabeth, Elizabeth Jones, and Sybil Kritchevsky. *Day Care As a Child Rearing Environment,* Vol. 2, p. 55, Washington, D. C.: National Association for the Education of Young Children, 1972.

A brother and sister playing together learn that there are differences between boys and girls.

Learning About Sex

We begin to learn about love from the time we are born. Learning begins in the family. Much that we do later will depend on these first family experiences of being loved and wanted.

Awareness of sex. The infant starts early to discover her or his own body. The baby sticks a finger in her or his mouth. This gives the infant a different sensation than does a bottle or rattle. The baby gets a dawning realization that it is "me." The baby discovers toes and fingers and plays with them. The infant touches all the parts of her or his body. They feel different. When a mother washes her baby's neck, stomach, or genitals, the baby gets different sensations. An infant is different in different parts of her or his body.

We let babies explore and discover their bodies in their own way. We avoid overwhelming them with too many body sensations, such as tickling them too much or almost smothering them with kisses. Babies may get excited and overstimulated with more sensations than they can manage. This leaves them upset and confused and somehow out of touch with their own bodies. They need time to come to know what their bodies are like and what they can do with them.

Young children often handle their genitals. This is part of the ordinary process of discovering themselves. Frequent handling of their genitals may mean that their clothes are too tight or that there is some irritation. It may mean that they are seeking comfort. They may lack a feeling of being secure and loved. We simply add to children's distress by reproving them. We need to help them feel better about themselves and their world. They are not being "bad" by touching their genitals. As they grow and find more activities that are satisfying to them, children gradually stop touching their genitals.

The baby becomes aware of differences between the sexes. Infants soon discover that there are differences among people. The way their fathers hold them is different from the way their mothers do. Their fathers' voices and the way they play with babies are different. From such experiences babies begin to *know* about sex differences long before they understand the words *male* and *female*.

Every child needs to have experiences of being cared for by a man as well as a woman as a basis for understanding the meaning of masculine and feminine.

Every child needs to have experiences of being cared for by a man as well as a woman as a basis for understanding the meaning of *masculine* and *feminine*. Children need these experiences in their childhood so that they may in time come to know what it means to be a man or a woman. Sometimes children grow up in one-parent families. In such cases it is especially important that they have a chance to be with male and female relatives, such as uncles and aunts or friends of the family. Experiences with people of both sexes are important to both boys and girls if they are to understand sex differences in a real way, not just as words.

Later children add to their understanding of sex differences through experiences with brothers or sisters or with playmates outside the home. The older child may watch mother caring for the new baby, bathing it or changing its diaper. The child may help to care for the baby himself or herself. The child observes and asks questions, and the mother helps the child find answers to what he or she is wondering about.

Nursery schools or other group experiences are a help to children who do not have brothers or sisters. As they play together and use toilets together, they observe the differences between the sexes. They are free to ask questions and find answers. We help young children when we provide them with plenty of opportunities to learn more about what people of both sexes are like.

Feeling comfortable about one's sex is important. Feeling comfortable about one's own sex is an important part of healthy growth and development. Accepting oneself as a boy or as a girl is not just a matter of discovering that one has a penis or a vagina. It is a matter of the "models" one has to follow. A child tries to model himself or herself after the people who are important to the child. These people need to be people who accept themselves as male or female, as the case may be, and who accept the child as he or she is.

What are some experiences that help or hinder the child in accepting his or her sex? Here are some examples:

Parents who help a child to accept its sex are parents who like their little boy because he is a boy and like their little girl because she is a girl. They treat them as boys or girls, respecting their sex. Sometimes we see a father who wanted a son very much but has a daughter. The child finds that she must act like a boy to get his approval. It becomes hard for her to feel good about enjoying feminine things. Sometimes we find a mother who does not really feel good about being a woman. She may have grown up in a family where girls were not valued. This made her wish that she were a boy rather than a girl. Her feelings are communicated later to her daughter, even though she does not put them into words. These feelings do not make it easy for the girl to want to be a woman. Sometimes we may see a mother who wanted a girl rather than a boy. She may dress her boy more like a girl and leave his curls long until he or his father protests. She is making it hard for her son to feel masculine. Fortunately, most parents who may have wanted a child of one sex or the other find that their feelings change when the baby is born. They like the baby and want it the way it is.

When we work with children, it is important that we like both boys and girls and accept them for what they are. We serve as "models" for them, and we need to feel comfortable about our own sex. We, too, need to like ourselves as we are.

Children learn from homemaking play. In their homemaking play, young children often try out different roles in the family. They pretend to be mothers or fathers, regardless of their sex. They want to understand more about what it is like to be a mother or a father. A boy may dress in women's clothes, or a girl may put on a man's hat and tie. This is natural and healthy. They are exploring and trying to understand roles. It is only if the boy continually dresses in girl's clothes, for example, or always wants to be the mother that we may suspect he is confused about his sex role. He may be having a hard time accepting himself as a boy. His parents need to think carefully about how they are treating him. They may need to consider how they have answered his questions about differences between boys and girls or where babies come from. In such a case we should make sure that we let him know how much we like little boys. We can encourage him when he takes the male role in play or does the kind of things boys usually enjoy, such as climbing up high, throwing balls, or building with blocks. But we will not make fun of him for dressing in girl's clothes. Feelings change from the inside, not the outside. He needs to have the chance to do his own changing and to discover satisfactions in being a boy.

Questions About Where
Babies Come From

Through infancy children lay the foundations for sex education. They come to know something of the difference between a man and a woman from their experiences with their fathers and their mothers. They absorb feelings about their relationship to one another. They discover their own bodies with different sensations in different parts.

As young children playing with other children, they observe physical differences between the sexes and begin to be aware of their own sex and have some ideas about sex roles. They communicate verbally and can ask questions.

By the time children are three years old some of their questions will be about where babies come from. They are becoming very much interested in the subject even if they are still unable to phrase their questions clearly.

It is important for children that we be ready with some answers. It may be helpful to read some of the good books on the subject that put explanations into words that young children can grasp, such as Karl De Schweinitz' *Growing Up: The Story of How We Become Alive, Are Born, and Grow Up;* or Marie Ets's *The Story of a Baby;* or Sidonie Gruenberg's *The Wonderful Story of How You Were Born.* There are also books to read to children about family experiences with a new baby.

The information that a child wants at first is simple. The child is not interested in anatomy at this point. It is usually enough to say, "You grew inside your mother, under her stomach." Later the child will want to know about the egg, or ovum, that was fertilized by a tiny sperm from the father and from which he or she started growing.

Most children imagine some fantastic things about prenatal life, in spite of all our efforts to make things clear to them. Selma Fraiberg, in her book, *The Magic Years* (chapter 7), points out that a large part of sex education is a matter of clearing up the child's misconceptions. Children have active imaginations at this age. They make up their own explanations and only slowly get things sorted out. It may be wise to ask, "What do *you* think?" when a child asks a question about babies. When we find out what he or she thinks,

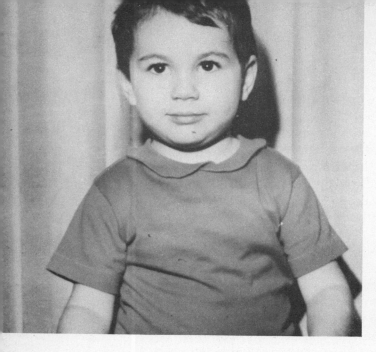

By the time children are three years old, some of their questions will be about where babies come from. It is important that we be ready with some answers.

we are better able to clear up misunderstandings. Also, we are less likely to give information in which the child is not much interested. It is also wise to avoid lengthy, detailed explanations with young children. When we tell children more than they want to know, they are likely to become confused. They are less likely to ask questions again. The important thing is to keep the conversational channels open. Children need to ask questions more than once before even the simplest facts of reproduction are clear to them.

Experiences that teach about growth and reproduction. There are many kinds of experiences that help extend the child's understanding of growth and reproduction. Children learn about growing things from experiences with animals—a cat with kittens, a rabbit with bunnies, a dog with puppies. As they watch animals caring for their babies and as they themselves share in the care of animals, they learn more about caring for young animals. With the arrival of a baby in her or his home or in the home of a neighbor, the child adds to what she or he knows about different kinds of care. A child can also discover that the egg may grow outside or inside a mother's body by watching the hen sitting on the nest and the bird building a nest and sitting on it after the eggs are laid—in contrast to the rabbit who makes a soft nest for the babies just before they are born.

Watching baby chicks coming out of the eggs and observing a bowl of tadpoles slowly changing into frogs are further experiences that bring questions. The child slowly comes to understand more about growth changes and the time it takes for growth.

The way in which various baby animals are nourished is another fascinating subject. The child may observe a mother bird feeding her baby birds and a baby lamb suckling from its mother. He or she may watch a human baby nursing or taking milk from a bottle. These are absorbing experiences for children. They will have comments and questions.

Some children ask few questions. When this is the case, we may wonder whether the child feels that his or her question may be about a "forbidden" subject. We may need to raise some questions ourselves so that the child can feel that it is all right to want to know about the subject in which he or she is sure to be interested. By the time children are five years old, they should have a reasonably good understanding about how babies grow and are born.

Sometimes we meet a child who is incessantly asking, "Why?" without giving much attention to our answers. We may wonder whether the child is afraid to ask the questions that are really on her or his mind. Such questions may be about reproduction. Instead of asking the real question, the child keeps demanding "Why?" seeking and not finding out, because she or he has not asked the right question. It may be wise to offer some comments on the subject ourselves to help that child.

Children love stories about what they were like and what they did when they were little or even what we did when we were little. Such stories help the child to learn something about the wonder of growth through time. The child begins to realize that one has a past and can look forward to a future—a significant thing for us all. Grandparents are usually good at telling such stories.

Sex experiences of the child. Occasionally a child's interest in his or her body or in reproduction may lead the child into explorations with other children, in sex play. It is probably important for us to be "preventers" of such sex play when possible. We should redirect children into other activities, but our redirection should be casual, without scolding or reproof. It is not "bad," for example, to try out taking a temperature rectally but it may do harm and it should be stopped with an explanation of why it should not be done. Children do not learn from unexplained prohibitions or disapproval. They may only become anxious or secretive. They need to understand reasons. Sex play is a natural outcome of an interest in finding out more about what people do. With more adequate supervision and explanation of what puzzles them, children can become absorbed in exploring the vast range of experiences presently within their reach. Our part is to protect them from experiences which leave them anxious and guilty about what they may do with their bodies.

If unfortunate enough to have a sex experience with an adult, a young child will need to talk over the experience many times with someone whom he or she trusts. Talking about it reduces the child's anxiety and makes it seem less disturbing. Fear and anxiety are poor feelings to associate with sex. Parents can explain that some people are "sick" in the way they behave. They can help to reassure the child that such things do not happen often.

Coping With Feelings of Jealousy and Rivalry in the Family

Members of a family love one another and help one another, but they also get angry with one another sometimes. They are jealous at times. Anger and jealousy are feelings that everyone has at times when living with others. A child must learn to manage such feelings. This begins in the family. The family is the "testing ground" for learning to deal with such feelings in constructive ways. There is no better place to learn.

Personal relationships in a family are not simple. From the start the baby is involved in a triangle of mother, father, baby. The baby must share the mother's attention with the father. The baby becomes aware that he or she is *not* the *only* important member of the family.

If children are secure because they are having a generous amount of loving care, they can face sharing attention without feeling left out. They can even share attention with brothers and sisters. They may not like this sharing and may sometimes resent it, but they can gradually accept it as they find their own special place in the family.

There will still be times when every child will feel jealous. The child will resent having to share attention. It is not easy to feel sure of one's place, especially when that place seems to keep changing. Parents help a child with this when they are happy in their relationship together, for then they do not need to compete for the child's affection.

Children in a family will quarrel with each other at times in the course of learning to manage the feelings of rivalry and jealousy which are part of growing. But if the climate of the home is warm and friendly, and if the situations are handled reasonably by the parents, the children gradually learn how to deal with strong negative feelings. The rivalry conflicts are usually most intense around the ages of three or four. Even in a favorable family situation the parents need to be especially patient and loving and firm with children through this period. When we are caring for children, we should avoid rousing jealousy in them by such things as showing favoritism or making comparisons. We need to be sympathetic with their struggle to learn to manage conflicting feelings.

Through quarrels and the reconciliations, children in a family develop strong bonds of affection. They become able to differ, to compete, and to face failure without feeling upset, lonely, or helpless. They have battled successfully within the safe limits of the family. They have coped with feelings of resentment and jealousy. They are readier to turn the strength of such feelings into the service of real accomplishments.

Play with other children helps a child cope with conflicting feelings. Companionship with other children helps both boys and girls weather the storms of this period. The problems a child has in relationships with her or his peers are not so intense and full of conflict as the problems the child has with adults. The child lives in a real world with other children—one that seems more manageable and less full of fantasies. Children can be successful in realistic ways. They learn with each other and have fun doing things on their own level. They work and accomplish their purposes. They explore and discover and make things.

Group play in healthy neighborhood groups or in organized play groups (provided these offer plenty of opportunity for self-initiated play) gives the child a chance for relationships with children who are not her or his brothers or sisters. In group play the child can enjoy companionship with peers without the intensity of feeling that exists within the family. Feelings of jealousy and rivalry are easier to cope with at this age when they occur outside the family. The conflicts between friends are not as difficult to resolve as those between brothers and sisters. The child can learn to assert herself or himself and yet remain friendly in the face of differences. All children need the chance to test themselves out in relationships with other children as they learn to deal with the feelings of jealousy and rivalry common to everyone.

In guiding children, we must be aware of all these feelings. We must be aware, for example, that a child will often be jealous when we give attention to another child. We must reassure that child that we also value and are concerned about her or him. We must avoid increasing needlessly the burden of jealous feelings. We must give instead the guidance that builds confidence, self-respect, and the capacity for close ties of affection and friendship.

All children need the chance to test themselves in relationships with other children.

Children need guidance that builds confidence, self-respect, and the capacity for close ties of affection and friendship.

ACTIVITIES

TO DO AND DISCUSS

1. Observe and record an incident in which two or more children are playing "house" and pretending to be grown-up members of a family, such as a father or a mother.
   a. How do they portray their roles?
   b. What seems important to them in the roles?
   c. How does the observation help you to understand better the way a child may be seeing the roles of different family members?

2. Recall some situations in which you and your brother or sister or a friend quarreled. Describe the situation.
   a. What was the immediate cause of the quarrel?
   b. What other things do you think may have contributed to the quarrel?
   c. How did such quarrels usually end, and how did you feel afterward?

3. a. Recall some misconceptions you may have had when you were young about where babies come from.
   b. How and when did you come to understand the facts about human reproduction?

TO THINK AND WRITE ABOUT

1. Discuss the possible ways in which a young child may add to his understanding about reproduction. How do you want your children to learn about sex matters? What reasons do you have?

2. Discuss the possible ways in which a young child adds to his or her understanding of the roles of a man and of a woman. What are some changes that have taken place in these roles in the last 25 years?

3. What are ways in which the community can be of help to parents in carrying out the role of a parent?

REFERENCES

GENERAL

Ginott, Haim
Between Parent and Child: New Solutions to Old Problems
New York: Avon Books, 1969

Harrison-Ross, Phyllis and Barbara Wyden
The Black Child: A Parents' Guide
New York: Peter Wyden, Inc., 1973

CHILD CARE

Day Care Facts
Women's Bureau Pamphlet 16, Revised
Washington, D. C.: U. S. Department of Labor, 16 pp., 1973

Fesler, Wendy
"Family Day Care Homes in Humboldt County"
Children Today, January–February, 1973

Keyserling, Mary D.
Windows on Day Care
New York: National Council of Jewish Woman, 1972

LaCrosse, E. Robert
Day Care for America's Children
Public Affairs Pamphlet No. 470
New York: Public Affairs Committee, Inc., 1971

Prescott, Elizabeth and Elizabeth Jones
"Day Care for Children—Assets and Liabilities"
Young Children, Vol. 18, No. 2, March–April, 1971

Readings in Homemaker Service
Selected papers presenting the background, uses, and practices of homemaker-
    home health aide programs
New York: National Council for Homemaker Services, 1969

Who will take care of your child when you are in training or on the job?
Children's Bureau Publication No. 467
Washington, D. C.: U. S. Department of Health, Education, and Welfare, 12 pp.,
    1969 (15 cents)

EDUCATION FOR PARENTHOOD

Badger, Earladeen
"A Mother's Training Program—The Road to a Purposeful Existence"
Children, Vol. 18, No. 5, September–October, 1971

Bromberg, Susan
"A Beginning Teacher Works with Parents"
Young Children, Vol. 24, No. 1, pp. 75–80, December, 1968

Education for Parenthood
Office of Child Development
Washington, D. C.: U. S. Department of Health, Education, and Welfare, 8 pp.
  (Single copies free from OCD)

Goldstein, Harriet
"Providing Services to Children in Their Own Homes: An Approach That Can
  Reduce Foster Placement"
Children Today, July–August, 1973

O'Keefe, Ruth Ann
"Home Start: Partnership with Parents"
Children Today, January–February, 1973
Pechman, Sylvia
"Seven Parent and Child Centers"
Children Today, March–April, 1972

Vvladimar de Lissovoy
"Child Care by Adolescent Parents"
Children Today, July–August, 1973

SEX EDUCATION

Berger, Allan S.
"Sex Education of the Young Child"
Young Children, Vol. 25, No. 5, pp. 261–267, May, 1970

De Schweinitz, Karl
Growing Up: The Story of How We Become Alive, Are Born, and Grow Up
New York: Macmillan Co., 1965

Fraiberg, Selma
The Magic Years, Chapter 8 "Education for Love"
New York: Charles Scribner's Sons, 1959

Levine, Milton
"Early Sex Education"
Young Children, Vol. 22, No. 1, pp. 11–15, October, 1966

Sex Education and the New Morality
New York: Child Study Association of America

Stumbling Blocks in Growing

9

After studying this chapter, you will be able to

1. Analyze your feelings of jealousy, anger, and resentment.
2. Recognize negative feelings in children.
3. Guide children in learning how to manage negative feelings.
4. Adjust to problems of bossing and being bossed.

In this chapter we shall discuss three of the common stumbling blocks in growing. Everyone faces these stumbling blocks at times, and everyone must learn to cope with them to grow in a healthy way. The three stumbling blocks we will discuss are feelings of jealousy and rivalry, feelings of anger and resentment, and problems of authority.

Why are these such universal problems?

What are constructive ways of coping with these problems?

It is important to remember that healthy personality growth does not depend on the absence of problems and conflicts. It depends on how we solve the problem or how we manage to deal with the conflict. Growth comes from reaching solutions to a problem. Solving one problem successfully enables us to deal better with the next problem. Sometimes we try solutions which block our growth and make it more difficult to deal with the problems which follow. One person, for example, wants to make friends with someone else. If not immediately successful, the person may be critical of the other person and blame that person for acting as he or she does. This response is likely to block the person in achieving the friendly relation wanted. Another person in the same circumstance may try a different approach and find it successful. It is easier for this person to make friends the next time. We grow as we overcome obstacles.

Feelings of Jealousy and Rivalry

One of the stumbling blocks to healthy growth is the jealous feelings with which we all struggle. These feelings are natural because we love and care about other people and want them to care, too, and sometimes we are not sure of our place with them or of the meaning of what they do.

Beginnings of jealousy and rivalry. Feelings of jealousy and rivalry have their beginning in the early experiences of an individual in the family. Because of this, they are strong feelings. They continue with us through life, motivating much that we do.

As babies become more aware of the world around them, they also become aware of the rivals they have for attention and affection. In the beginning as infants they felt as though they were the center of the universe. But with time and experience there comes the awareness that attention has to be shared, that one must compete with others for it, that others have important places, too. Perhaps we are never entirely sure of our place in any group. Relationships keep changing. It takes time to build enough assurance to be confident that we will have a place with which we can be satisfied. It often takes painful effort on our part to achieve this.

It is natural for the young child to be tremendously concerned about the place he or she holds in the parents' affections. The child is sometimes resentful of the time and attention they give to household tasks, the time they spend at the telephone, with a casual visitor, or, even more, with a good friend. Children often do not like their parents' best friends because of the struggle with jealous feelings which are aroused by seeing parents with them.

But the most important rival for attention at first is the father. The child becomes aware of how much of the mother's attention is given to the father. The child wants to hold on to the most important place herself or himself, but senses that the mother and father are interested in each other in ways which do not include her or him. The child is confronted, too, with the fact that feelings are mixed or ambivalent ones. The child is jealous of the father, but also wants attention from the father very much. The child must struggle with this conflict. Slowly young children must resign themselves to knowing that they cannot have the most important place, that they must cope with their jealous feelings somehow and find places for themselves in the affections of both their mothers and their fathers. The young child does not accomplish all this without great effort. She or he may be fussy and irritable and act unreasonably as a result of the struggles to cope with these feelings. Parents help by not provoking any unnecessary jealousy. They help by being patient and kind and loving, but the child will still have some unhappy moments.

Mothers and fathers help children as they steadfastly maintain their love for the children as well as their love for each other. The children are reassured by the fact that the parents' love is not disturbed by the children's feelings. It is harder for children if there is serious friction between parents. The children do not find reassurance. Their jealous feelings may frighten them and leave them tied to one parent. They are less able to find a healthy resolution of their conflicts. If fortunate, the child gradually manages to cope with his or her feelings and to become sure of his or her place as a child in the affections of both parents.

It takes time, patience, and wisdom on parents' part to help a child resolve the conflicts he or she feels over a new baby's arrival.

Another real occasion for jealousy, especially for the first child, is the coming of a new baby. The child's place in the family is changed. Attention necessarily centers on the new baby. We have begun to appreciate the strength of the jealous feelings which many children have. It takes time and patience and wisdom on the parents' part to help a child resolve the conflicts he or she feels. It is not wise to deny them. The readjustment is hard, but in making it in constructive ways the child gains strength and is better able to cope later with competitive situations he or she meets in life. It would be serious if the child showed no jealousy over a new baby's arrival. It would suggest that the child did not value his or her place in the family. The *way* the child manages feelings is important.

The child who lives with brothers and sisters has many opportunities to grow through coping constructively with feelings of jealousy and rivalry. In the family the child has a chance to find ways of managing love and hate feelings. The particular type of sibling rivalry the child experiences will influence adjustments in personal relations throughout her or his lifetime. The child has gone through a training and should emerge better able to feel comfortable about rivals. The child who has no brothers and sisters has fewer chances to learn how to cope with feelings of rivalry and jealousy. That child must learn to deal with these feelings in experiences with playmates.

In dealing wisely with the friction between siblings, parents make one of their most significant contributions to the personality growth of their children. If parents manage to deal with each child in individual ways, without favoritism, leaving each as free as possible to work out problems but stepping in when the conflicts are too intense or one-sided, the children will have confidence that disagreements and conflicts with those they love can be managed. Good sibling relations are a source of great support to children. They are the result of the efforts of thoughtful parents and fortunate circumstances.

In coping successfully with feelings of jealousy and rivalry, the children face these feelings and turn them into constructive channels, using their energy to accomplish things in the world of work, to create, to be people who do important things, and to care for and be concerned about others who need care. Children do this when they use the love side of their jealous feelings. They have

Some children want more attention than others do.

harnessed the energy and drive of jealousy and channeled it to constructive uses.

This is a summary of the origins of jealousy and rivalry which arise out of our earliest and deepest relationships. Now let us look at ways in which we may recognize these feelings in children and help a child deal with them.

Sharing attention. Many people have a good deal of trouble at times in sharing the attention of a person who is important to them, like a parent or a teacher or a best friend. They don't like it when a good friend spends time with someone else. It makes them uncomfortable and unhappy. It is likely that when these people were children they were not successful in resolving the conflicts which come with sharing attentions. They may not have had the kind of guidance then which would have helped them find a place for themselves even with rivals present. They feel resentful and hurt. Perhaps they may be the kind of individual who always seems to need a great deal of attention, more than is available. Some children want more attention than do others.

Paul is an example. He is very quiet and is just beginning to make friends at nursery school. He plays with Wendy one day and they have lots of fun. He is very happy. Later Paul sees Wendy playing with Helen, laughing and talking. He says to Wendy, "Are you her friend?" Wendy nods yes. Paul says sadly, "Then you aren't mine." He has not yet reached the point of feeling that one can be friends with more than one person. He has been very jealous of two older brothers who, in their turn, are very competitive. No one in his family feels sure of his place.

One needs to feel valued even when one is not the center of attention. It takes self-confidence to realize that one is still a person of value and worth even though one is not always chosen first or played with exclusively, even by a good friend. It takes confidence to realize that people are our friends even when they prefer someone else at the moment. Too often we turn away and act unfriendly when this happens, thus making other people less friendly to us.

Every parent has had the experience of having a child climb all over her or him and demand things when the parent was talking on the telephone. Every parent has had the child act naughty (and thus get attention) when there was an important visitor.

When young children act this way, they are trying to hold on to their places. It is easy to feel annoyed with them, but a parent needs to understand what a child is saying by acting this way. The parent needs to take time for an explanation such as, "I will soon be through telephoning and then I'll come with you. You may play with your cars while you wait." The child may feel more satisfied if the parent gives him or her a kiss or a loving pat while saying these words. The child's doubts are over then.

As long as children feel they are still important to their parents, they can be less demanding. They can share attention. Later when the parent has more time, she or he may make it clear to the child how the parent would like the child to behave while the parent is telephoning. The child can be prepared ahead of time. It helps, too, to approve when a child does behave well.

Children usually are jealous over sharing the attention of any person who is important to them. If you are caring for a child, you may find the child dislikes having you give attention to any other person or thing. The child may be concerned about his or her place with you. You can try to manage in a way which will help reassure the child.

When a new baby arrives. A really critical time comes when a new baby arrives and the child's place changes. The child can grow very anxious and may suffer a lot. He or she needs help in finding that the child *has* a place even though it has changed. The mother needs to show the child by really giving him or her some special attention or some time that belongs just to that child, that she still cares just as much for him or her as before. She can help the child learn to be comfortable and not feel less valued because of having to share attention. It takes time to learn this.

One mother kept a cookie in her pocket when she was nursing the baby at first, so that when the two-year-old came up she could give her something to eat and thus make it possible for her to feel less upset about seeing the mother feed the baby.

What children need is help in feeling satisfied. They can also begin to realize that they do not really have to depend as much on attention as they grow older. We can help by explanations such as, "The baby takes a lot of time. You want me to play with you. I'd like to and will later. You are my big boy now. I'm glad to have a big boy." The world changes as we get older. It holds new possibilities.

At this critical point fathers play a very important part. A father can give support to the child by spending time with him or her on excursions and by sharing work and play experiences with the child. The child finds a new and wonderful place with the father. Sharing experiences with a young child may be the start of a companionship which is rewarding to both father and child.

We can also put into words what we expect of the child so that she or he is clear about this, too. "When we go into the bedroom where the baby is sleeping, we will both walk quietly and just whisper. I'm sure you can do it just the way I do."

It is important that we feel sure ourselves that jealous feelings are natural and that they can be managed. Then we can help the child by our confidence, or our casualness and our firmness. If we are not afraid of these kinds of feelings we are more likely to feel sure that the child, with time, can behave in acceptable ways.

A place in the group for everyone. If you happen to be caring for a group of children, you need to be aware of the jealous feelings with which all children have to struggle at some times. When you hold one child in your lap, you may need to take care that the other children feel as sure as possible that you care about them, too.

Children are very sensitive to what is happening in situations like these. If a child is being held because of being hurt and needing comfort, the other children will usually feel good about this. It is reassuring. It is what they would want to have happen to them, so they feel safer as they watch the child.

If the child is there just because the adult enjoys having that child there and it makes the adult feel good, the children feel left out. They may wonder, "Doesn't teacher like me?" They feel jealous, and no wise adult provokes jealous feelings. These are not good feelings to have. The children may act "naughty" to get attention, or they may retreat from trying to get attention. Any way it happens, there is trouble. We have to use our very best judgment and be aware of the feelings of all the children. They need to be sure of their place with us.

Rivalry in groups. When young children are together in nursery school groups or Sunday school, they are often concerned about their place with the teacher. They may want to sit next to the teacher at story time or be first in doing what the teacher asks. It is sometimes hard for the teacher to manage but it may be impor-

One needs to feel valued, even when one is not the center of attention.

tant to arrange the situation if possible so that there isn't a "first" or that no one is "next" to the teacher. Sitting facing the children may help, for example. This reduces the occasion for rivalry. It is also important to find ways of showing each child that he or she is important in some way and has a place. Children need reassurance in their first group experiences that they are important as individuals. They need attention, even the quiet ones who never ask for attention. These may be children who are just too timid to demand it.

> **Observe a group of children with a teacher and see what you think they may be feeling about their place in the group. How sure are they that the teacher values them and thinks they are important? What did you observe?**

Learning to share a place in the group is a very important learning for a child. Teachers need to be aware of the way children are feeling, so that they can be careful to show that they like *all* the children even when doing something for an individual child. Teachers need to help children grow in their capacity to share attention with others without pushing them toward this goal.

Misbehaving to get attention. Bobby, a three-year-old who was covered with mud from play outdoors, was being helped to clean up by his nursery-school teacher. Two children began to run noisily around the room; they tipped over the table on which there were some paint jars, making a mess. Why did this happen?

We might call them naughty, but if we are trying to understand them, we would suspect that they were jealous. They did not like seeing the teacher so busy with Bobby. They wanted a share of attention. Here is what had happened earlier.

When Bobby came in covered with mud, they had noticed him and were interested. They asked questions of the teacher and wanted to go to the coatroom to watch him get cleaned up. Perhaps they wished they had had fun in the mud, too. But the teacher told them to go back to their play and went on to the coatroom with Bobby. They felt left out. So now Bobby had the teacher all to himself! By misbehaving they did something to get the teacher to pay attention to them.

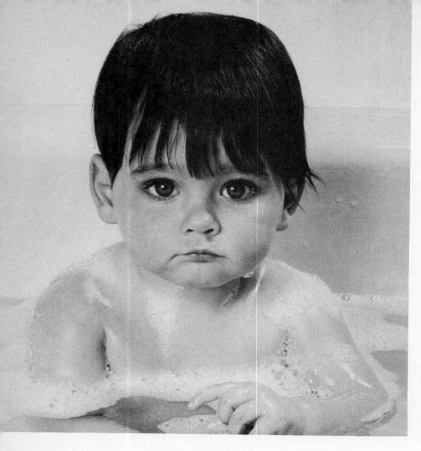

Children need attention, even the quiet ones who never ask for it.

In this case, the teacher might have prevented the naughtiness of these two children by including them and making cleaning up Bobby an experience in which they shared. The teacher might have said, "Bobby certainly needs some washing up! My, how muddy. We'd better help him get washed. What were you doing, Bobby?" The two children could have gone to the coatroom with Bobby and the teacher. There they could have had a part in helping him wash, change his clothes, and get cleaned up. They would have been satisfied that the teacher was interested in them as well as in Bobby.

Children often misbehave to get our attention when they feel they have been left out, or that others are getting much more attention than they are. We should never scold a child for feeling jealous or try to make the child feel ashamed. Feeling ashamed only makes matters worse. It is harder to like people when one is ashamed of oneself. A child is jealous because he or she cares and wants to feel that the adult cares.

Feelings of Anger and Resentment

Feelings of anger and resentment are also feelings which everyone has. The infant may cry in discomfort and rage when she or he wants feeding. The toddler may have a temper tantrum when we take something from her or him. Angry feelings are strong feelings. They may be a strong force in constructive efforts or in destructive ones, depending on how we manage them. They may be stumbling blocks in growing unless we can accept them and then can deal with them with understanding.

Everyone feels angry sometimes. Everyone knows what it is like to feel angry. We have all felt angry and resentful at times, and these feelings make us unhappy. Angry children are unhappy children.

Accepting feelings. Many children, not all, who are quiet and don't join in the play with others are really afraid of the bad feelings they have inside them. They have become too afraid of these feelings to act at all. They feel it is very bad to be angry. They feel that no one will like them. They are afraid to act for fear these feelings will come out and other people will know about their anger and hate.

Mary played by herself in nursery school, doing the same thing over and over. She hardly ever spoke and always did what the teacher asked. She wasn't any trouble but was missing out on a lot of fun in the group. One teacher made friends with her and spent time with her. Soon Mary showed that she didn't want the teacher to give attention to anyone else. This was a good sign. It showed that Mary cared about the teacher and that she was beginning to dare to demand something. The teacher explained carefully whenever it was necessary to leave Mary. The teacher tried to give Mary all the attention she wanted.

One day when Mary was in the sandbox and teacher was near, another child came up and gave the teacher a pan to hold. Mary threw some sand directly at the teacher. Although startled, the teacher took time to think what it meant. Mary had been very afraid to express feelings in the past. Because the teacher felt it was good that at last Mary had been able to show her displeasure directly, the teacher did not reprove her at this point. The teacher only said quietly, ''Next time throw it at my feet.'' Mary played more freely after that.

The next day Mary tried to take a favorite tricycle from another child who was using it. The teacher stopped her, saying, "No, she's using it." Mary hit at the teacher's dress, not really touching it. The teacher said, "I know you really want it. You're mad at me because I won't let you take it. But you can have it later." Then Mary ran to the jungle gym and climbed up on it, the first time she had done any climbing. She felt freer and better able to do things now because she had shown her teacher how she felt and the teacher had not been angry with her.

Because Mary trusted herself to show how she really felt in a good relationship with a teacher who understood, she became less afraid of herself and her anger. She could play. She began to change into a more active child who could enjoy herself. Mary no longer did exactly what the teacher said but began to live with the whole of herself and feel that she could be liked by others for what she was—a real person. She began to enjoy playing with others. She got angry with them and was less upset when they got angry, too.

Paul, who was also quiet and passive, took this way of feeling freer. He began to call everyone, "Hi, rotten apple." After he had done this, he seemed able to play more actively. He dug in the sand, threw sand over a ball, and covered it. Soon he shouted to everyone and anyone, "Hi, you *big* rotten apple." Then, no longer a passive child, he began making friends with people.

A child has to be sure that aggressive feelings are all right, that the responsible adults will stop him or her without getting angry when the child is aggressive in unacceptable ways. Then the child can play freely and can feel it is safe to make friends. The child can be creative and make things.

Managing feelings. The way in which we manage our feelings may be a big stumbling block in the healthy growth of personality. There are different ways to manage feelings. Perhaps the first step is to recognize that feelings can be managed.

We can try to hide our feelings, denying that we feel the way we do or we can express our feelings, bringing them out in words or in action, doing something about them or with them.

There are differences in patterns for expressing feelings. What we do can be destructive or constructive, harmful, harmless, or helpful. We can guide children in learning to manage feelings so that these feelings will not act as stumbling blocks.

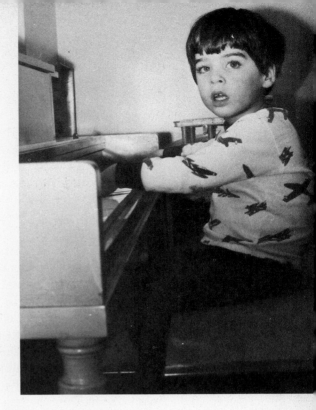

Many children who are quiet and don't play with others are really afraid of the bad feelings they have inside them.

We all develop patterns or ways of managing uncomfortable feelings. These patterns start when we are small children. Since these patterns influence the kind of living we do, it is important to understand how to manage difficult feelings in healthy ways. We can help children, and ourselves, manage feelings in ways that will help rather than hinder the process of growth.

One way to help a child manage feelings well is to make sure that he or she is not overwhelmed by having to face too many difficulties. Children need to be protected, not from all difficulties, but from too great a load of trouble. It is a matter again of being presented with the world in "small enough doses" so that they can master it. It is a matter involving some mutual regulation. We avoid doing things which make children feel jealous. *We avoid teasing.* We avoid making children feel angry needlessly. We avoid adding to the burden of uncomfortable feelings children have to carry.

Another way to manage feelings in a constructive way is to be honest about the way we feel. When we are jealous, the worst thing to do is to pretend that the jealous feeling isn't there. To say, for example, "I don't care" (if we really *do* feel hurt), when we see a friend enjoying someone else will never solve the problem. It just piles up more bad feelings.

Since it is hard to be very clear about what happens with feelings, we may prefer to think that our unhappiness or resentment is actually *caused* by the other person rather than our own feelings of jealousy. We blame other people and we get very mixed up in our relationships with people. Of course, some of the trouble may lie with the other person who is thoughtless and inconsiderate or not loving. But people who have denied to themselves that they have certain feelings lose sight of the part their *own* feelings play in their behavior. They haven't much chance of changing their behavior and improving the situation when this happens.

It is very important to help children start out being honest about the way they feel. When they are jealous or mad, they need to say so. Later, they will learn that there are times when one doesn't tell others but is just clear about it with oneself.

We really need to stop and say to ourselves, "I don't like it a bit." Just doing this helps. We need to be honest with ourselves. It is all right to have all kinds of feelings. All people do. That is what it is to be human! The thing we are concerned with is managing well the feelings we have, not just wishing them away, like magic. They exist and they are much more likely to be managed well if we look squarely at them.

If we say, "I don't like it a bit when Jane talks to Mary," we may be free to think about it and say, "Gosh! That's funny. I like to talk to Mary, and Jane shouldn't get mad at that, so I guess I really shouldn't get mad at Jane." It seems different then.

If Jane is mad, we may think about it and say, "Maybe I've done something she doesn't like and she's really mad at me." She may be behaving like the children who spilled the paint when they felt left out because Bobby was getting all the attention from the teacher.

In this case the thing to do would be to ask Jane, "What's happened? I felt badly when I saw you talking to Mary. Are you mad at me?" That's getting to the heart of the matter and things can get cleared up. It shows you trust yourself and your feelings and trust your friend and can be honest.

Because the things we do when we feel resentful, for example, often get us into trouble, we are likely to cover up the way we feel. We try to pretend even to ourselves that we don't have these feelings. If we have been scolded for being mean to a brother or sister, we hide the feelings even from our family.

One way to help a child manage feelings well is to be sure that he or she is not overwhelmed by having to face too many difficulties.

The need to express feelings. One of the most important things we have learned about feelings is that they need to be *expressed.* They need to be expressed, not blindly, but with awareness.

It is a long process to learn about ourselves, what we feel and how we can express feelings in satisfying and constructive ways. It is a process that should begin in the first years. People are fortunate if they have been helped to be clear about their real feelings rather than having had to hide them and grow confused. They are fortunate if they have been helped to be clear about the feelings behind their actions.

Feelings can be expressed in actions. At first children are not able to put feelings into words. They may need to tell us how they feel through the way they act. We need to understand their language.

A baby cries when hungry, unhappy, or hurt. Crying is a way to express feelings. A child cries, too, and isn't a "crybaby." The child is telling us how he or she feels, trusting us enough to believe we care about knowing. Children who have not had parents to care for them sometimes do not cry much even when they are badly hurt. This is a poor sign. They have stopped feeling that someone cares.

Feelings are also expressed through vigorous activities like hitting, throwing, kicking, running. Children need plenty of chances to do all these things. Vigorous action drains off strong feelings that become too much to manage. Who hasn't felt better, less angry about something, after a good hard game outdoors? All of us need this kind of an outlet for our strong feelings.

We only need to keep the action safely "channeled" with children. The hitting should not be done at a person, only at an object such as a pillow or punching bag or a dummy figure. Throwing at a target, throwing a bean bag at a wall, banging something hard, pounding clay, all help drain off anger.

Encourage children to express their feelings this way. You can say, "It feels good to do this when you are angry." If children feel free to hit objects and drain off their angry feelings, they can play with other children more peacefully.

Feelings can be expressed in words and also changed through words. As soon as children learn to talk, they can put their feelings into words. Words are the most useful way to be clear about what is happening inside us and to let others know, too. We should be careful not to discourage children from using words to express their feelings. They can't manage feelings well if they keep them inside themselves.

By the time they are five, children should have developed both an awareness of social relations and an ability to manage their feelings in a variety of ways. "I hate you. You're mean," they say. We can say, "I know that's the way you feel. I guess you didn't like what I did." We never say to a young child, "Don't talk like that. It's bad to say such a thing." We let children of five or six know how we feel about what they say. We let them know that we understand how they feel when they say it. If we need to, we direct them to other outlets for their feeling. We make sure that they realize that they can be honest with us, but that people outside the family may resent open expression of feeling or the use of certain words.

We all know that no one is kind and loving all the time. We all get angry. We get tired and discouraged and we are impatient with other people. We are jealous or envious or selfish or cruel at times. Everyone is! People are hard to live with. Some are harder to live with than others. Sometimes the hardest person of all to live with is yourself.

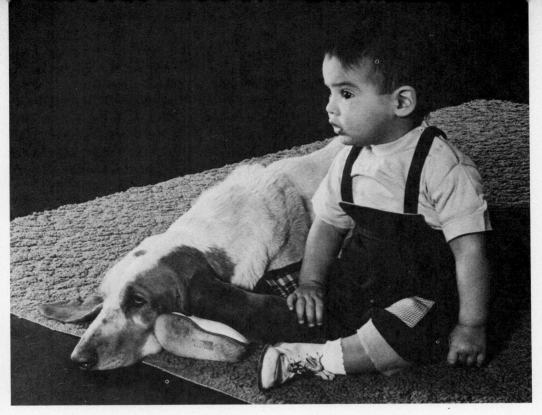

Learning about ourselves—what we feel and how we can express feelings in satisfying and constructive ways—takes a long time.

We find it easier to live with ourselves if we *like* ourselves and are comfortable about all the feelings we have. We like ourselves better when we can accept *all* our feelings. We are helped in living with people if we are comfortable about all the kinds of feelings they may have.

If a parent is comfortable about the fact that his or her child gets angry with the parent sometimes or that brothers and sisters don't like each other all the time, the parent makes it easier for them to modify these feelings with time. The parent may not like the fact that the feelings are there, but accepts them and doesn't make the children hide them from him or her.

Every little child will wish at times that baby brother or sister had never been born. It's a pretty good thing if the child can say it. It will make it easier to be glad about the baby at other times. It will make it easier if the child knows the parents understand the way the child really feels. It is no help if parents say, "Don't feel like that." Then the child can't share his or her thoughts with them.

Every child will be angry at times with a brother or sister. It helps if his or her parent says, "I know you are cross with him right now. It is hard to have someone else use your train without asking. I know how you feel. A mistake has been made, and I hope we'll remember another time. We all make mistakes. Remember when I forgot to leave a piece of cake for you? I was sorry about that. Remember when you forgot and used my scissors and I got very cross?" A child can face a situation better with this kind of help.

Just talking can do a lot to help draw off angry feelings. It is a good pattern to use in learning to manage these feelings. They begin to disappear when we put them into words.

Feelings can be expressed creatively through music, art, poems, and stories. The child who goes to the easel and paints is expressing feeling. An angry child may cover the paper with black and only a bit of red or blue. At another time when the child is happy, mostly yellows or reds may be used. The child who sings while playing is usually expressing contented feelings. These are creative and constructive ways of expressing our feelings. Feelings expressed in these ways are no longer stumbling blocks to growth—our growth or the growth of others.

Creative people are people who can express *all* of themselves. They aren't afraid of the dark sides. It takes both the bright and the dark sides to make a whole person. Both sides are manageable, the good and the bad. We need to begin to learn as children what we are like and how to live with ourselves in ways which make use of all of our capacities. Feelings can provide energy for getting really difficult things done or for being creative, or they can keep us from accomplishing what we should.

Channeling anger constructively. When we try to hide our anger, we find it appears again in unexpected ways. We are familiar with the stories of the man who is angry with his boss and comes home and criticizes his wife's cooking—or of the woman who gets mad with her husband and goes out and kicks the dog. We may have had an experience in which we were very patient through a difficult, trying day and then suddenly exploded with anger over a trivial incident, to our own surprise. All the anger we had piled up earlier and had not had a chance to express spilled out at this trivial incident.

It may be dangerous and it is always disturbing to have feelings spill out where they do not belong. We can give children no greater help in emotional growing than to help them learn to be aware of the feelings they have, to be aware of what is causing them, and to do something about them at the time they occur, even if the doing is no more than realizing that these feelings exist. Anger does not just disappear, but it can be drained off.

Guiding children so that anger does not remain a stumbling block means identifying anger whenever we are aware that the child feels angry. It also means putting the anger into words for her or him, "I think you are mad at someone because of something," and then helping the child drain it off in ways that do no harm. Anger turned against oneself can be very damaging. Children often turn anger inward, feeling it is safer to feel angry at themselves than with their parents or other people. Children cripple their growth this way.

Anger is a strong feeling. It can be channeled into avenues which lead to constructive accomplishments which take energy and drive. If it is left to work out its course blindly, it destroys much that is of value.

We find it easier to live with ourselves if we like ourselves and are comfortable about all the feelings we have.

Some children have stronger feelings and impulses than do others. They may have more of a struggle in learning to cope with these feelings. We have a greater challenge in guiding them wisely and with skill. The rewards may be great for they are likely to be people of energy and drive who will assert themselves as leaders wherever they are.

We Have Feelings, Too

While we can accept the fact that a child may feel angry at us or friends and we can accept the fact that it is important for the child to be honest about feelings, we do not necessarily need to put up with what the child may do. We have a right to our feelings, too.

If the child keeps on telling us that he or she doesn't like us we may say, "I know how you feel now, but that's enough. Try telling me something else." Children learn from our responses to them. We can show them that we accept our feelings and do not deny the way we feel.

Recognizing anger in children is the first step in helping children cope with it.

The Problems of Authority

Another stumbling block in growing lies in the problems having to do with authority or of bossing or being bossed. There are healthy ways and unhealthy ways of meeting these problems.

Bossing and being bossed. Healthy people need and want to be individuals, to assert themselves, to do things in their own way and in their own time, and to work toward goals that are important to them. But they also need and want to be with other people and have them as companions and friends. They want things that come only through working with other people.

When any of us live and work with people, we must take directions and follow some rules. We must fit into the group as well as be an individual. A successful balance in this is not easy to achieve. Often, the closer the relationship with people, the more difficult is the balance and the more important it becomes.

For a society to be a good one its members must come to terms with the matter of authority. They must not be afraid of it or feel resentful about it. They must understand its value. They must feel responsible for it, deciding when to lead or to follow, knowing what is involved when they make these choices. They may conform, or they may rebel, but they should not do it blindly. They must be able to live with satisfaction as individuals within the framework of a social order.

Learning about authority. The extent to which anyone finds a good balance in coping with matters of authority will depend partly on what she or he has learned about authority as a child. If children are bossed around a lot, they are likely to grow up disliking authority or trying to escape from it. They are likely to get into trouble when they themselves try to be a boss someday.

People in authority may be strict, or they may be indulgent. They may be arbitrary or reasonable. They may be concerned, or they may be busy or indifferent. They may explain things, or they may not. From the kinds of experiences children have with people who are important to them they may learn to respect authority or to resent it. They are sure to develop ways of coping with it or living with it. Their way may be cheating and lying and fighting it in some way. It may be by taking it too hard, or it may be by facing it comfortably. Fortunately there are usually a good many people who are important in a child's life. His or her experiences are seldom all good or all bad. A child is fortunate when most of his or her experiences with people are with those who use authority in responsible ways.

Because children are dependent on other people when they are young, they have difficult tasks in finding a balance between fitting into a group and asserting themselves. They must depend on their parents and then on their older brothers and sisters and later on their teachers. They have to discover who they are and what they can do within the framework of what all these people will permit. They must do this while they are quite dependent on adults and quite inexperienced. Is it surprising that people have trouble understanding the problems of authority?

When we live and work with people, we must take directions and follow rules. We must fit into the group as well as be an individual.

The right kind of discipline will encourage a child to meet the problem of authority with a good balance of self-respect. If adults are sympathetic and loving as well as firm, they help a child. The child sees adults being responsible for doing what needs to be done without making it seem harsh or frightening.

We have discussed other aspects of discipline in an earlier chapter. Children need wise discipline if they are to cope well with problems of authority.

Children are also helped to cope with the problem of authority by the way the adults around them make them feel about being little. If they feel of no value because they are little, they are helpless to defend themselves. "You can't have this because you might break it," or, "You can't go because you're too little," or, "You do as I tell you. No questions!" Children can only wish for the time when they will be big enough to push people around.

One of the important things anyone needs to learn is that authority means responsibility—not just control and pushing people around. If we treat children with respect even though they are little and dependent on us, we show them that we do not have to take advantage of size and strength. They can see authority used in fair and responsible ways which leave others with feelings of self-respect. They themselves are free to grow more independent, too. Wise parents use authority in these ways.

Learning through playing with others. As we watch them in their play, we can see the way children are working out the problem of achieving a good balance for themselves in giving and taking directions. Let us take as an example the behavior of two four-year-olds in a nursery school and see what a teacher does in helping them with this problem in their relationship.

Janice and Jerry play together constantly. Janice takes the lead, giving Jerry directions which he seems to enjoy following. She has good ideas, uses language well, and is skillful socially. Jerry is slower in speech and movement and depends on her. They play happily together day after day, paying very little attention to anyone else.

If one observes carefully, one notices that Janice is really pretty "bossy" and that Jerry occasionally resists in a mild way and even plays with another child. Janice gets upset when this happens.

Should they be separated? How would you feel if someone tried to separate you from your best friend?

We should remind ourselves that they are playing together because they *want* to. Being together really satisfies a need for them both. Jerry may still need to be dependent. He may have a lot of "unfinished business" left in this task of growing to be an independent person on his own. If we separate him from Janice, he may just find someone else to depend on. Janice needs to find out from Jerry, not us, about how people feel about being bossed. She may really need to do this bossing.

Jerry is the one who must assert himself in their relationship. When he is ready to try it, there will be opportunities to help him. For example, Janice was already there when he came to school one morning, playing in the housekeeping corner where the two usually played together. She called to him, but he answered, "I'm going outside." Janice protested to the teacher, "Jerry shouldn't go out when I don't go out." Jerry said uncertainly, "But I want to go out. I'm going to play with Timmy."

The teacher encouraged Jerry to carry out his wish. "It's all right to go out, Jerry. It's a nice day. I'm glad you are going out. You can come in and play with Janice later." In this way the teacher helped him stand up for himself.

Jerry did go out and joined Timmy at play. It was his own decision. He was ready to separate himself from Janice, and the teacher helped him. He might not have been able to do it by himself for Janice was his best friend. He liked her, but the teacher's support helped him feel more certain that it can be all right to pay attention to one's own wishes, to assert oneself, and to do what one likes. Acting this way does not need to mean that one is less friendly.

When Jerry was younger, at home, he may have been disapproved of when he began to show more independence. He may have gotten the idea that the only way to get along with people was to do what they wanted. But we know that this is not always a desirable way to get along. Now the teacher is helping him learn differently.

Janice, too, needs help. Perhaps she is unsure of herself with others unless she is "boss." She may only feel sure that people like her when they do what she wants them to do. Unless she can control matters, she may feel as though she is pretty helpless.

When she was younger, she may have been expected to be more competent and grown-up than she really felt. She may have felt that she should be able to make things happen. She may not have been accepted as she was, a little girl who was not yet big and able to manage everything. So, to make herself more acceptable, she tried to manage things and people and felt she was failing if she could not control them.

She needs help from the teacher in learning another point of view. In this case, the teacher said, "You like having Jerry with you, I know. But he's going out now. He'll be back later. You and he will play together again." The teacher gave Janice something else to think about by adding, "I wonder what you are going to do with those dolls." Janice seemed satisfied and continued her play. She seemed to feel more comfortable alone, without someone to boss. Later the teacher helped Janice again by finding another child to join her.

People who are responsible about matters of authority do not assume authority when it is unnecessary. They do not avoid assuming it when it is necessary.

It will take more than one time for these children to learn the lessons they need to learn: 1) that one can stand up for oneself and still be friendly, and 2) that one can feel comfortable and liked even when one is not controlling and bossing. These are good things to learn. They help in all relationships.

These are lessons which are part of learning to live with the realities of authority, with bosses and rules and restrictions. These lessons go along with learning that one can give in with no loss of self-respect and that at times one cannot. They go along with learning to decide wisely how to act independently and be responsible for one's own decisions.

People who have learned to feel responsible about matters of authority do not assume authority when it is unnecessary. They do not avoid assuming it when it is needed. They make the kind of citizens needed in a democracy.

ACTIVITIES

TO DO AND DISCUSS

1 a. Observe a child over a period of time and make notes of the situations in which:
   (1) The child expresses anger or resentment.
   (2) The child bosses others.
   (3) The child accepts authority.
   (4) The child tries to get attention from adults.
   b. In what ways did the child handle these things? Which ways were constructive and effective? Which were not?

TO THINK AND WRITE ABOUT

1 How have you been influenced by the position you have in your family, such as being the oldest child, the middle child, or the youngest? In what ways can parents help in relations between siblings?

2 Why is it better for a child to express feelings rather than hide them? Describe how a child's feelings might be expressed:
   a. When the child has a great many difficulties.
   b. When the child is jealous of someone.
   c. When the child is really angry about something.
   What do *you* do when you have these feelings? How many different ways do you use to drain off such feelings?

3 How can you help a child who is too afraid of feelings to play freely?

4 How can an adult use *words* or *ideas* to change a child's feelings in these situations?
a. When the child says, "I hate you. You're mean!"
b. When the child expresses antagonistic feelings about a new baby brother or sister.

5 How would you help young children find a balance in the following authority-dependency situations?
a. William is continually being requested to do as he is told and ask no questions.
b. John, a vigorous, energetic boy, feels he should be able to assert himself and do what he likes at all times.
c. Helen feels that the only way to get along with people is to do what they want.

6 How do words like these affect a child's ideas and feelings about authority? "You come in when I tell you to. I don't care whether you are ready or not."

7 How do you feel about being bossed? Discuss this question in class and see how many different ways there are to feel about it. Which ways are most helpful, or lead to the best results?

8 How do you feel about doing the bossing yourself? Discuss this question as you did Number 7.

9 What are some examples of responsible attitudes and actions toward authority on the part of an adult?

REFERENCES

Nicolaysen, Mary
"Dominion in Children's Play: Its Meaning and Management"
Young Children, Vol. 22, No. 1, pp. 20–28, October, 1966

Read, Katherine
The Nursery School, Chapters 17, 18, and 19
Philadelphia, Pa.: W. B. Saunders Co., 1971

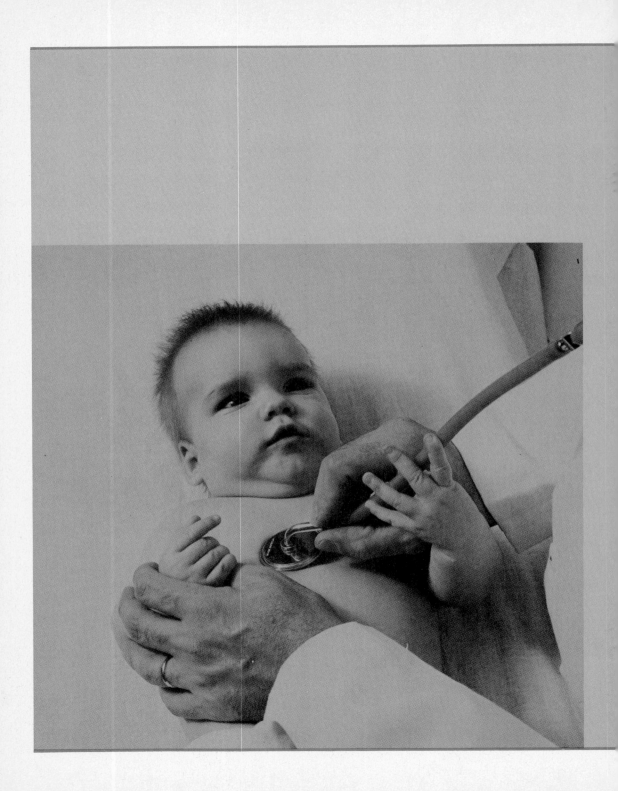

10

Handicaps and Crises

After studying this chapter, you will be able to

1. Analyze special handicaps that certain children face.
2. Accept need for well-run child care centers.
3. Resist the temptation to be harsh at times with children.
4. Appraise suitable arrangements for children who are blind, mentally retarded, or in other ways handicapped.

Everyone has some difficult situations to face in life. We may say, "If only I didn't have this problem or that problem." But problems keep popping up and we keep having to find ways of meeting them.

Children have crises and handicaps to face. Some children we meet may have only one parent, because of either death or divorce. They may have mothers who work outside the home, leaving the child with a succession of baby-sitters A parent may be ill and unable to give the kind of care which parents usually give to children. The family may be of a different nationality, race, or religion from the neighboring families. The family may have more money or less money than other families around them. The child may be adopted and feel different from others.

Many factors may be important in determining how a child feels or acts. Any one circumstance is only a factor among many others. But these make a real difference, depending on the circumstances and on what the individual child is like. Heredity and environment both influence a person's reactions to circumstances.

Some children we will meet are handicapped physically by injury or disease such as crippling polio or cerebral palsy. They may often be sick. Or, they may be handicapped by being blind or deaf. They may be mentally retarded and unable to learn at the same rate at which most children of their age can learn. Some children may be brain damaged, or they may be emotionally ill and unable to react the way most children do.

It is important for all these children that the people they meet avoid adding to their difficulties by lack of understanding and sympathy. Everyone has problems, but some children carry a heavier burden than others. They need more understanding. We can lighten the burden if we are more aware of what can be done to help them grow and develop.

An only child has some problems, but the problems need not be greater than those of other children, just different.

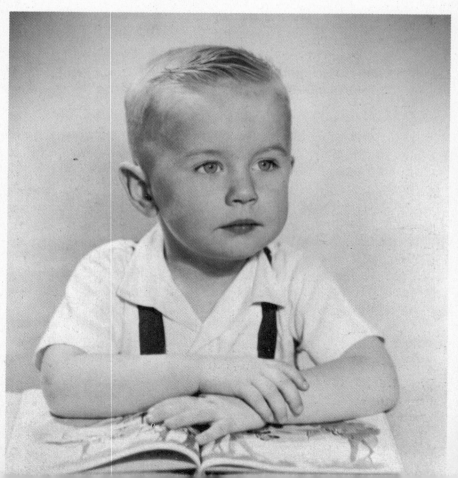

An Only Child

Jane was an only child. Her parents loved her very much and she was a delightful child, friendly and intelligent. Her parents felt sorry that they could not have more children. They knew that only children have some problems, but they felt that the problems need not be greater than those of other children, just different.

They spent a lot of time with Jane because they enjoyed her, but they had time for their own friends, too. When they went out, they left Jane with a baby-sitter whom she knew well. They sent her to nursery school when she was three. She was happy there for she liked people and entered into all activities easily. Jane's parents encouraged other children to play in their yard. When they went on drives or trips, they almost always took one of Jane's friends along. Jane did not feel different from other children. Her parents were firm in their discipline and expected her to take responsibility, but they did not expect her to act like an adult as parents of only children sometimes do. They gave her time to be a child and did not push her into growing up.

Not all parents of only children are able to be this understanding. Some only children are pushed and indulged and do not grow up into happy people unless they receive a good deal of help from someone else.

Adopted Children

Peter and Steve were twin boys who had been adopted when they were infants. They were lively, healthy boys and their adoptive parents were very happy with them. When they were three years old, they went to nursery school. Here they made friends readily and fitted into the group well. They liked each other's company but they spent as much time playing with other children as with each other. They were sturdy and independent.

After they had entered public grade school the parents adopted a little girl of two named Helen. She was plump and moved slowly. She seemed to find it hard to fit into this busy, active family. Her adoptive mother found Helen more difficult to manage than she did the boys. Perhaps she preferred boys to girls. Perhaps the mother and Helen did not "fit" well together as happens sometimes even with children born into a family. Their interests and their tempo of living differed.

Helen found it hard to play with other children when she went to nursery school. Her greatest joy came from pets, the rabbit and the chickens. She was resistant to routines, and no teacher ever got very close to her. At home she did not get much attention from the two boys. Her adoptive father enjoyed her more than the other members of the family did, but he was a busy man and was not at home a great deal. Helen went through school feeling lonely and apart from others and full of resentment. She felt people were against her. As soon as she was old enough, she left home and found a job in a distant city. Peter and Steve kept in close touch with the family.

The problems of adopted children are always somewhat special. Both parents and children have adjustments to face in their feelings about adoption and the reasons for it and other people's attitudes toward it. When these adjustments are made well, the relationships of adoptive parents and their children are as close and warm as those of natural parents.

When adjustments are made well, the relationships of adoptive parents and their children are as close and warm as those of natural parents.

Children with only one parent have special problems Much of their security must come from the one parent.

A Child With Only One Parent

Bill was a bright, alert four-year-old. His mother had died the year before. There were no relatives nearby and his father was caring for him alone. During the day Bill was left with a woman in the neighborhood. His father picked him up on the way home from work and took him back to the trailer where they lived. Sometimes they had supper in a restaurant on the way. Bill and his father were depending on each other. They both carried a heavy burden. Bill tried hard to do everything his father told him to do. His father tried hard, too, to be both mother and father to the little boy.

They managed this way for several years. Bill played with children in the neighborhood, but he had a feeling that he was different from the others somehow. When he entered school, he was much happier for he did well in school and a motherly, understanding teacher meant a great deal to him.

It is more common for a child to be brought up by a mother alone than by a father. The problems are similar, for boys and girls both need two parents if they are to understand the role of a man and of a woman. This was discussed earlier under identifying with one's sex role. The child being raised by a mother alone may not seem to have much difficulty at first, but problems may become greater at adolescence. Children such as these are helped by the fact that there are men interested in elementary education today as teachers and principals. The school, too, may be a help to these children, as it was to Bill.

Children with only one parent have special problems. They have a special need to share experiences with friends and teachers who are understanding. Much of their security must come from the one parent. Every child gets mad at a mother or father at times, but when a child is mad at one parent, he or she can feel good about the other parent. The child with one parent is less free to feel this way and more likely to bury the feeling inside himself or herself where it sometimes causes trouble. The parent, too, has no one to turn to in relieving his or her feelings. The relationship of the child and the parent has to bear strains which are "diluted" in the ordinary family by the variety of relationships possible for the members.

Some communities have an organization called "Parents Without Partners." Its members are parents, either mothers or fathers, who are bringing up a child or children alone. They meet to talk over their special problems and give help to one another in carrying the load of raising children without the help of a partner. Parents Without Partners recognizes the need these parents have to share their problems with others who understand.

When there is a death in a family with children, or a parent is ill for a long time, an understanding "homemaker" provided by an agency in the community can often help keep the family together while the other parent has time to work out more permanent plans. In such a case children do not lose the secure feeling that there is a place for them where they can feel truly at home.

Children Whose Mothers Work Outside the Home

John and Betty are children who have been left with a succession of baby-sitters. John is three and a half, and Betty is only six months old. Their mother works as a secretary while their father has a job as a mechanic in a garage. His work is often irregular. When the father is home, he cares for them. When he has to go to work, he leaves them with a neighbor or gets a young girl down the street to come in. It is not easy for any member of the family.

John cries a lot and finds it difficult to settle down to play. He seems always to be seeking someone or something. He runs out to the sidewalk and talks to people who are passing by. He gets into trouble because he takes small things he finds. He has no children of his own age to play with. It seems likely that John's problems will increase. His restlessness and irritability may make school difficult and he will not know much about making close friends.

Children need their mothers especially in the first two or three years of life. When mothers work outside the home while their children are young, the children should be cared for by someone who can be a real parent-substitute. The parent-substitute should like children and should care for them on a regular basis in either her or his home or the children's home. Only if there is a real parent-substitute, liked by both the children *and* the parents, can the children develop in healthy ways.

Foster day care services and day care centers can meet these children's needs if they are well-run places. Children under three years of age are usually better cared for under a foster day care plan. In this plan a social agency supervises foster day care homes where a qualified person cares for two or three young children in her or his own home. In most cases this person is paid a regular salary by the agency. The parents pay the agency an amount based on their ability to pay. The children are assured better care than if they are left with a baby-sitter whom the parents do not really know well.

Day care centers usually care for children of three, four, and five years. In a good day care center the groups are small, so the child can feel he or she has a place in it. There are perhaps 12 to 15 three-year-olds and 15 to 20 four-year-olds in a group. Sometimes the groups are of mixed ages. A large center may have several separate groups, each with a professionally trained director. There are two adults in every group. The child has a place for his or her own clothes, his or her own bed, and a nourishing hot meal is served at noon. The day is planned with periods of active play outdoors and with periods of rest. Good day care centers provide an educational program such as nursery schools offer. These centers give the child a chance to grow and learn in healthy ways as children do in homes.

The need for day care centers is much greater than the number of centers available. There are many places where children are cared for in groups which do not meet even the minimum standards for children's health and social and emotional welfare. Parents need to protect their children by a careful investigation before they leave a child in any center. They need to be informed themselves about what a good center is like and what they should expect.

Citizens should be aware of the kinds of group care for young children being provided in their community. Learning in the first years of life is so important that provisions for group care of children should be the concern of all citizens.

Not all children both of whose parents work outside the home have the kind of care which adequately supplements the care a mother and father can give. As a result, these children will have behavior problems which can be met only by a good deal of understanding help.

The Neglected Child

Mary's mother had been very ill at home for many months. Mary was the youngest in a large family. Her sisters, who were much older, helped in nursing their mother. They took responsibility for managing the household duties. But Mary was only two. She was not allowed in the sickroom and played quietly by herself. She was a good child. She spent much of the time outdoors. Sometimes she would cry at the closed door of her mother's room. She could not understand what was happening. Everyone in the family gave her some attention but no one had much time for her. They all felt anxious themselves and were kept very busy.

Mary's mother died after nearly two years of illness. The family carried on as they had been doing. The father was often away and left things to his oldest daughter. Mary was looked after by a neighbor most of the time. She caused no special trouble except that she sometimes ran away.

But Mary had more and more trouble as she grew up. She had not been sure of her place in the family. She had felt pushed out

Children who have been neglected for any reason usually need special understanding and help.

when she was growing up. Her mother's closed door stood for rejection to her. She had misunderstood things that happened. She was never sure that anyone really liked her. In those beginning years, she had not mastered the first task in personality growth, that of gaining sufficient trust to overcome her mistrust. As a sensitive child, she was unable to take the ordinary rebuffs and failures which came with living. She was a lonely, unhappy person.

No one had been really aware of how she felt or had made much effort to take the place of a mother. A child must have reassurance and someone to depend on in the beginning. Children who have been neglected for any reason usually need especially understanding help.

Bill was one of a family of three children, Bill and his two sisters. When the mother died, the father could not manage alone so he placed them in an orphanage. Bill kept hoping that his father would come for him someday. He ran away from the orphanage once but was brought back and punished severely. Someone offered to take the three children, but Bill refused to go. His sisters left, but he stayed on for he felt so sure that his father would want him back. That time never came, but fortunately when Bill left the institution he found a place in the home of a kindly minister and his wife. They treated him like a son and helped to heal the wounds left by years of disappointment. Because Bill was a strong, resourceful child he had survived. With their help he became an active member of the community and finally married and established a home of his own.

"Battered" Children

Today we sometimes hear the term "battered" children. It refers to children who have been harmed by the adults caring for them. A better term might be "child abuse" or "nonaccidental injury." The children may be infants or preschool children or older. Their parents, or the adults involved, are so upset and unstable that they beat the children or abuse them physically or inflict severe deprivations. The results are tragic for them and for the grown people as well.

The adult who abuses a child is usually someone who has been mistreated as a child, who has lacked the warm loving care everyone needs. The adult has learned little or nothing about loving. From childhood on she or he may have lived in an unfavorable environment where people were indifferent to her or his needs. When facing strains and frustrations later in life, this adult was not prepared to deal with them. He or she broke down.

In such cases the mother may be a young woman who is overburdened with caring for a child or children whom she may be ill-prepared to care for. She may live in poor surroundings—away from family and friends, with no time for herself away from the family, and few satisfactions. In the end she loses control of herself and takes out her hopeless, despairing feelings on the child. Possibly a good child care center or a center with a play group where she could have found friends and some recreation might have prevented this kind of breakdown.

Sometimes a father from an unfavorable loveless background abuses a child out of jealousy and irritation at the child's demands for attention because of strains he feels at work or in the family. There are always very real emotional problems of long standing behind such abnormal behavior in parents.

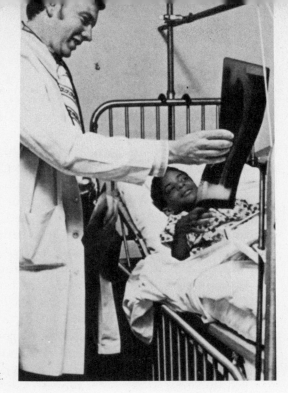

When they face a serious crisis, children need reassurance and support from the people they trust.

Everyone gets tired and impatient sometimes but, fortunately, most people are able to control their actions. Better housing, better economic conditions, better community services for health and welfare and particularly for child care facilities and recreation would certainly help prevent many of these tragedies. All children need to live in environments favorable for good growth and development.

Society needs to prevent these unfavorable beginnings. Society also needs to take responsibility for protecting children when it becomes apparent that they are likely to suffer abuse of any kind.

A Child Acutely Ill

Bobby was suddenly taken acutely ill. His parents rushed him to the hospital. There the doctors diagnosed the illness as serious and immediately began treatment. He was in great pain. His mother remained with him day and night at first, and then she and his father took turns staying so that one of them was always with him until he was well on the road to recovery. Young children desperately need to have a parent with them when they are ill.

When he woke crying in the hospital, one of them was there to reassure him. They explained things to him, prepared him for the "shots" and comforted him. As he began to feel better, he sometimes said he didn't like anyone or anything. But it was safe for him to bring out his feelings because his parents understood. He didn't have to keep them inside himself.

When he left the hospital, his doctor wisely instructed the parents to let him be as active as he wished. He told them to trust the child to know when he needed to rest during the day. He said that anxious warnings about the danger of getting too tired would only result in his taking less responsibility for himself.

Bobby was able to make a remarkable recovery from what had been a serious illness. He had had reassurance and support from people he trusted when he was most in need of it. In the time following his illness, too, he was not overprotected or indulged. His parents trusted him to regulate his activity to his strength. In this they had the backing of understanding doctors.

Bobby entered school eager and interested in it. He was a leader among the children in his neighborhood, absorbed in the projects they all engaged in. He may have gained self-confidence by having mastered a serious crisis with his parents' help.

A Blind Child

Alice entered a nursery school at three and a half. She was blind. Her blindness was the result of too much time spent in an incubator as a premature infant. Fortunately we know enough today so that this type of blindness does not often occur. Alice's parents had help from a person on the staff of their state department of health, trained in work with blind children. She helped them make plans for Alice's future. She also helped them understand more about how they could encourage Alice to grow and develop, letting her do things for herself and play with other children.

Most important of all, she helped them talk about their feelings. It is hard for loving parents to face the fact that their child is different from others and must live with a handicap. Sometimes parents are not able to talk about these things. They keep their thoughts to themselves where their fears and anxieties multiply. But Alice's parents were helped to talk freely about how they felt.

Because they did, they felt more comfortable about Alice and with Alice. They could help their friends feel more comfortable with her, too. They could explain to the other children in the neighborhood about blindness, how it was like having your eyes closed and how Alice depended on feeling with her hands and feet and on words for descriptions of what things were like.

With only a little extra supervision, Alice could play outdoors. She entered nursery school, eager for the new experience, and made a place for herself among the children. The teachers learned, through the help of the trained worker who visited the school and talked with them, to be careful not to do things for Alice that she could do for herself and to treat her as a person who was learning and growing and finding her way as the other children were doing.

Alice is now doing well in grade school, spending five days a week at the special school for the blind and returning to her home for the weekends. She travels by herself on the bus. She plans to attend the regular high school in her own hometown when she is older. Alice has had understanding help and has made progress in mastering her tasks in growing.

A Mentally Retarded Child

Philip had seemed like such a wonderful baby at first. He was placid and good and a lovely looking infant. He seldom cried. He was nearly a year old when his parents were forced to admit to themselves that he had not developed as he should. He was making no effort to sit up or talk. Philip's family found it very hard to face the diagnosis that he was retarded mentally and would not grow like other children. Their dreams of what he might someday become would have to be changed.

They were very unhappy. His mother did not want to see her friends. It was painful to her to see their babies who were active and busy. She hardly wanted to see Philip at times. Philip's mother and father took him to many different doctors. Some of them suggested remedies, but there was no cure. Finally they talked with an understanding counselor. With the counselor's help, they began to think about how they might plan for Philip's future, and help him grow in his own way.

Fortunately there was a school not too far away which was for children who were too retarded mentally to enter the public school. When Philip finally learned to walk, his mother drove him back and forth to school each day. She met other mothers whose children were like hers. She then began to talk about her problems with the director. She watched the teachers work with the children with patience and kindness and firmness. The teachers expected things of these children. Philip seemed happier. She could see some changes in his behavior. He was slowly learning to do some things for himself.

His mother's feelings began to change. She could share the responsibility for his care. She was happier, too, as she watched him begin to learn. She loved him, and now she could face the future with some hope.

If Philip's parents had had other children to care for, they might have decided to place Philip in the state institution for mentally retarded children because they might not have had time to meet his special needs. They could have continued to see him regularly and bring him home for visits. He would have been with people who understood and accepted his rate of growth. He would have had a place with other children like himself just as he has in the special class at the school he attends.

Common Problems

We will meet children who have not faced any of the difficulties we have mentioned, but who still are having a difficult time in living with other people and liking themselves. They are in trouble even though the reasons are not clear to us.

When we are trying to understand children's behavior, we need to be aware that they may have had many kinds of experiences which have special meaning for them, either helpful or harmful.

Many seemingly unimportant experiences may cause real disturbance in people's lives. Moving to a new community is an example. It may be very hard to leave one's friends behind at certain points in one's life and go to live in a strange place and find new friends. It may be easier to do this when one is eight or nine than when one is thirteen or fourteen. It may be easier for some people than for others. It may be easier if one happens to find a new friend quickly or if people in the new school and community welcome strangers.

The "timing" of an experience is important. If a child has to adjust to a new house and yard just after having had to accept a new baby in the family, for example, the child may find the move more difficult than he or she might otherwise have found it. Mary, who was separated from her mother at two, might not have found it so difficult if this had occurred when she was six years old. The year-old child is more seriously disturbed by a parent's absence than the four-year-old is.

ACTIVITIES

TO DO AND DISCUSS

1 Read an article on homemaker services and report on it to class.

2 If there is a social agency in your community which offers a homemaker service, find out how the homemakers are selected and trained, how they are paid, what services are offered, and what types of families are served.

3 Report on one or more children who may be the victims of serious neglect. (a) What is the reason for the neglect in each case? (b) What personality weaknesses may a child have as a result of long and persistent neglect?

4 Contact a local social agency which places children for adoption and request information concerning the procedures to be followed and the criteria for selecting adoptive parents. Get a pamphlet or brochure, if possible.

TO THINK AND WRITE ABOUT

1 List several things that parents of an only child can do:
   a. To insure adequate socialization.
   b. To provide opportunities for play with other children.
   c. To prevent the child from becoming overindulged.

2 What type of arrangement is best for each group of very young children when mothers work outside the home?
   a. For children under three years of age.
   b. For children three, four, or five years of age.

3 In what way can each of the following assist a child with only one parent?
 a. Men teachers in the elementary schools.
 b. Sharing experiences with friends and teachers who are understanding.
 c. The organization, Parents Without Partners.
 d. A homemaker provided by a community agency.

4 How can the relationships of adoptive parents and their children become as close and warm as those between natural parents and children?

5 What role must be played by parents when a child has a serious illness?

6 What is the best way to help a blind or otherwise handicapped child develop properly?

7 What are some typical symptoms which may lead parents to suspect that their child is mentally retarded?

8 What constructive steps should be taken by the parents of a retarded child?

REFERENCES

PAMPHLETS AND PAPERBACKS

Bloch, Judith
"A Preschool Workshop for Emotionally Disturbed Children"
Children, Vol. 17, No. 1, January–February, 1970

Caddan, Vivian
"Crisis in the Family"
In Coplan, Gerald, *Principles of Preventive Psychiatry*
New York: Basic Books, Inc., 1964

Galaway, Burt
"Clarifying the Role of Foster Parents"
Children, May–June, 1970

Galen, Harlen
"A Matter of Life and Death"
Young Children, Vol. 27, No. 6, August, 1972

Grey, Catherine
"Four Children"
Children Today, July–August, 1972

Meyer, Margaret
"Family Ties and the Institutional Child"
Children, November–December, 1969

Millar, T. P.
"The Hospital and the Preschool Child"
Children, Vol. 17, No. 5, September–October, 1970

Morse, Joan
"The Goal of Life Enhancement for a Fatally Ill Child"
Children, Vol. 17, No. 2, March–April, 1970

Ogg, Elizabeth
When a Family Faces Stress
Public Affairs Pamphlet No. 341
New York: Public Affairs Committee, Inc.

Rafael, Berta
"Early Education for Multi-Handicapped Children"
Children Today, January–February, 1973

11

A Look Ahead
to Life's Work

After studying this chapter, you will be able to

1. Accept the importance of the work ethic.
2. Examine your feelings about the type of career you would like to choose.
3. Appraise your suitability for child care work.
4. Analyze the career ladder and lattice in child care programs.
5. Consider whether a career in child care services is the field for you.

You have come to the last chapter in this book on understanding and guiding young children. You have learned many aspects of this field of study. What are you going to do with the understanding and insights you have gained?

Will you use your new competencies as a parent? Will you use your new competencies as a child care worker? The skills you have learned are useful in both areas—personal living and earning a living.

When you were a child the adults around you supported and took care of you. Now the time is coming when you will have to support and take care of yourself and others. To do this you must make a vocational choice.

The field of child care is an area of work which you may wish to consider. In this chapter various aspects of child care work are explored. The purpose is to help you find out about the career possibilities and problems and to help you decide the following two questions:

Are child care services the vocation for me?

Am I the person for child care services?

Preschoolers and Careers

Little children are learning about the world and about the people in it. They learn about families from their own families. They learn about school by going to school. And they learn about work from their parents, from school, and from the experiences which they have.

At home parents talk about the work they do. They also get across the idea that one of the reasons they work is in order to earn money. Money is needed to buy the things children want and need. Money buys food or ice cream, clothes or toys.

The preschool years are the time when children are developing their value systems. This is the time when they learn that work is necessary for earning a living in order to provide life's necessities.

Sometimes children live in families where they do not learn this concept at home. For children such as these, it is particularly important to have opportunities to learn career awareness in school.

At the preschool level career awareness is very simple. Children learn what members of their own family do and what members of the school community do. These are stated in very simple terms, such as "Daddy goes to work. He sells shoes," or "Mommy is a nurse. She helps sick people."

A second concept at the preschool level is that people who work get paid. They use the money to buy the things they need.

A third concept which children must learn early in life is that there are many different ways one can earn a living.

When little children are taken on walks through the neighborhood the teacher should point out the many things people are doing to contribute to the world's work. "This is the grocer who sells food for your dinner." "There is someone repairing the telephone. That person fixes telephones so we can talk to people who call."

A fourth concept is that school is part of the preparation for a career. In school one can learn about the many things that people do to earn a living. In school one can learn the actual skills needed for the career of one's choice. These are ideas which little ones should learn even at the preschool level.

Is it selling school to little children? Yes, it is. It helps them learn at a very early age that school will play an important part in their futures as well as in their present lives.

Why Work for a Living?

There are many reasons why people work. Earning money is a primary one, but it is not the only reward one gains from working.

There is also personal satisfaction in doing something one enjoys. Not only the work itself, but the opportunity to be with other people, all working toward a common goal, is a source of satisfaction. Even griping together about a job problem becomes a shared experience and a basis for friendship.

Supporting oneself through having a job and doing worthwhile work is a source of satisfaction and helps one build a feeling of self-respect. Any healthy person needs some sort of activity to occupy her or his time.

When people are having problems from which they would like to escape, they are often told, "Your work will never let you down." This emphasizes the idea of work being a source of satisfaction and a way to occupy one's time constructively.

Life-Styles and Careers

Nowadays people are able to choose from a variety of life-styles. Some people like to work the hours of nine o'clock to five o'clock and have the evenings free for relaxation or recreation. Others say they would rather sleep late and work on into the evening. Some say they would prefer to work a very long day four days a week and have three free days instead of two. Then they can pursue other interests.

Some people want to work indoors; some outdoors. Some say they want to earn a lot of money. Others prefer a simpler life. Some people want to travel a lot. Others are homebodies who want to be with their families or take care of their gardens.

When you choose a career, you are also choosing a life-style. If you choose to be a traveling salesman, you are committing yourself to being away from home much of the time. If you choose to be a ski instructor, you are choosing an outdoor, physical life, in a cold climate.

Many people choose a career and after a few years find they must change to something else. However, in many careers there is a great deal of study and preparation involved. Therefore, it is wise to do as much thinking as possible ahead of time. It is wise to become acquainted with as many career choices as possible early in life. Talking to people, seeing them at work, reading about careers, taking a variety of courses in school—all are ways which will help you choose a career.

Working With Children

In selecting a field in which to work, there are many factors to consider. Does one want to work with people or alone; indoors or outdoors; at a desk or doing physical things? Does one want an immediate job? Is the person willing to study for a few years or for many years in order to prepare for a career?

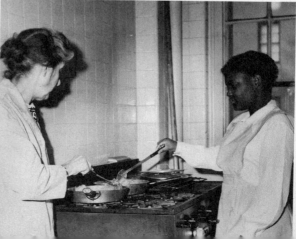

Within the field of child care there are many different opportunities and jobs.

Within the field of child care there are many opportunities and many different jobs. This is a field where one can start at an entry level immediately after high school. By combining experience and more education, it is possible to climb the career ladder.

This is a career ladder in which there really is no top either in education needed or in money earned. The person who opens his or her own nursery school has no limit to the amount of money that can be earned, depending on the success of the school. The person who likes to study can go on to become a professor of child development or early childhood education. It is even possible to become a member of the Cabinet of the President of the United States with a job as Secretary of Health, Education, and Welfare. The field of child development presents a complete ladder—starting with entry level jobs and continuing to climb with no top limit. Later in this chapter the career ladder and lattice in this field will be described.

The career possibilities are open to both men and women, with room at the top for both. Reaching the top depends a great deal on how much you are willing to study and how hard you are willing to work.

Someone interested in children and ice skating might enjoy teaching children to skate as an occupation.

What Employees Need

There are certain skills that are needed by all people who want to get and keep a job. The ability *to get along with other people,* including one's boss, is necessary to getting and keeping a job. One must be able to work toward the achievement of common goals. This is necessary in any type of work. If one is working with little children, it is especially important to like children and to enjoy them.

In almost any kind of work, *good health* is a big asset. A person who feels well is better able to do the work that the job requires. Excessive absence makes it impossible to hold almost any job. If one is working with little children, it is very important to be in good health. One will then have the strength and patience required for the job. Good health is necessary also in order not to spread disease.

Personal appearance and good grooming count. A clean body, clean hair, and clean clothing are required in most jobs. They are absolutely essential for anyone who is working with little children. Children learn from the adults around them. Cleanliness and good health habits are among the things they must learn.

Attitudes toward work are very important. They always show. A person who is interested in doing a job well and who is willing to accept direction and correction is more likely to be the one who gets and keeps the job. When you are working with little children, your attitudes are catching. If you are cheerful and cooperative, the little ones will learn the same spirit from you.

Dependability is necessary in any job. You are counted on to be at work and to get there on time. If your attendance is irregular, or if you come late frequently, the work cannot get done. In the case of child care, there are parents who depend on you to take care of their children so that they can go to their own jobs, where other people are counting on them. You are in a very important post when you are working with children. Many people depend on you.

Character traits such as honesty, loyalty, and high ethical standards are necessary to keeping any sort of job. If you are working with little children, you must be the kind of person whom they can trust. You must be the kind of person who remembers promises and keeps them. You must know right from wrong and act accordingly.

Patience is a virtue. This is an old proverb which applies to almost any kind of work. In child care it is more than a virtue; it is a necessity. Little children need understanding, love, kindness, and, above all, patience.

This sounds like a long list of desirable qualities to expect from one person. Perhaps it can be considered a standard of perfection. No human being is perfect. We all falter at times. But standards are necessary, so that we know what it is that we are trying to achieve. If the standard seems absolutely impossible for you, then you should consider work in a different field. Of all the traits listed, liking children is most important. If you don't like children, don't go into this field of work.

The Need for Child Care

At one time most people felt that a mother had to be at home with her children. Now most people are used to the idea of mothers working outside the home. Nearly one half of all mothers with children under six years old are working at any given time. This number is growing steadily.

There are many reasons for this change. A growing number of women enjoy their work outside the home. They do not want to give it up when they become mothers. Many families need the money earned by both the father and mother to support the family. Some mothers must support their families by themselves. Sometimes this may be because the fathers are ill or have died. Sometimes the parents are divorced. Divorce rates have increased. There are also more unmarried mothers than there used to be.

Working mothers need care for their young children during the parents' working hours. Most mothers of young children who work do so because they need the money. These mothers need help with child care. This is happening all over the nation. It has resulted in great pressure on the government to provide child care services. This is the *economic reason* that child care has become a public issue.

A *political reason* for more child care services deals with welfare reform. More people than ever before are receiving welfare. This is very expensive. Taxpayers are concerned about the cost. They feel that something should be done to cut down on these costs. They feel that just giving people money keeps them in poverty. A better way would be to help them earn money and support themselves.

Welfare costs are steadily rising. Politicians of all types are looking for better ways to help the poor. Almost every plan they suggest includes some kind of child care. If parents on welfare are to receive job training and hold jobs, their children need care during the hours that their parents are training and working.

Some people have jobs which do not pay much money. They must also have child care arrangements which do not cost more money than they can afford to pay. As it stands now, the price of child care for two children may cost more than the total take-home pay for a working mother. So government help is needed to pay part of this cost.

There is also a *social reason* for child care becoming a public issue. There is increased demand for child care and early childhood education by minority groups, and by people who feel that they cannot give their children all the opportunities that some other parents can give their children. These parents want day care for their children.

Many people feel that early childhood education and care may be an important way to break the poverty cycle. They feel that a really good child care center can make up for opportunities which children may be missing at home.

A really good child care center must meet many different needs. This includes care by doctors, dentists, and nurses when needed. It provides good nutritious food to help children grow and be healthy. It helps children also with their social and emotional development. Many people are working for the continued growth of child care centers that meet these different needs. These people are now a very strong and growing force. Politicians know this.

For many children, *growth opportunities* are greater in an organized setting. Recent research in child development points to the importance of helping mental growth and learning during a child's early years. It has been found that a child's intelligence is developed during the earliest years of life. The more growth opportunities the child has during these preschool years, the greater will be the child's chance for full mental development.

A good child care center can make up for opportunities children
may be missing at home.

The give and take of a day care center provides interaction with
other children. Learning to get along with other children helps the
social development of the child. This is just as important as intellec-
tual or mental development.

Some families may be able to provide enough opportunities
for social and mental growth for children to reach their fullest de-
velopment. Many other families find their children develop better
in an organized setting where there are facilities, equipment,
supplies, trained workers, and, above all, other children of the
same age.

These are four of the reasons for the growth of the need for
child care centers: working mothers, welfare reform, equal oppor-
tunity for all, and learning opportunities.

Types of Child Care Facilities

With the growth in the number of child care centers comes the growth of job opportunities for those with training.

At one time this care was referred to as day care. However, these are becoming the wrong words to use. Women do not always work during school hours. Many women work during odd hours, or evening or night hours. Their need may be for night care. Therefore, there is now a trend for child care centers to be open on an around-the-clock basis.

Family day-care homes regularly care for children other than those who live there. Usually, these are homes where the mother is caring for her own children and decides to care for a few others for a fee. Or, perhaps a retired couple decide to open their home to a few children of working mothers for a fee. They can accommodate any age children, including infants, toddlers, and preschoolers. The quality of care or education or concern varies with the person who is doing the care. It is usually low cost and conveniently located for working parents. This type of care provides socialization for the children. But some kind of supervision really is needed to be sure that the homemaker does indeed stay home and provide some sort of educational program other than television. Also, what would happen if there were an emergency, and the homemaker needed some sort of assistance?

The *family day-care system* was started to fill this need for supervision and some kind of help in emergencies. This is a community-wide system. Member families become part of a helping network. Some families join as providers of day-care homes; others join who need care for their children. Standards are set by the group. An adult training program is part of the setup. Paid educational aides are employed to relieve the home-center homemaker who is otherwise tied down without relief from the moment the first child is delivered in the morning to the moment the last one is called for at night. This system provides medical care, nutritional advice, and around-the-clock availability in case of emergency.

A newly developed idea is that of mixed home care with day-care systems. The basic idea is to attach home care centers as satellites to a child care center. In this way, children, parents, and caretakers have the advantages of both kinds of systems with child care available fifty-two weeks of the year in a flexible time arrangement.

A fourth type of home-based program is the home visiting program. Here children and parents remain in their own homes. A visiting education aide helps parents with child development problems. This is an attempt to help parents to grow together, to learn better, to improve themselves. Some welfare programs operate this way with periodic visits from the social worker.

In addition to home-based educational programs for preschool children, there are educational programs in child care centers. These are growing rapidly throughout the United States. There are four main preschool curricular models. These are the child-development approach, the verbal-cognitive approach, the sensory-cognitive model, and the verbal-didactic model. All the day care programs are dedicated to helping both parents and children, but the approaches differ.

The *child-development approach* stresses a natural program with plenty of freedom and play and time to develop naturally in the sequence which nature provides.

The *verbal-cognitive approach* places great stress on educational development and reading readiness. Words are taught and there are many charts showing sizes, colors, numbers, and words.

The verbal-cognitive approach places great stress on educational development and reading readiness. Words are taught and there are many charts showing sizes, colors, numbers, and words, as in this Arab school.

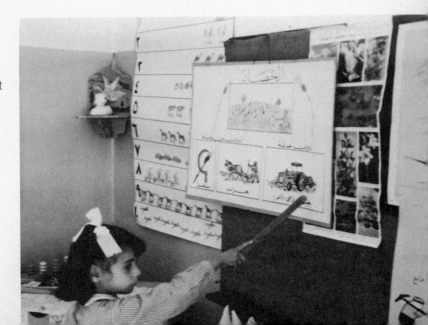

The sensory-cognitive model, often known as the Montessori method, allows children to learn through exposure to many kinds of materials and experiences.

The *sensory-cognitive model,* popularly known as the Montessori method, allows children to learn through exposure to many kinds of materials and experiences. Playthings are also tools of learning, such as laces to tie, buttons to fasten, and animals to feed.

The *verbal-didactic method* stresses hard-core teaching and drill. Children are taught to repeat words, sounds, numbers. They are taught to answer questions such as they might later be asked in a traditional school. They are also taught the type of discipline and control which would prepare them for a traditional school.

If you have the opportunity to serve as a student aide, it will be your responsibility to follow whichever method is used in the child care center to which you are assigned. You should understand what is happening, but you would not be in a position to change the system at this time. However, you should discuss your experiences both with the field site teacher and your own teacher when you get back to your own school.

The verbal-didactic method stresses hard-core teaching and drill. Children are taught the type of discipline and control that would prepare them for a traditional school.

A Special Life-Style

In Israel there are some people, about three percent of the total population, who live in a special type of community called a kibbutz. (The plural of kibbutz is kibbutzim.) This is a special life-style.

On the kibbutz there is a special children's house. The children live here with others of their age group. They are cared for by a special house mother called a metapelet (me ta pel' et). As the children grow older they move to a house for older children. Here also they are cared for by another metapelet.

The children visit their own parents daily for playing, loving, and spending time together. However, their needs are taken care of in the children's house. This is comprehensive child care in the fullest sense. It is also an example of a different life-style which has proven successful over a period of two generations.

On the kibbutz, all men and women work a full eight-hour day. After work, generally during the hours of 4–7, the children visit their own parents in individual apartments. At this time they receive their parents' undivided attention.

After family visiting hours on the kibbutz, parents take their children back to the children's house to put them to bed.

During these hours, parents are not under pressure to prepare meals or wash dishes or do other household chores because these are all taken care of centrally. After the family visiting hours, the parents take their children back to the children's home and put them to sleep, and then go on to the big dining room for their own evening meal.

In the children's house a few children of the same age share a room and grow up in a very close emotional relationship. From infancy until they join the army, they live, play and study together. Thus, they have close emotional ties with both their families and their age mates.

Job Opportunities in Child Care

Ladders and lattices. There are many opportunities in the child care career ladder. They vary with the amount of education the worker has. The greater the education, the more responsible the job, and the larger the salary.

By taking a child development or child care course in high school, you may qualify for a job as a child development aide in a nursery school or child care center.

With a child development or child care course in high school it is possible to get a job as a child development aide in a nursery school or child care center. An aide works with children under the direct supervision of a professional person. On-the-job experience and continuing education lead to the next rung of the career ladder.

With about two years' experience, high school, and a year or two of community college training, a young man or woman can get a job as child day care assistant, child day care worker, child care leader or nursery school teacher. At this level, the worker leads activities of children under the supervision of a child development supervisor or as a teacher if in a smaller center.

A family day care mother is licensed to care for up to five children in her own home. This includes her own children. With an assistant, she may be licensed to care for ten to twelve children. This type of work usually requires a high school diploma and some study and training beyond high school.

Progressing up the career ladder is the teacher of child development, kindergarten, or early childhood education. This generally requires a bachelor's degree, state certification, and some experience. With additional experience the teacher may become a child development director or nursery school director. The teacher's job requires working with children. The child development director plans work schedules and supervises teachers, child development assistants, and aides.

Near the top of the child development career ladder come the assistant director and finally the director of a child development center. This job carries responsibility for the business and personnel of the center. It includes planning and directing the educational program. A master's degree is usually required in addition to the bachelor's degree, plus experience and certification. Other professional jobs working with children are that of child psychologist, social worker, or director of a children's program.

Obviously, as one progresses up the career ladder, the amount of necessary education increases, and so does the amount of responsibility and pay. The education and the jobs are open to both men and women.

In addition to these jobs which climb the career ladder, there are possibilities for switching to slightly different jobs at the same level of responsibility and pay, but with different work emphasis.

These include such diverse possibilities as department store selling in children's clothing or toys, catering children's parties, or making children's clothing or toys. Work is available in children's summer camps, the pediatric ward of a hospital, or in home or schools for handicapped children. Recreational centers, such as parks and clubs, frequently have jobs for someone who can organize programs for children. There are also job opportunities in private homes or in institutions to take care of well or sick children.

Field Site Experience

Learning to work with children is best done through actual work with children. Book learning is not enough.

There are many ways of gaining this actual experience. Babysitting helps. Perhaps you will work with Cub Scouts or Brownies. Perhaps you will teach a Sunday school class. Best of all ways is to take a course in your school where you can have supervised work experience in a local day care center. Some high schools and colleges have a nursery school or child care center right within the

Learning how to work with children is best done through actual work with children.

building. Other schools and colleges make arrangements for you to work under your teacher's supervision in a nearby child care center. Your teacher will visit you at the field site and will later discuss your experiences with you when you come to class.

In order to make the most of this learning experience, it is necessary for the high school student to establish good rapport with the field site teacher.

Also, the field site teacher should have good communication with the high school or college classroom teacher. Thus, all together can form a team to provide the greatest learning experiences for the trainee.

Every child care center has a unique character of its own. This is based in part on the personalities of the people working in it, on the personalities of the children attending, on the facilities and equipment available, and on the wishes of the parents whose children are attending the school.

However, there are also certain factors which all day care centers or nursery schools have in common. These common factors require definite skills on the part of the workers and aides.

Throughout the country there are many junior and senior high schools, junior colleges, and other agencies where Occupational Education courses are taught. These include Child Care Services. In some schools these courses are in the Home Economic Department, while in other schools these courses are listed as Health Careers. These courses have two parts, classroom instruction and supervised work experience in a nearby child care center. The supervised work experience is a very valuable part of the training.

This training is important because it prepares students for either of two roles with young children, the role of parent or the role of paid worker. Understanding and guiding young children is a basic component of either role.

On the first day of your field site experience, which is also called work-study experience, you will be in entirely new surroundings. This may be the first time you are in a preschool setting since the time of your own preschool days. Or perhaps you never had preschool experiences and now will have your very first exposure to this type of classroom.

Look around you. There is much to see. The room is divided into several distinct areas. Try to identify each of them. Probably your teacher will have given you an observation form to help you observe the different parts of the room and their uses.

You will observe several centers for group and individual activities. Each has its own appropriate equipment and furniture.

As you enter you will see a line-up of individual "cubbies," or open lockers. Here is where the little children hang their coats and place their hats and overshoes.

As you look around the room you will see areas for block building, housekeeping and dramatic play, creative art, science, and a book corner. You will see equipment, such as puzzles, for quiet play and large toys, such as bicycles and jungle gym, for active play.

You will see movable tables and little chairs. These can be used for play activities and also for eating lunch. You will see stacks of light-weight cots for use during the rest period. You will probably see that the classroom has its own lavatory for toileting and washing up.

On the walls you will see many bulletin boards, posters, and other learning materials. You will see exhibits to help children learn such things as colors and numbers and days of the week or months of the year.

It is almost as exciting for you as it is for the little ones to make discoveries about this classroom.

As you participate in the supervised work experience, you will be required to fill out certain forms. Included are observation sheets and lesson plans. On the pages which follow are sample sheets which are now being used in several high schools. You and your teacher may wish to use these as they are or as a basis for developing other forms which may be more appropriate for your own use. Even the schools where they are now being used find it necessary to change these forms from time to time in order to meet changing conditions.

A child care center is an interesting place.

Observations

Report on the following topics on your notebook paper from your experience at centers.

Observation #1.
  Physical Setup

  a. Size—number of floors, rooms
     Size—classroom you are observing

  b. Furniture
     Lavatory facilities
     Clothing lockers
     Cots

Observation #2.
  Safety of Children
     Interview the classroom teacher at an appropriate time.
     a. Safety on trips and outdoor play.

     b. Safety rules explained to children?

     c. Areas for special activities designated?

     d. Special instructions for safety drills—How can student assist?

     e. Appropriate toys and equipment?

Observation #3.
   1. Observe a child in the classroom:
   a. Describe the child's appearance

   b. Describe what you observed about the child's physical development. (How active was she or he? What did the child do which showed you something about his or her motor coordination, large muscle coordination, and small muscle coordination?)

   2. Describe what you observed about social development.
   a. Did you observe the child learning something? Describe it.

   b. Give some examples of his or her speech.

   c. What did the child's interests seem to be?

   d. What else did you notice about this child?

Student's Name _____
Date _____
Group Observed _____ Teacher _____
Center _____

Diary of Activities

Keep a record of every visit at Child Care Center. The records will be collected and later returned to you.

Activities of children	I did the following today
Menu	Comments: Children's behavior, speech, reactions

Lesson Plan — Activity Experience

Type of Activity —

Lesson —

Purpose of lesson — What will children learn from activity?

Procedure
1. Equipment needed —   Supplies in classroom

2. How will you introduce activity to children?

3. Safety and hygiene reminders

4. Description of activity
   a. What will you do?
   b. What will children do?

5. Plans for cleanup

6. Evaluation — Children's reactions

Special Skills Needed for Working With Young Children

1. The most basic job skill required is protecting the physical health and safety of children. People who work with children must be scrupulously clean, and in good health, so that they do not carry diseases to the children in their care. The area occupied by the children must be kept immaculate. Eating areas, play areas, sleeping areas — all must be kept clean.

Appropriate clothing is also necessary to protect the health of children. This includes pants which cover the knees in case of falls. Clothing should protect against the elements, such as cold, rain, or snow.

A daily routine health examination is necessary when children arrive. Children who are obviously sick should be sent home with their parents. Sometimes illness develops during the day and it is impossible to contact the parents. In this case an isolation room provides the opportunity for the child to lie down and rest and not infect the other children.

In any child care facility provision must be made for sufficient sleep and rest and for an adequate diet. Usually the nursery school or child care facility sends home its menus for the week. This guides the family in preparing meals which avoid repetition and provide variety and complete nutritional balance. Many centers use disposable paper or plastic goods for serving food. If real china and flatware are used they must be washed thoroughly in water of at least 190 degrees to prevent the growth of germs.

Physical care and the aide. The aide in a child care center contributes to the physical health of the children in many ways. One way is to supervise the use of play equipment to be sure of safe practices. For example, when children are using the swings, other children should not be permitted to run in front of, or in back of, the moving swing.

The use of the sandbox must be supervised. Children must be taught not to throw sand in each others eyes, or on the floor surrounding the sandbox, and not to urinate in the sandbox.

The child care aide may have a role in preparing and serving food. This is another occasion demanding scrupulous cleanliness. It provides the opportunity to help children develop good eating habits and to broaden their food tastes. Good nutrition is founded on a well-mixed diet. Nutrients, vitamins, and minerals not found in some foods are found in others. A well-mixed diet, drawn from the four basic food groups, helps to ensure good nutrition.

An aide or assistant in a child care facility has the responsibility for recognizing and reporting early signs of illness to the director. When a normally pleasant, happy child is cranky, there is usually a reason. It may mean there is trouble at home, or it may be an early sign of illness. A flushed face, coughing and sneezing, rash, loss of appetite, or running eyes are signs of illness which cannot be ignored.

Safety practices are always a big concern when working with children or in any job. One must be constantly vigilant to prevent hazards affecting the safety of children. A cluttered work and play area, toys with sharp or broken edges, slippery or unclean floors are common hazards. Unprotected windows, or windows open at the bottom should be avoided. Unsafe toys such as BB guns, firecrackers, plastic bags, ropes, and cords do not belong among the playthings of young children. Medicines or household cleaning agents should never be kept within the reach of young children.

Safety is promoted by reducing hazards in children's work and play situations.

Fire protection and civil defense drills are a necessary precaution in any situation involving groups of children. They must be taught to obey signals, remain calm, and to line up for safe exit in case of emergency. It is the responsibility of all who work with young children to know how to operate the fire extinguishers and how to call in a fire alarm. However, it is more important to remove the children to safety than to try to extinguish the fire. In case of an actual fire, the adults working with the children must act very calmly. This helps the children to feel calm and prevents panic. It is a good idea to role-play the nursery school during a pretend fire so that children can become familiar with coping in case of an actual emergency situation.

A child care aide is not expected to be a doctor, and would certainly call a doctor in case of real trouble. However, there are little emergency situations with which one must deal on a daily basis. These include taking care of minor cuts and bruises, nosebleeds, burns, and foreign bodies in a child's eye. In a real emergency a doctor must be called.

A child care worker must be prepared to give physical care in many situations. These include providing and maintaining a safe environment, recognizing illness and assisting in emergency situations, helping children develop good habits of eating, cleanliness, and other health habits, and setting a good personal example by practicing good health habits.

2. Getting along with little children is a basic requirement for working with them. An adult who doesn't like and enjoy little children should find some other area of employment. Little children know whether the people around them like and enjoy them. It can be taxing and trying to one's patience to be with little children all day. So unless one can really enjoy the work, it is better for everyone concerned not to go into this career. A person who can show warmth and understanding in relationship with children is likely to be successful with them. A crying child needs help and comfort and a little loving attention. Some need more of the teacher's attention, while others prefer to be independent for most

Being able to get along with little children is a basic requirement for working with them.

of the time. Some like to play with others, while some like to play alone. Individual differences show up at an early age, and must be respected.

Children are helped to feel secure when discipline is consistent. They then know the rules and know what is expected of them. An adult who allows misbehavior one day and is angered by it another day confuses the child. The rules should be simple and clear and consistently enforced. This is done quietly and kindly, by saying, "This is the way we do it here." Rules are stated positively, "We put the blocks away after we use them," or, "We always taste a little of each food," or, "We wash our hands after we play with clay."

It is a thrilling experience to work with children and to notice their growth and development from month to month. Physically, socially, emotionally, and intellectually they show a great deal of growth during the preschool years.

Children differ. Each is an individual. Some are quick and some are slow. Some are active and some prefer quiet activities. Some are strong and healthy and some are frail. Some are quick to accept new situations and others are fearful. Some are friendly, while others are shy.

Children come from different religious, ethnic, and economic backgrounds. They have different family customs and traditions. But each child is an important individual. As you work with children, you must remember that each one needs your love, affection, and approval.

Children grow best when they are allowed to grow at their own pace. Each child performs a little differently from each other. It is not fair to children to compare one with another. One may be better at running and climbing. Another may be better at talking or singing or painting. Each child is himself or herself and can never be anyone else. The earlier children, and adults too, can learn to accept themselves as they are, the happier they can be.

Children thrive on warmth and approval. It is necessary to help a child feel accepted whether he or she succeeds or fails. It really doesn't matter whether the tower of blocks stands or topples over. But it does matter to the child to know that you appreciate his or her efforts at building with blocks. Each child must have a feeling of adequacy and accomplishment.

Each child is an important individual. As you work with children, you must remember that each one needs your love, affection, and approval.

A pleasant nod, an approving remark, a pat on the shoulder, a smile of encouragement help the child feel your acceptance.

Listen carefully when the child speaks to you. Answer questions, even though they seem unimportant to you. Treat the child with the same courtesy that you would treat a valued friend.

When a new child arrives, greet that child with extra friendliness. Be sure to use his or her name several times, so the child knows that you know who he or she is.

Help the new child remove outer clothing, and show where they are to be kept. The child's "cubby" will have some distinctive sign that can be recognized. Perhaps it will be a flower, or toy, as well as the child's name.

Show the parts of the room to the new child so that she or he can become familiar with them. Hold the child's hand while walking around the room. When feeling secure, the child will withdraw her or his hand from yours.

It is to be expected that children will be timid in a new situation. You can help them to feel secure by showing affection and friendly interest. It is helpful to introduce a new child to one other child who may serve as a buddy on the first day.

3. Helping young children to play is a job responsibility of those who work with them. Play is the work of children. It has many values. Play aids in physical growth through the development of motor skills and coordination. It helps children get along with others, including helping them learn to share and cooperate. It helps children learn how to solve problems, such as putting puzzles together or making things go. It helps children express themselves through talking, singing, music, and art. It serves as an outlet for excess energy. Successful play experience helps children develop self-confidence.

Within the child care center, equipment is usually arranged according to activities. There are usually separate areas for block building, housekeeping and dramatic play, art, science, reading, and music. Usually there are separate areas for quiet play and for active play.

As part of the play activity, children must be taught to put away equipment when they have finished using it. This is necessary for safety and as good housekeeping practice. It also trains children in habits of neatness.

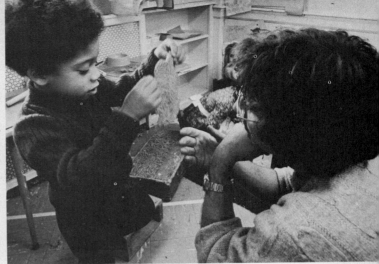

Helping young children play is a job responsibility of those who work with them.

4. Communicating with parents and other adults is one of the skills required of a child care worker. By keeping an open relationship with the adults who care for the child, you help to create a child care team. This is good for the child.

Always greet the parents or other visitors in a warm and friendly manner. Friendliness is contagious. It will help the parents feel good about the center, and also will teach children how to be friendly and polite to visitors.

Parents may have doubts or guilt feelings about leaving the child at the center when they go to work. As a child care worker, you must show sensitivity to the way parents feel and help them to feel that their child is in a safe and desirable place.

If parents tell you confidential things about their child or family, you must respect their confidences. They are told to you in order to help you understand the child. Confidential information must not be treated as gossip.

Business Activities

If you are working in child care services, your basic responsibility is to the children. However, there are also certain skills which are necessary in any type of business activity.

Answering the telephone is a task common to any work. The telephone is the first contact a person has with the child care center. Making a good impression is important.

The telephone should be answered promptly and courteously. Identify the center and yourself. A typical greeting is "Good morning, Sunny Day Center. Elsie speaking." On a pad of paper beside the telephone, write down the name of the caller, the time, and the message. If it is necessary to refer the caller to another person for further assistance, this should be done courteously. A typical expression might be "Please hold the phone while I call Miss Smith. Thank you." As in all contacts with other people, "please" and "thank you" are key words.

If someone leaves a message, write it down on your pad. Check the spelling of names with the caller. You are not expected to know how to spell all names the first time you hear them. However, you are expected to get the message straight. This means asking.

Handling money may be one of your tasks. Any money which you receive or pay out must be carefully recorded. You are handling other people's money, and are held accountable.

Sometimes as parents drop off their children, they may also wish to pay their weekly or monthly bill. Although they may be in a hurry to get to work, you must take the time to make a neat record in the proper book and also to give them a neatly written receipt.

Most places insist on payment by check or money order, so that there is less possibility that money may be missing. However, whether you are handling checks or cash, you must be very careful to keep an accurate record.

Keeping records is a part of any business. These records are of many types. They include records about the children, their attendance, supply inventories, food costs, where to reach parents in case of emergency, information about employees, and many other types of necessary information. No office can operate without records.

These records are kept in files, which are alphabetically arranged by topic. Each topic has its own file, or its own drawer, and within the drawer file records are arranged alphabetically.

In a large center the office staff is responsible for all the record keeping. But in a small setup, you may find this is one of the tasks which is assigned to you. It must be done with care and accuracy.

In a child care center, as in many other types of work, you are part of a team. Everyone works together to create a good environment for the children. As in any team effort, it is your responsibility to put the welfare of the group ahead of your own interests of the moment.

Members of the team include not only the teachers and supervisors, but also many other people. A maintenance crew, porters, cooks, clerks, social workers, nurses, visiting doctor or dentist, parents, aides — all are working together to have a smooth operation.

At one time or another you may find yourself assigned to various different tasks. This gives you the opportunity to learn more than one job and will be very helpful to you in several ways. It makes you more employable, since you are eligible for more than one type of job. Also, it helps you explore exactly which kinds of jobs you like and do not like to do.

When you are working as part of a team you must be willing to accept common goals, and to work cooperatively with others. Problems frequently arise and it is necessary to try to understand the points of view of others. If you have problems which you cannot handle yourself, you should discuss them with your supervisor.

Working Conditions

It has been constantly repeated that a warm attitude toward children is important. However, no matter how much one likes children it is impossible to maintain one's warmth, friendliness, and patience without fairly good working conditions.

Caring for young children requires energy and effort. It is an emotional as well as a physical strain. There is a limit to the number of young children with whom an adult can work.

The lower the child-staff ratio, the easier it is to work well with the children. Including teachers, assistants, aides, and volunteers, an ideal ratio might be one adult for each five children. State licensing laws rarely allow more than ten children for each adult.

In selecting a place to work, one must consider whether the working conditions seem to be reasonable.

Finding a Job in Child Care

Developing the skills needed to hold a job is only part of the task before you. Finding a job also takes time and skill.

There are various ways of locating a job. You may hear about an opening through your school employment counselor or by going to an agency or from a friend who is already employed. You may find out about the job opening through newspaper want ads. You yourself may place a newspaper ad under the positions wanted column. It is helpful to use the yellow pages of the telephone book to find organizations which may have the kind of opening you are looking for. There are special techniques for getting a job after you know about the vacancy. You must be able to write a letter of application. You may be able to prepare your first letter in school with the help of your teacher. You will also need a résumé. This is a summary of your experience, education, and interests. When you are young and have not yet done very much in the world, every little bit counts. A sample letter of application and a sample résumé follow.

The Interview

After you have located an opening, you may be invited to come for a job interview. You must be ready to go out immediately when a job call comes.

Your appearance and grooming are important when you are looking for a job. Whether you are a boy or a girl, you must be freshly bathed or showered so that you have no body odor. Your teeth should be brushed and clean. In order to be sure your breath smells fresh, do not eat highly seasoned foods before an interview. Be sure you are wearing clean underwear as well as clean outer wear. Your hair also must be clean and well brushed.

Looking for a job is an adult thing to do, so dress like an adult. A girl should wear a clean blouse and skirt. A boy should wear a clean shirt and slacks. You may wear blue jeans to school, but many employers would hesitate to hire someone who comes to an interview dressed so informally. If there are several applicants for one position, the decision may be made on the basis of conservative dressing.

20 Midway Road
Streamline, New York 00025
January 17, 1976

Ms. Annette Jones
Streamline Center
17 Western Boulevard
Streamline, New York 00038

Dear Ms. Jones:

In response to your advertisement in today's Evening
Herald, I am applying for the position of Child Care Assistant.
My resume is enclosed. I have letters of recommendation from
my previous employers.

I shall be graduated from Vasco de Gama High School at
the end of this month and will be seeking immediate employment.

I am available for an interview any afternoon at your
convenience.

Sincerely yours,

Elsie Smith

Telephone: 000-1234

Résumé

Elsie Smith
20 Midway Road
Streamline, N.Y. 00025

Telephone: 000-1234
Social Security #000-00-1234
Height 5'6" Weight 110 lbs.
Date of Birth: January 17, 1958,
Philadelphia, Pa.

EDUCATION
Vasco de Gama High School, graduated January 1976.

Home Economics Occupational Education:

Majored in Child Care Services and received a certificate
of competency. I expect to work during the day and attend
Streamline College in the evening and on Saturday.

EXPERIENCE

1975-76: part-time child care aide at Sunny Day Center

Summer, 1975: children's counselor at Little Camp in the Woods,
                Little Forest, N.Y.

1973-75: Girl Scout Leader

Summer, 1974: tray girl at Kingstream Medical Center

1972-1976: Baby sitter for several families in my neighborhood.

SPECIAL SKILLS

Play the flute and guitar

Write simple rhymes, which fit popular tunes

Sing folk songs

Ski, ice skate, swim, and excel at all sports

FAMILY BACKGROUND

I am the youngest of five children. Both my parents work for
Con Edison.

Be sure to eat a good breakfast or lunch before your interview, so you will have the energy to make a good impression.

When you go for a job interview, take with you your social security card, diploma, and letters of recommendation.

Be sure to arrive for your interview a few minutes ahead of time. This will give you a chance to catch your breath, straighten your hair, and relax for a bit before going into the employer's office.

Both smoking and chewing gum make a poor impression. They are unsuitable activities during an interview.

At the start of the interview men usually shake hands. Women usually do not. However, if a woman does extend her hand, be sure to do likewise, whether you are a man or woman.

If you think you will feel nervous at your first interview, practice talking to yourself out loud looking into the mirror. It helps you get used to the sound of your own voice.

If you are interviewed for several jobs, you will find that each time is easier because of the experience you have gained.

Locating a job, applying for it, and being interviewed are all steps along the way to your goal. Getting the job is also only a step. Keeping the job and advancing up the career ladder is the real goal.

In the field of child care services there are many opportunities for advancement. The steps up the career ladder are for those who work hard and continue to study. Although you may start as a high school graduate, consider going to college either full time or part time, so that you may become a professional person in the field of early childhood education.

ACTIVITIES

TO DO AND DISCUSS

1 Visit a local nursery school or day care center. List how many different kinds of workers you can find. Make two lists:

              Job title   Kind of work performed

1.
2.
3.
4.
5.

2 Make a class list on the chalkboard combining all the job titles gathered in problem one above. Compare the type of preparation and education needed for each job title.

3 Observe children at play in a day care center. List ten types of play which you observe. Next to each, write the type of growth experience this play activity provides for a child. For example, bicycle riding helps to develop large muscles.

4 List twenty personality traits which you consider desirable for a person who is working with young children. Rate yourself in regard to each of these characteristics. Use a form similar to the one which follows:

Desirable Trait   Self-rating

                                   Excellent   good   fair   poor

1.
2.
3.

5 Visit a child care center. Try to write a running account of the instructions or directions given by preschool teachers to young children. When you come back to your own class, analyze and discuss the type of language used and the clarity of the instructions.

TO THINK AND WRITE ABOUT

1 Think back to the time when you were of preschool age. Can you remember any mistaken ideas you had about situations or people? Write about one and tell, if you can remember, how you learned the correct idea.

2 Make a floor plan that you would consider an ideal classroom for a group of three-year-olds. Try to fit it into an area of 20 feet by 30 feet.

3 In your local preschool center, observe two children at play. Write down their conversation. How does it differ from a conversation you might have with a friend of yours.

4 Think back to your own childhood and try to remember how your development was influenced at a crucial moment by the guidance of an adult.

Typical Situations

Circle the number of the best solution.

1. Alice is graduating this June and will look for a job. Her best chance to find a job would be through
    a. her school principal
    b. the school guidance counselor
    c. the State Employment Service
    d. her friend who has a job

2. John will have his first job interview. The best outfit for him to wear would be
    a. blue jeans, a sweatshirt, and sneakers
    b. red slacks, a flowered shirt, blue vest
    c. blue fringed suede jacket, blue jeans
    d. blue jacket, blue shirt, red necktie, blue slacks

3. Patricia has heard there is an increase in the number of jobs available for child care workers. The reason for the increase is due to
    a. a decrease in the demand for skilled workers
    b. an increase in the number of women in the labor force
    c. an increase in the birthrate
    d. shortage of toys in private homes

4. Of the following applicants the one who would have the best chance of getting a job as a child care aide is
    a. Barbara who has had baby-sitting experience
    b. Angela who has taken a child care course in high school
    c. Estelle who is the oldest of seven children
    d. Ruth who dropped out of high school to get a job

5. When Mrs. Norton, director of a day care center, wants to hire a teacher aide, she will try to find someone who
    a. likes to work with little children
    b. is interested in working outdoors
    c. is unemployed and needs a job
    d. is neat and well groomed

6. Some experts recommend that all children should have pre-school experience mainly because it provides
    a. clean surroundings
    b. nourishing food
    c. experiences with other children
    d. attractive toys

7. When Richard and Ann are assigned to work in a local child care center, their main goal is to
    a. have fun playing with children
    b. display their knowledge of children
    c. talk very frequently with children
    d. gain experience working with children

8. A new child has come to the child care center where Bob works. Bob should
    a. teach him all the rules
    b. help him play with other children
    c. ask him a lot of questions
    d. show him where the games are kept

9. In order for the children at the child care center to eat their lunch most readily, Alice should be sure that
    a. there is a centerpiece on each table
    b. the food is well spiced
    c. mealtime is calm and pleasant
    d. meals are nutritious

10. As Nancy watches her class of three-year-olds, she realizes that
    a. all three-year-olds are alike
    b. all children respond the same way
    c. each child is an individual
    d. all three-year-olds cry a great deal

REFERENCES

Andrews, Margaret E.
The Job You Want
New York: McGraw-Hill, Inc., 1968

A Study of Child Care, 1970–71
55 Wheeler St., Cambridge, Mass.: Abt Associates, April, 1971

Career Education
U. S. Department of Health, Education, and Welfare Publication No. (OE) 72-39
Washington, D. C.: U. S. Government Printing Office (20 cents)

Career Ladders and Lattices in Home Economics and Related Areas: Possibilities for Upgrading Household Employment
2010 Massachusetts Ave. N. W., Washington, D. C.: American Home Economics Association

Exploring Careers in Child Care
Bloomington, Illinois: McKnight Publishing Co., 1973

Hershenson, D. B.
"A Life Stage Vocational Development System"
Journal of Counseling Psychology, Vol. 15. pp. 23–30, 1968

Home Economics Occupational Education: Child Care Services
The State Education Department, Bureau of Secondary Curriculum Development
Albany, N. Y.: The University of the State of New York, 1966

Illinois Teacher for Contemporary Roles
Vol. XV, No. 4, March–April, 1972

Kruger, W. Stanley
Programs in Education for Parenthood
Undated report issued by Director, Interagency Taskforce on Comprehensive
    Programs for School-Age Parents
Room 2181, H. E. W., 400 Maryland Ave., Washington, D. C.: U. S. Office of
    Education

La Crosse, E. Robert
Day Care for America's Children
Public Affairs Pamphlet #470
381 Park Ave. S., New York, N. Y.: Public Affairs Committee, 1971

Lang, Joyce
"Nursery School Lab Part of Career Course Focusing on Child Care Aide as
    Vocation"
Focus on the Family, January, 1973
1802 Moss St., Eugene, Oregon: E. C. Brown Foundation

Lang, Joyce
"Pre-Schoolers Provide Child Development Lab as High Schoolers Study Parent-
    ing Role"
Focus on the Family, May, 1973
1802 Moss St., Eugene, Oregon: E. C. Brown Foundation

Lang, Joyce (Editor)
A Selected Bibliography on Child Development, Preschool Nursery, and Child Day Care
1802 Moss St., Eugene, Oregon: E. C. Brown Foundation (single copy 16¢)

Mayer, Rochelle S.
"A Comparative Analysis of Preschool Curriculum Models"
in Robert H. Anderson and Harold G. Shane, *As the Twig Is Bent: Readings in Early
    Childhood Education*
Boston, Mass. Houghton Mifflin Co., 1971

Procopilo, Mary A.
A Guide for Teacher Aides in Early Childhood Education
Peabody Early Childhood Education Project
Salem, Massachusetts: Salem State College, 1970 (pamphlet)

Resources for Day Care
1401 K Street, N. W., Washington, D. C.: Day Care and Child Development Council
   of America

Rettig, Jack L.
Careers: Exploration and Decision
Englewood Cliffs, N. J.: Prentice-Hall, Inc., 1974

Stapleton, Constance
"Teaching Youngsters to Be Parents"
Reprinted from *PARADE,* March 11, 1973
by H. E. W., Office of Child Development

The National Standard Career Education Model, Kindergarten Through Adult
P. O. Box DX, Irvine, California: Educational Properties, Inc. (chart)

The Public Responsibility
Massachusetts Early Education Project, Child Care in Massachusetts
Washington, D. C.: The Day Care and Child Development Council of America,
   Inc., 1972

Index

INDEX

A Manual of
HOUSE MONSTERS

A Manual of
HOUSE MONSTERS

STANISLAV MARIJANOVIC

To my daughters—S.M.

Published in the United States of America in 1999
by MONDO Publishing

For information contact:
MONDO Publishing, 980 Avenue of the Americas, New York, New York 10018
MONDO is a registered trademark of MONDO Publishing
Visit our web site at http://www.mondopub.com

Text adaptation by Howard Goldsmith
Design by Mina Greenstein
Production by The Kids at Our House
Printed in Italy by Grafiche AZ, Verona
First Mondo Printing, May 1999

99 00 01 02 03 04 05 06   HC   9 8 7 6 5 4 3 2 1
   01 02 03 04 05 06   PB   9 8 7 6 5 4 3 2

Library of Congress Cataloging-in-Publication Data
Marijanovic, Stanislav, 1935-
A manual of house monsters / Stanislav Marijanovic.
    p.   cm.
Summary: Presents descriptions of monsters that cause all sorts of bad behavior.
ISBN 1-57255-718-4 (hardcover : alk. paper). — ISBN 1-57255-717-6 (pbk. : alk. paper)
[1. Monsters Fiction. 2. Behavior Fiction.] I. Title.
PZ7.M33847Man   1999
[E]—DC21
                                           99-20138
                                            CIP
                                            AC

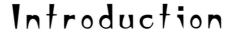

Introduction

House monsters are creatures that live in your home. They are not guests. They were not invited to live there. But they move right in anyway and cause all sorts of trouble.

House monsters are always planning mischief. They tug at you and trip you up. They make you do strange things. They make your life more difficult than you would like.

A Manual of House Monsters introduces the most common household monsters. These monsters are found in almost every home. They like to hide, so you may have to search for them. This manual tells you how to spot them all.

If you don't find any house monsters, don't worry. They will surely find you!

AHCHOO

the monster of sneezing

AHCHOO likes to curl up in snug, warm places for the winter. As soon as the weather starts to turn cold, Ahchoo begins his search for a winter home. Once he moves in, he seldom moves out before spring. He sniffles and sneezes giant, ear-splitting sneezes. Soon everyone nearby catches the sniffles. Choruses of *Ahchoo! Ahchoo! Ahchoo!* are heard everywhere. If you don't want a red, runny nose this winter, carry a pack of tissues and run when you see Ahchoo.

REFLECTUS

the mirror monster

REFLECTUS hides behind the mirrors in bathrooms and bedrooms. The moment you see your reflection, Reflectus holds you in her spell. She delights you with her songs as you stare at yourself for hours. *How cool I am,* you think. Reflectus also keeps you stuck in front of the bathroom mirror when Dad is in a hurry to finish shaving or your sister is waiting to wash her hair. So the next time you pass a mirror, don't stop and stare. Reflectus may be hiding there.

FIDGETS

the monster of impatience

When FIDGETS attacks, you lose your patience completely. You pace up and down. You grumble and whine. You just cannot sit still. But when properly trained, this monster can actually help you. You learn to enjoy the excitement of being impatient—for your birthday to come, for snow to fall, for summer vacation to start. Just don't let Fidgets give you the fidgets.

ALLMINUS

the monster of selfishness

Be on your guard against the sly ALLMINUS. She attacks unexpectedly with her familiar cries of "It's mine, all mine," and "I don't want to share." Some people say only children fight over things such as toys and candy. But Allminus attacks grown-ups just as much. Say "no" to selfish Allminus. It's much more fun to share.

CHATTERBUG

the telephone monster

CHATTERBUG moves into your home as soon as the telephone is installed. He cleverly hides inside the receiver. He feeds and grows on thick, juicy bits of conversation. Hot, cold, salty, or sweet—any conversation will do. Every time you use the phone you end up spending hours feeding him. Unfortunately, the phone company doesn't warn you about Chatterbug. You may not realize he is there until your mom receives the phone bill.

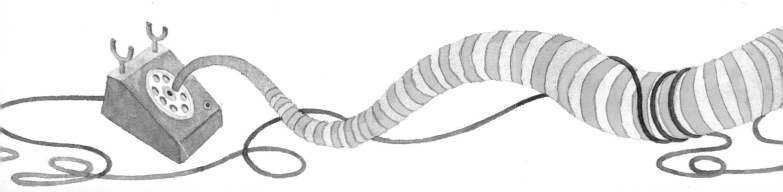

STUMBLETUMBLE

the tripping monster

STUMBLETUMBLE loves to watch a good stumble, tumble, or fall.
He hides under rugs, chairs, tables, and stairs, waiting to trip you. He
will chase the dog under the ladder when you climb up to the attic.
And he'll untie your shoelaces as you run to tell your brother to put
away his skates. Ooops! Too late. There goes Dad taking a slide.

OHNO

the monster of surprises

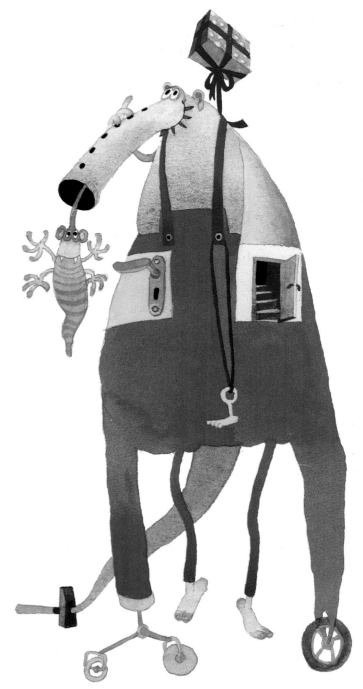

The thing OHNO likes best is a good surprise, usually at your expense. When no one is around, Ohno will get you to flood the bathroom. And if the walls in your home are painted white, they won't be for long. Not after your baby sister splashes orange juice, scrambled eggs, and ketchup on them. Not after she draws pictures on them. Who do you suppose gives your sister such ideas? Don't be surprised if it's Ohno.

DR. MISPLACE

the take-away monster

DR. MISPLACE is very nice, but troublesome. She follows you from room to room, snatching up things and tossing them where you seldom look. She takes away your pens and pencils, single socks, toys, and even the last piece of a jigsaw puzzle. She collects coins, keys, important notes, and electronic gadgets like remote controls. So be extra careful about where you put things, or Dr. Misplace will grab them.

TANTRUMELLA

the monster of yelling

TANTRUMELLA is the monster that makes you scream and shout, jump up and down, and yell at anyone who tries to talk to you. Sometimes you do this for no good reason at all. That's when adults will say you're having a tantrum. When you feel a tantrum coming on, take three deep breaths and count to ten. Then run if you see Tantrumella is still lurking around.

GOBBLEGOBBLE

the snacking monster

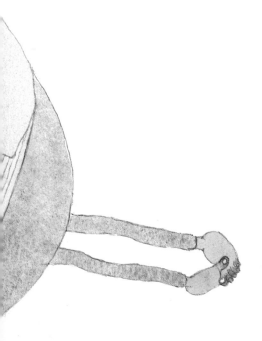

GOBBLEGOBBLE hides in the kitchen, particularly in the refrigerator and other places where food is kept. He strikes at almost any time, making you ready to snack. It could be in the morning, right after a meal, between meals, or even in the middle of the night. When Gobblegobble really gets naughty, he might make you munch on everything in sight—chips, ice cream, popcorn, cookies, pickles, meat loaf. This will surely spoil your appetite for your next meal.

SIZZLE

the monster of burns

SIZZLE is a very dangerous monster. She lurks behind the stove, under hot bowls and cups, and near other hot places. The sight of burned fingers or toes makes her glow with pleasure. She pushes your fingers toward the oven door and makes you lean against hot radiators. So the next time you're near something hot, stay alert, and watch out for Sizzle.

OOPSALO

the monster of spills

OOPSALO will do anything to cause a spill. He usually hides in the kitchen and bathroom. He makes you knock over the new bottle of shampoo, hold a mug full of cocoa with one finger, stir your soup too fast, or look away while pouring a glass of juice. Sponges, washing machines, and detergent make it easy to clean up, but Oopsalo is still a big nuisance to have around.

TOSS N. TURN and WORRYWART

the keep-you-awake monsters

TOSS N. TURN and WORRYWART strike the moment you lie down to go to sleep. They fill your head with thoughts and ideas. *Where did I put my homework?* you ask yourself. *Am I still hungry? Did I feed the cat? Do I need to go to the bathroom again?* After worrying for a while, you call your mom to get some answers.

Try to avoid these monsters or you will never sleep a wink. If you think they are near, hum a tune, close your eyes, and stretch your arms and legs. Soon you'll be sound asleep.

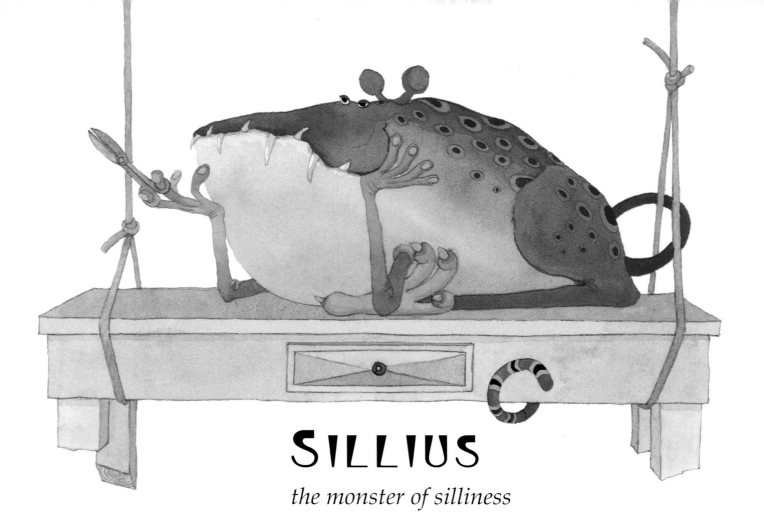

SILLIUS

the monster of silliness

SILLIUS takes over when you are feeling bored. Suddenly you start doing silly things like trying to hang your clothes from the ceiling of your room. Then you might start bouncing a basketball on the kitchen floor. When this happens, stop and get some fresh air. Sillius hates fresh air, so ask someone to take you to the park immediately.

SHADOWY

the monster of the dark

SHADOWY comes out when you turn off the lights. She swirls and whirls through the dark, making everything in the room terribly frightening and scary. If you listen carefully, you will hear her singing, "A haunting we will go, a haunting we will go, . . ." But Shadowy is really a harmless old monster. If you switch on the light, she runs and hides. So just say, "Good night, Shadowy," and quietly go to sleep.

TEEVEE

the television monster

     TEEVEE looks harmless enough, resting between the sofa cushions or on a chair. But the moment you sit down he hands you the TV remote control. He forces you to turn on the television and sit there, eyes glued to the screen. He keeps you there for hours, watching show after show after show. You forget about everything else. You're stuck! The best defense against this monster is the simplest one. Turn off the television as soon as your favorite show is over.

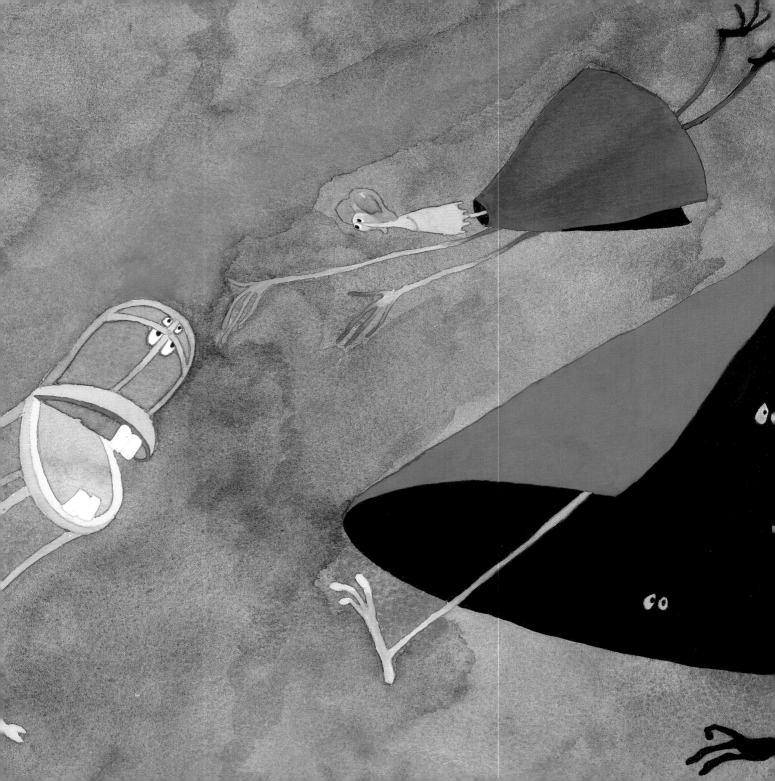

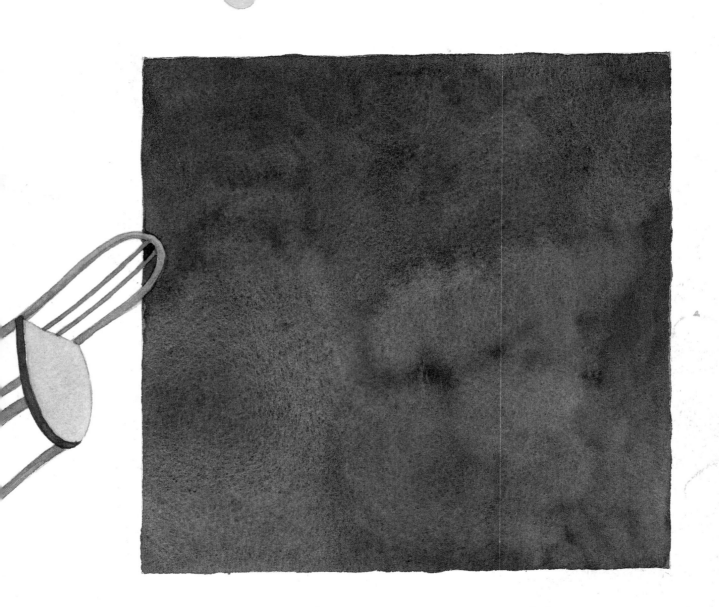

Turn this page at your own risk.

THISORTHAT

the clothing monster

THISORTHAT strikes in the morning, especially before school. You stare at your clothes and wonder, *Should I wear this or that?* Whatever you put on first looks wrong. Your shirt looks too red, your pants look too blue, and your socks don't match anything. Thisorthat keeps handing you other clothes to try on and does not stop until everything is piled on the bed. The only remedy is to pick out what you will wear the night before.

NOWINKS

the monster of tiredness

You feel grouchy and cranky. You yawn and drag your feet.
You can hardly keep your eyes open. This can mean only one
thing—NOWINKS has struck. Nowinks is a clever monster
who works her mischief at night. She keeps you up well past
your bedtime playing video games, watching television, or just
fooling around. The next day you feel tired from head to foot.
So when Nowinks strikes, there is only one thing to do. Go
straight to bed and sleep, sleep, sleep. You will wake up feeling
happy and fresh. And that's a good thing, because tomorrow
is sure to be full of new house monster adventures.